India
and the
Global Financial Crisis

India
and the
Global Financial Crisis

Managing Money and Finance

Y.V. Reddy

Orient BlackSwan

ORIENT BLACKSWAN PRIVATE LIMITED

Registered Office
3-6-752 Himayatnagar, Hyderabad 500 029 (A.P.), India
E-mail: centraloffice@orientblackswan.com

Other Offices
Bangalore, Bhopal, Bhubaneshwar, Chennai,
Ernakulam, Guwahati, Hyderabad, Jaipur, Kolkata,
Lucknow, Mumbai, New Delhi, Patna

The publishers gratefully acknowledge the Reserve Bank of
India for permission to reproduce the speeches in this book.

ISBN 978 81 250 3694 4

Typeset in Veljovic Book 10/13 by
Eleven Arts, Keshav Puram, Delhi

Printed in India at
International Print-o-Pac Ltd.
Noida 201305 (U.P.)

Published by
Orient Blackswan Private Limited
1/24 Asaf Ali Road, New Delhi 110 002
Email: delhi@orientblackswan.com

To
Pranav, Rohan, Diya & Uma

Contents

III Banking-Sector Reforms

IV Monetary Policy in a Globalising World

V Organisation and Communication Policies of the RBI

VI Managing Capital Account Liberalisation

VII Global Financial Imbalances and Crisis

Abbreviations

ADB	–	Asian Development Bank
ADR	–	American Depository Receipts
AFS	–	available for sale
ARCs	–	asset reconstruction companies
ARDC	–	Agriculture Refinance and Development Corporation
ASEAN	–	Association of Southeast Asian Nations
ATM	–	Automated Teller Machine
BCs	–	business correspondents
BCSBI	–	Banking Codes and Standards Board of India
BFS	–	Board for Financial Supervision
BIS	–	Bank for International Settlements
BPO	–	business process outsourcing
BPSS	–	Board for Regulation and Supervision of Payment and Settlement Systems
CAAP	–	capital adequacy assessment process
CCIL	–	Clearing Corporation of India Ltd
CGAP	–	Consultative Group to Assist the Poor
CHI	–	Chiang Mai Initiative
CHIC	–	Central Huijian Investment Company
CIBIL	–	Credit Information Bureau of India Limited
CRA	–	credit-rating agencies
CRAR	–	capital to risk-weight assets ratio
CRR	–	cash reserve ratio
CSF	–	Consolidated Sink Fund

DFI	–	development finance institutions
DICGA	–	Deposit Insurance and Credit Guarantee Corporation
DTL	–	Demand and Time Liabilities
EC	–	European Commission
ECB	–	European Central Bank
EMEs	–	emerging market economies
ETF	–	exchange traded funds
EU	–	European Union
FCNRB	–	foreign currency non-resident bank
FCCBs	–	Foreign Currency Convertible Bonds
FDI	–	foreign direct investment
FEMA	–	Foreign Exchange Management Act
FERA	–	Foreign Exchange Regulation Act
FIIs	–	foreign institutional investors
FIMMDA	–	Fixed Income Money Market Dealers' Association of India
FIPB	–	Foreign Investments Promotion Board
FRBM	–	Fiscal Responsibility and Budget Management Act
FRL	–	Fiscal Responsibility Legislation
FSAP	–	Financial Sector Assessment Program
G-7	–	Group of Seven
G-10	–	Group of Ten
G-20	–	Group of Twenty
GCC	–	General Credit Cards
GDP	–	gross domestic product
GDR	–	Global Depository Receipts
GFD	–	gross fiscal deficit
GIC	–	Government of Singapore Investment Corporation
GIV	–	Government-owned Investment Vehicles
HFC	–	housing finance companies
HFT	–	Held for Trading
HTM	–	Held to Maturity
IBA	–	Indian Banks' Association
IBL	–	inter-bank liability
ICT	–	Information and Communication Technology
IFR	–	Investment Fluctuation Reserve

IIFCL	–	India Infrastructure Finance Corporation Ltd.
IMF	–	International Monetary Fund
IIP	–	international investment position
KIC	–	Korean Investment Corporation
LAF	–	Liquidity Adjustment Facility
LTV	–	loan-to-value
MAS	–	Monetary Authority of Singapore
MBS	–	mortgage-backed securities
MFIs	–	micro-finance institutions
MFP	–	Multifactor Productivity
MFP	–	multi-factor productivity
MoU	–	memorandum of understanding
MPC	–	Monetary Policy Committee
MSS	–	Market Stabilisation Scheme
NABARD	–	National Bank for Agricultural and Rural Development
NBFCs	–	non-bank financial companies
NBFIs	–	non-bank financial institutions
NCF	–	Natural Calamity Fund
NDS	–	Negotiated Dealing System
NGOs	–	non-government organisations
NHB	–	National Housing Bank
NPAs	–	non performing assets
NPLs	–	non-performing loans
NRI	–	non-resident Indian
OECD	–	Organisation for Economic Co-operation and Development
OMO	–	open market operations
OTC	–	over-the-counter
PAIF	–	Pan-Asian Bond Index Fund
PBC	–	People's Bank of China
PDAI	–	Primary Dealers' Association of India
PDs	–	Primary Dealers
PPP	–	purchasing power parity
RBI	–	Reserve Bank of India
RBS	–	Risk Based Supervision
RIDF	–	Rural Infrastructure Development Fund

RRBs	–	regional rural banks
RTGS	–	Real Time Gross Settlement
SARFAESI	–	Securitisation and Reconstruction of Financial Assets and Enforcement of Securities Interest
SBI	–	State Bank of India
SCBs	–	scheduled commercial banks
SDLs	–	state development loans
SEBI	–	Securities and Exchange Board of India
SHGs	–	self-help groups
SIVs	–	structured investment vehicles
SLR	–	statutory liquidity ratio
SMEs	–	small and medium enterprises
SPV	–	Special Purpose Vehicles
SRC	–	Securitisation and Reconstruction Companies
SRP	–	supervisory review process
SWF	–	sovereign wealth fund
TAC	–	Technical Advisory Committee
TFP	–	total factor productivity
TFPG	–	total factor productivity growth
UAE	–	United Arab Emirates
UCB	–	urban cooperative banks
UNCTAD	–	United Nation Conference on Trade and Development
WMA	–	Ways and Means Advances
WPI	–	Wholesale Price Index
WTO	–	World Trade Organization

Acknowledgements

cknowledgements are due to the Directors of the Board, officers and staff of the Reserve Bank of India for the benefit of their guidance, advice and assistance in the art and science of central banking for well over a decade. The insights I gained from them find expression in the speeches. Dr Bimal Jalan, my immediate predecessor and a close friend for three decades, has been a pillar of support to me in several ways. Dr C. Rangarajan initiated me into the mysteries of central banking and never hesitated to educate and enlighten me. I am thankful to Dr D. Subba Rao, Governor Reserve Bank, for his support to this venture. Mr S.S. Tarapore, economist and central banker, has been a teacher, friend, philosopher and guide to me. Deputy Governors, Dr Rakesh Mohan, Mr V. Leeladhar, Mrs Shyamala Gopinath and Mrs Usha Thorat have all been valuable colleagues, and continue to contribute to the thought processes expressed in the book. There are a host of other professionals of the Reserve Bank who have, from time to time, rendered valuable assistance but they are too numerous to be listed here—I am grateful to each one of them.

Since September 2008, several organisations have invited me to deliver lectures or participate in their seminars, and that has been a great source of education for me. These include Bank for International Settlements; Bank Negara Malaysia; Chairman, International Monetary and Financial Committee; Committee on Global Thought, Columbia University; Government of Federal

Republic of Germany; Government of Singapore; The International Development Economics Associates, United Nations (Department of Economic and Social Affairs); United Nations Conference on Trade and Development; University of Hyderabad; World Bank and World Economic Forum. During this period, the greatest source of inspiration and education has been my association with the distinguished members of the Commission of Experts of the President of UN General Assembly on Reform of the International Monetary and Financial System, under the enlightened and scholarly chairmanship of Professor Joseph Stiglitz. I remain grateful to Professor Stiglitz.

I am thankful to Mr C. Rammanohar Reddy who encouraged me to bring out this volume and helped me in the process. Mr A. Premchand, a friend, philosopher and guide, always offered support, encouragement and commented on my drafts. Dr Rajiv Ranjan provided invaluable and continuous support by commenting on the drafts and in editing the volume. Mr K. Kanagasabapathy went through the Introduction and Epilogue to make sure that I did not make serious mistakes. Among others who helped me in the process are Ms Alpana Killawala, Mr K. Damodaran, Mr Durgananda Swamy, Mr A.K. Misra, Dr Partha Ray, Dr A. Prasad and Mr Vaibhav Chaturvedi. Special thanks are due to Ms Gayathri Vadrevu who has been a one-person office providing unstinting and continuous support to me while working on the book.

I must place on record my deep appreciation of the outstanding work of the publishers, Orient Blackswan. Ms Nandini Rao spared no effort to bring out the volume in time while maintaining high standards. Ms Mimi Choudhury coordinated the efforts admirably well. Ms Proteeti Banerjee, copy editor, has done an excellent job going through the dense and often abstruse language to make it readable.

This book is dedicated to my grand children Pranav, Rohan, Diya and Uma whose love helps me carry on with my life and work cheerfully and gainfully.

Introduction

This book is a compilation of twenty-three select speeches delivered by the author during his tenure as Governor, Reserve Bank of India (RBI), from September 2003 to September 2008—a very eventful period for both the global economy and for India. The lectures were selected keeping in mind the significance of intent, context and, in some cases, the impact expected of and created by them. They provide insights into the challenges, as they emerged from time to time, facing the management of India's calibrated integration within the global economy. In the epilogue, the author discusses the possible causes and potential consequences of the global financial crisis that began in mid-2007, and the challenges being addressed by the Indian economy.

EVENTFUL PERIOD

The period 2003–4 to 2007–8 (the fiscal year in India ends on 31 March) witnessed India's emergence as a significant player in the world economy. India's contribution to both global output and growth and stability of the global economy has been monitored closely by both analysts and academics. The period witnessed what was possibly the highest average growth rate ever achieved by India, contributed essentially through domestic saving and investment, and the lowest average inflation since Independence. There was further removal/relaxation of foreign exchange restrictions in the capital account, a process that began in the mid-1990s. Unprecedented investments were undertaken by India's enterprises abroad, leading to India's presence in the global economy being one that involved two-way capital flows. Similarly, the financial sector was considerably strengthened by carrying forward reforms in micro-structures, which promoted operational efficiency and soundness of financial institutions, and stability of financial markets.

It is interesting to observe that the period initially witnessed a pick-up from a slow growth of credit followed by very strong credit growth, leading at a later stage to percipient signs of over-heating. India benefited from the growing integration with the global economy at a time when there was expansion in global output and trade combined with overall stability, although some felt that there were persisting global imbalances that needed to be corrected. During the period, there were also huge oil price shocks, followed at later stages by shocks on account of food prices, both caused by global factors. In 2008-9, the global financial crisis impacted India, transmitted essentially through volatile capital inflows as well as a dampening of real sector activity. It is interesting to note that India continued to clock the second highest growth rate after China even during the ongoing global crisis, and has remained one of the islands of relative stability in financial and external sectors in what otherwise could be termed a sea of global turbulence.

It is also noteworthy that the *de facto* trade and financial integration of the Indian economy with the world economy has progressed steeply. The significant growth in trade over the five years from 2003-4 to 2007-8 has enabled India to achieve a ratio of exports plus imports of goods and services to gross domestic product (GDP) of about 48.4 per cent during 2007-8, as compared with 30.8 per cent during 2002-3. The ratio of current receipts and gross capital inflows plus current payments and gross capital outflows to the GDP, a broader measure of openness, averaged around 49 per cent during 1997-8 to 2001-2, and rose to an average of 80 per cent during 2002-3 to 2007-8. In fact, the ratio of gross inflows and outflows on current and capital account to GDP stood at 120 per cent in 2007–8, as compared with around 50 per cent in 2002–3 and 60 percent in 2003–4.

The global economy also witnessed unprecedented growth in output during 2003–8. At the same time, a significant achievement in maintaining price stability was evident, although the relative contribution of the monetary policy and productivity increases due to the integration of the world economy is difficult to estimate. The period also coincided with a significant shift in the relative contributions of emerging market economies (EMEs)[1] and others to global output growth. There was at one stage a severe impact of sudden and huge increases in oil prices, soon followed by increases in the prices of other commodities, including food items. These shocks necessitated appropriate policy responses, recognising the limitations of monetary policy in tackling supply shocks and influencing inflation expectations. There was, however, concern about the persistence of global macroeconomic imbalances, and about the possibility that there could be under-pricing of risks by financial markets. There was an eruption of financial crisis in 2007–8, which originated in the US and spread to other advanced economies. The financial crisis has seriously affected the growth prospects of emerging market and developing economies, also resulting in recession or slow down in growth in almost all economies of the world. Despite the determined and coordinated efforts of central banks and governments, the crisis intensified in the latter part of 2008–9, making the global financial crisis spill over into a serious economic crisis with unprecedented challenges for policymakers. The challenge before India's policymakers, therefore, shifted at this stage from managing the successful integration of the Indian economy with the global economy to managing the impact of the global financial crisis on India, although India did not contribute to the global imbalances. This book provides insights into the process of managing integration while being equipped to mitigate the threats to stability and medium-term prospects for growth from globalisation.

The twenty-three speeches have been grouped thematically into seven parts, each containing a minimum of two and a maximum of four speeches. We have broadly attempted to set out, chapter-wise, the context, intent and analytical content of each speech, particularly any important message contained as an integral part of central bank communication. It is hoped that readers will benefit from reading these introductory observations before turning to the respective chapters in the volume.

INDIAN ECONOMY: REVIEW AND PROSPECTS

The speech titled 'India and the Global Economy' aimed at moderating the commitments and enthusiasm in both policy circles and financial markets for an accelerated financial integration of the Indian economy with the global economy, in particular the faster opening up of the Indian banking sector to foreign banks. The logic behind a calibrated approach and resetting the then proposed pace of financial integration with the global economy was sought to be explained. Furthermore, a comprehensive policy framework for financial integration was articulated, and the policy regarding the opening up of the Indian banking industry placed in this overall context. A pointed reference was made at that time to the global economy also having to reckon with the impact of India's integration within it. The speech was delivered on 17 July 2004 at the Lal Bahadur Shastri National Academy of Administration, Mussoorie, the national training institute for the elite civil services, although the intended audience was far wider.

The context in which this speech was delivered was significant. The Budget Speech of the Finance Minister for 2003–4 announced that the ownership of Indian banks was being thrown open to foreign investors up to 74 per cent. This was to facilitate the setting up of subsidiaries of foreign banks, as well as inviting investment in private banks. The budget speech also announced that the Banking Regulation Act, 1949 would be amended to remove the restriction on voting rights to 10 per cent, irrespective of the investors shareholding in a banking company. While the original intent of the provision relating to the ceiling on voting rights was to ensure a diversified ownership of banks, one of the purposes of the proposed amendment was to remove such restrictions, thereby facilitating foreign banks to acquire dominant ownership in a domestic bank and expand their operations through the inorganic route. A bill to this effect was introduced in Parliament. The government was committed to implementing the budget announcement before the end of the fiscal year.

During the second half of the fiscal year, the RBI reviewed the proposed policy changes in light of the overall compulsions of reforms in the financial sector, especially the domestic banking sector. The RBI indicated that the issue of foreign ownership in banks should be viewed in two distinct terms: first, foreign ownership, as distinct from the presence of foreign banks, and that the whole process of ownership should be linked to progress in ensuring compliance with the fit and proper criteria for larger shareholders in banks; and second, sound governance and consolidation in the domestic banking sector. Furthermore, the public sector was functioning under severe constraints, and easing those constraints should be a priority for improvements in the banking industry, and for ensuring genuine competition. The RBI did not subscribe to the view that foreign banks or foreign capital are critical to enabling improvements in the domestic banking industry, which was (and continues to be) dominated by public-sector banks. The RBI was of the view that among the private-sector banks, there were some vulnerable banks which were best addressed initially and as a priority through regulatory rigour without necessarily invoking the assistance of foreign banks. The government, after some discussions, made some moderation in the framework of the proposed liberalisation. This was reflected in a press release issued by the RBI on 3 February 2004, in the form of guidelines for the acknowledgement of transfer or allotment of shares in private-sector banks beyond 5 per cent. The procedure for acknowledgement of share transfers required the approval of the regulator. The regulatory criteria for acknowledgement were set out, and were equally applicable to residents and non-residents. The continued applicability of restrictions on voting rights was reiterated. The Bill seeking amendments to the Banking Regulation Act to remove the ceiling on the exercise of voting rights was allowed to lapse.

The government revisited the issue in June 2004, and took the view that public policy was already committed to the approach of expeditious reforms in terms of foreign ownership of banks, and expanded the presence of foreign banks in India. Furthermore, it was held that there was a consensus already built around the matter in favour of such a reform, and that any backtracking would erode the global credibility of public policy.

After considerable discussion, it was agreed that there would be no backtracking from achieving the objective of liberalisation as originally contemplated, but that in view of the strong reservations expressed by the RBI, a roadmap could be drawn up which would give the RBI time to bring about the preconditions that would be favourable before implementing the decision.

The intention behind this speech was to focus on the fact that while the gains from trade liberalisation were evident, there was a need to weigh the risks and rewards of a rapid opening up of the financial sector. It highlighted the importance of ensuring progress in the reforms in fiscal and real sectors, such that the environment of domestic industry and trade would become consistent with a more liberalised financial sector. The speech explained, in a comprehensive manner, the logic behind the timetable and roadmap for the opening up of the Indian banking sector. In February 2005, a roadmap for the presence of foreign banks in India and guidelines on ownership and governance of private-sector banks were issued by the RBI, in consultation with the government.

The speech on 'Importance of Productivity in India' stressed the need to analyse productivity trends in India while framing appropriate public policies. For example, while studies on the measurement of poverty have been of world class standards, a similar coverage or quality of studies on issues relating to productivity in India were not evident, even though higher productivity is critical to poverty eradication. This speech was delivered on 27 December 2005 as the inaugural address at the Annual Conference of the Indian Economic Association, and was intended as a plea to economists to devote greater attention to studies on productivity at a time when India's integration with the global economy was taking place at a rapid pace. There were several reasons, some of which contextual, for articulating the issue of productivity in India. The immediate provocation was the view expressed in some influential circles that India was on the verge of double-digit growth; however, it was not clear how such assertions could be made without reference to productivity trends, along with saving and investment trends. Similarly, there was a view in some influential quarters that a strengthened currency enabled by expanding capital inflows would be appropriate, but such a view would only be credible if it was based on some assessment of relative inter-country comparisons of growth in productivity.

There were many other considerations in the articulation of the issue. In a deregulated environment, for the conduct of a sound monetary policy, especially in an economy undergoing structural transformation, a reliable fix on productivity trends is critical. In India, the dominance of the services sector made assessments of productivity further complex, and hence there was a need to pay attention to the contribution of information and communication technology (ICT) to productivity.

The speech titled 'Reflections on India's Economic Development' intended to place before the global audience the overall approach of gradualism in economic policy in India, within the broader socio-political context in terms of changes in the balances of several factors. It was also considered necessary to explain the rationale behind a calibrated approach to reforms in the external and financial sectors. The speech was presented at the Council of Foreign Relations in New York, on 12 May 2006, keeping in mind the fact that the perception among influential circles in the US and some market participants and analysts in India was that the RBI was being less than cooperative in bringing about the desirable reforms in financial and external sectors in an expeditious manner. There was a strong feeling, particularly in public policy circles and among large financial institutions, that the Indian policy of opening the banking sector to foreign banks was restrictive. The prevailing view in the US was that India's impressive development was almost exclusively due to reforms that had taken place since 1991, a view that ignored the contribution of institution-building and other policies that preceded and moved in tandem with the reforms.

In the presentation, attention was drawn to the extensive groundwork that had been done by Indian policymakers well before the reform period, based on which the impressive performance of the Indian economy had been achieved in recent years. In particular, differences between the regulatory challenges for developed and developing economies and the special challenges for the latter in balancing efficiency and stability in the financial sector were pointed out. There were references to the importance of broader issues of governance, which needed to be taken into account while considering factors that might impact economic growth and financial stability. In particular, an analytical framework on what constitutes the country-context for India was given as a background for appreciating the reforms in the financial sector. In this context, the fact that reforms in the financial and external sectors in India were impressive, and the need to harmonise these reforms with the progress in the fiscal sector and the real sector, such as physical infrastructure, were highlighted. The presentation explained the rationale behind a calibrated approach to the liberalisation of the financial sector in preference to a more rapid one in the Indian context.

The purpose of the speech on 'India: Development and Reform Experience; and Prospects' was to highlight the performance of the Indian economy before the global community, in particular the role of the RBI. The speech was delivered as an address at the Bank of Mexico on 12 September 2007, and was part of a series on the subject in other countries, in particular Chile and Argentina. There were several aspects of the Indian economic performance and its integration with the global economy that attracted the attention of other countries, especially in Latin America, which had paid a heavy price in the past for instability and fiscal profligacy. By 2007, there was significant interest in the unique features of the Indian economy, which had enabled high growth along with stability in prices and in both the financial and external sectors despite the huge public debt, persistent fiscal deficits and, for the most part, current account deficits, too. For several years, this performance was considered by some leading economists as the Indian rope trick, and hence was not expected to last.

The speech sought to explain how reforms progressed in India while building special defences against such vulnerabilities through what has been described by a rating agency as the unorthodox, but largely successful, policies pursued by the RBI. The speech also reached out to the domestic audience to caution them against excessive enthusiasm in expeditiously implementing measures such as introducing futures markets on an extensive scale, further opening up of financial markets, especially debt markets, to foreign investment, issuing a foreign currency denominated sovereign debt, etc. The intention was to explain the appropriateness of a policy of reform of the RBI, which could deliver growth with stability while being sensitive to social concerns. This was achieved by persevering with gradual reforms in view of the perceived forces of vulnerability prevalent in the economy. One of the major messages related to the importance of enhancing the standards of governance to assure efficiency along with stability, while placing greater reliance on market participants. There was a deliberate reference to the responsibility of business to strengthen rather than undermine public policy.

FINANCIAL-SECTOR REFORMS

The speech 'Reforming India's Financial Sector: Changing Dimensions and Emerging Issues' was a comprehensive narration of the reforms undertaken, and the main features of the work in progress before the global economy and financial community. The speech was delivered at The International Centre for Monetary and Banking Studies, Switzerland, on 9 May 2006. The purpose was to explain to the globally influential audience the iterative nature of reform and the complexity of the tasks undertaken to ensure a domestically driven but strong financial sector. The emphasis was on the work in progress and the socio-economic context within which the measures were undertaken. The fact that the RBI's reform agenda included developmental orientation was deliberately brought to the fore. While the progress and the features of financial-sector reforms were of general interest, the areas flagged continue to remain relevant and engage the attention of policymakers. These relate to capital account convertibility, fiscal management, consolidation in the banking sector and the role of foreign banks. The speech elaborated the importance of financial inclusion and customer service as part of the emphasis on the banking services that are relevant to India's socio-economic conditions, and contribute to both growth and stability.

The developments in financial markets have not been adequately and comprehensively documented, although the actions taken were recorded in the annual and mid-term policy statements. By and large, the measures reflected a definitive progress in liberalisation, but with considerable caution and safeguards against excesses. The RBI's perception had been that in emerging markets like India, in view of the vulnerabilities to volatile capital flows, fiscal deficits and current account deficits, there is a need for some caution in the pace of liberalisation of financial markets. The RBI continued with its presumption of its responsibility for maintaining financial stability, and hence the dialogue with the government, which was keen that the agenda for more rapid liberalisation of financial markets be accorded greater weight in the interests of higher growth. The government actively participated in arriving at an approach to reform and developments in financial markets. There was full agreement on the ultimate objective—the healthy development of financial markets—but the pace of the actions to be taken in that direction and the relative emphasis on different components were the topics of discussion. The RBI placed high priority on the development of money markets, government securities markets and forex markets, while the market participants' focus was on the development of bond, currency and derivatives markets. With regard to the development of corporate bond markets, the RBI had a stake in it, in view of its importance in the transmission of monetary policy and financing of infrastructure; however, the RBI emphasised healthy regulation and development of the domestic bond market before opening it up further to foreign investors. Moreover, the RBI had in 2003 banned the operations of overseas corporate bodies of non-resident Indians

(NRIs) in the Indian financial sector in view of the opacity of their operations. These actions had no adverse consequences, and hence, on similar grounds—placing the need to 'Know Your Investor' on par with 'Know Your Customer'—the RBI sought in an unequivocal manner a ban on Participatory Note. These notes were instruments issued by foreign institutional investors registered in India, but holders' identities were difficult to establish in real time. These notes were traded outside India, and hence were substantively beyond the tax and regulatory regimes of India. Furthermore, the RBI had a preference for diversification in foreign ownership in the systemically important institutional infrastructure for financial markets, such as stock exchanges, credit information bureaus and mortgage companies.

The RBI was not comfortable with proposals to encourage, and in some instances permit, banks to be overly active in particularly risky activities like equity markets and venture capital, given the limited skills and risk-management capabilities of banks. In the context of the integrity of financial markets, the RBI was especially sensitive to the existence of conflicts of interest and had commissioned a report on the subject, which was placed in the public domain in 2006.

The speech titled 'Global Financial Turbulence and Financial Sector in India: A Practitioner's Perspective' was an address delivered at the meeting of the Task Force on Financial Markets Regulators, organised by the Initiative for Policy Dialogue, Manchester, UK on 1 July 2008 at a time when the initial impact of the financial crisis was already being felt. The objective was to narrate the perceptions relating to global developments in 2007–8 in the financial sector, in particular market and regulatory failures in some advanced economies, and contrast it with the regulatory policies adopted in India. At the same time, the measures taken for financial-sector development were explained to provide a balanced view of the overall policy or framework of the RBI, which sought a balance between efficiency and stability.

Some of the regulatory actions taken by the RBI related to counter-cyclicality in prudential regulation; comprehensiveness in regulations to cover systemically important non-banks; seeking governance standards in banks; prescribing appropriate rules relating to mark-to-market; according importance to systemic liquidity and depending on a process of supervisory review. There were a few other actions not articulated in the presentations that would warrant mention in this context. The operations of conglomerates were brought under the supervisory review of inter-regulatory coordination mechanisms. The RBI, however, recognised that even if the multiple gearing of capital through holding companies could be effectively eliminated through the consolidation of supervision, the challenging issue of excess leveraging by downstream affiliates would continue to warrant concern in some circumstances. Further, banks were closely monitored to avoid excessive dependence on sources other than traditional sources of retail deposits. The compensation of the chief executive officer has to be approved by the RBI, and the bank refused to approve entry bonuses and severance packages. The fit and proper criteria for directors on the boards of private-sector banks were defined and generally enforced by the RBI. The mechanism for corporate restructuring by banks was streamlined and guidelines issued. Above all, while there was no formal mechanism to certify the safety of any financial product, the RBI issued guidelines to banks regarding various aspects of transparency and appropriateness. For example, banks were advised to assess the capabilities and understanding of a corporate before offering a product for hedging a forex exposure.

The RBI took the stand that reforms in the financial sector have to be undertaken in light of the progress of reforms in related areas. First, the scope of the administered interest rate regime, which had shown a decrease in the years prior to 2004, had shown a reversal in subsequent years. Second, the difference between what could be construed as market-based interest rates and administered interest rates actually widened during most of the period. Third, the management of capital flows resulted in excess capital inflows, warranting intervention and sterilisation since the tolerance for large movements in exchange rate was severely restricted. The government was transparent in bearing some of the costs of sterilisation through the Market Stabilisation Scheme (MSS). These developments compelled the RBI to increase the cash reserve ratio (CRR), reversing the trend of reduction of previous years. Fourth, the preemption of resources by the public sector through extra-budgetary means, especially to manage oil price shock, placed constraints on increasing the role of markets in financial sectors without threatening stability. Fifth, directed lending by banks, especially public-sector banks, both at formal and informal levels, had increased during this period. The reforms in the public sector, both in terms of legal framework and governance, had not taken place in the expected directions. Sixth, the tax regimes and other policy actions were tilted in favour of equity markets and mutual funds as well as non-banking financial companies (NBFCs), while the burden of taxes, regulation and macro-imbalances continued to fall disproportionately on the banking system.

In the move forward, several factors would favour the greater global integration of the financial sector, in particular the banking sector, over the medium to long term, despite some short-term issues arising out of the global financial crisis of 2008–9. The Indian economy and its financial sector are in a strong position now in 2009–10 to manage such integration, and support growth while minimising the risks of such integration. There are two reasons for such optimism: one, globally there is a better appreciation of the need for rebalancing market freedom and regulatory scope as well as rigour; and two, domestically there are opportunities and the time to reform real and fiscal sectors to equip the economy to ensure a smoother alignment of the Indian financial system with global financial markets.

BANKING-SECTOR REFORMS

The speech 'Rural Credit: Status and Agenda', delivered at the Administrative Staff College of India on 16 November 2004, should be viewed in the context of an announcement made by the Finance Minister in his Budget Speech for 2004–5. The budget speech expressed the government's resolve to double the flow of credit to agriculture in three years. The RBI accepted the compelling need to increase the flow of credit to agriculture, but also had to articulate the need for public policy to address certain fundamental issues, failing which the short-term measures to increase credit could result in a choking of the credit flow over the medium to the long term. There was a brief mention of the need to enhance the flow of credit to agriculture, and of the steps already initiated by the RBI. The agenda for the future related mainly to reforms in the rural cooperative credit system and strengthening of regional rural banks (RRBs). Many rural cooperative credit institutions were insolvent; yet, they were permitted to continue with their banking business. They were subject to regulation and supervision by multiple agencies, namely the RBI, the National Bank for Agriculture and Rural Development (NABARD) and the concerned state governments. Similarly, many RRBs, owned jointly by the Government of India, the concerned state government and the sponsoring public-sector banks, have been languishing in terms of their overall performance despite the capital infusion in many cases in earlier years. They were meant to be major instruments of credit delivery in rural areas and were not constrained by the need to enhance shareholder value, since by the relevant statute, the shareholding pattern was frozen within public sector, and shares were not tradable. More importantly, the credit culture in rural areas and the urgent issue of risk mitigation in farming were not generally addressed. The RBI did assist in the full realisation of the government's commitment to double the credit for agriculture in three years from the date of announcement in the budget.

The speech 'Banking Sector Reforms in India: An Overview' was delivered at The Institute of Bankers in Karachi, Pakistan, on 18 May 2005. The objective was to narrate the contours of India's banking reforms; explain the process by which the reforms were managed and focus on the elements of continuity and change over the years. The speech had particular relevance for Pakistan, which had followed a more traditional path to the reform of the banking sector, namely privatisation, greater access to foreign banks and emphasis on micro-credit to cater to the needs of the poorer sections. Contextually, there was a more general purpose, namely to indicate that the focus of financial-sector reforms was changing to non-traditional areas of banking regulations. These relate to the ease of usage of banking services by the common person, strengthening credit delivery, issues of governance and ownership of banks, and financial inclusion. Of particular interest to the banking community was a policy to encourage the operations of those banks that were responsive to the banking needs of the community through the exercise of powers of branch licensing. It is noteworthy that on almost all these issues, the government extended its full support. Many state governments in particular extended collaboration with regard to financial inclusion, reforms of urban cooperative banks (UCBs), expansion of rural credit, etc.

An update on banking-sector reforms since this presentation of May 2005 would be in order. The policy statement of 2006 concentrated on some issues that subsequently gathered significance, namely the rapid expansion in credit, whereby what had been described as 'lazy' banking at the beginning of the decade was being replaced by what could be described as 'crazy' banking, with rapid growth in credit. A contentious issue in internal debates related to the stand taken on the use of enhanced provisions, and the according of higher risk weights for lending to or investment in select sectors. The generally accepted wisdom as part of financial-sector liberalisation was that a regulator was not equipped to take a view on asset values, and in any case the data available was inadequate to take a considered position. The RBI was of the opinion that there was no view being taken on asset values as such, but that the effort was only to protect the banking system by insisting on additional capital since uncertainties and risks appear to have emerged. The RBI issued guidelines on securitisation, but they were considered conservative at the time they were issued, in 2006.

It must be recognised that the banking sector in India witnessed unprecedented strengthening during this period and that in this process, the unstinted support of the government was critical. Some examples would be in order. First, a newly licensed private-sector bank, which was not large but was systemically important, had to be placed under special directions, and a merger with another bank brought about over a weekend. Despite the high profile of promoters, the government extended support to the action of the RBI, which sent a strong signal to the banking community regarding the intent of public policy vis-à-vis the regulation of banks.

Second, the government supported the RBI in implementing measures to ensure the end of weak scheduled commercial banks through several steps. These included processes of amalgamation, the injection of additional capital, prescribing stringent norms for fit and proper ownership of banks and membership of their boards.

Third, coordinated efforts at reforming the banking system and regulatory effectiveness ensured that there were no large-scale frauds or scams during the period, despite a very high growth in credit and the expanded operations of banks in financial markets.

Fourth, the recommendations with regard to appointments to full-time executive positions at the board level in public-sector banks were honoured by the government.

Fifth, a large segment of UCBs faced serious problems of solvency, governance and transparency. In accordance with prevailing statutes, they were under the dual control of state governments and the RBI. Exercising its jurisdiction, the RBI stopped issuing fresh licenses for bank branches till a memorandum of understanding (MoU) on reform was entered into with the concerned state governments. This innovative and very productive strategic initiative was implemented smoothly with the support extended by the government.

Sixth, the non-banking financial sector also required the attention of the regulator. There were attempts to restrict the regulatory jurisdiction of the RBI to non-banking deposit-taking institutions only, thus ignoring other systemically important ones, but the government concurred with the RBI and dropped the proposed legislative changes.

Seventh, despite intense pressures, the government was supportive of several of the RBI's initiatives in regulating systemically important financial institutions, in particular two large residuary NBFCs.

Eighth, there was one somewhat systemically important issue relating to the soundness of the financial system. The government approved select foreign investments in a holding company structure with respect to a large private-sector bank, which was itself a conglomerate with commanding foreign ownership; however, this was subject to the approval of the RBI. The latter had concerns about the institutional framework implied in the approval of the government, which related to the potential for excessive leveraging and dilution of regulatory effectiveness in such a conglomerate. Hence, the RBI appointed a working group to study and report on the global best practices and the Indian context to take a view on the regulatory approvals for such an innovative structure. The report clarified several issues, including the desirable legal framework.

Finally, there were very few exceptions to the general practice of non-interference by the government in the RBI's exercise of its jurisdiction in according clearance to the appointments of chief executives in private banks and branches of foreign banks in India.

In the future, there is a vast scope and compelling need for significant reforms in the banking sector in India. The country is well-endowed with human skills, technological capabilities and indeed, the capital. Unlike most other economies, India has not experienced a banking crisis that needs immediate attention, although the impact of a slowdown in the economy due to the global financial crisis of 2008–9 may have the potential to increase the non-performing assets (NPAs) in banking in the short term. The banking sector may have to undergo significant and urgent reforms to sustain the growth needed to eradicate poverty, and the reform may have to reflect the new realities of financial-sector management consequent upon the global financial crisis of 2008–9, as well as the developments in several areas related to the financial sector that are also linked with reforms in the fiscal and real sectors. A large part of reform would no doubt involve public-sector banks, and consequently legislative actions.

The speech 'Micro-Finance: The RBI's Approach' addressed several complex issues at a micro-finance conference (6 August 2005) in Hyderabad, capital of the state of Andhra Pradesh, which accounts for the largest share, almost a third of the national activity, in micro-finance. The success of the traditional approach of the RBI had to be explained, efforts to strengthen the movement indicated and, at the same time, the implications of the government's proposed legislation on micro-finance had to be articulated. The thrust of the presentation was that informality and flexibility were assured in the existing framework of micro-finance through self-help groups (SHGs) and non-government organisations (NGOs), mainly through the banking system. Furthermore, any financial intermediary which could access deposits and is subject to a softer regulation, say relative to commercial banks, had serious arbitrage possibilities, as shown by the RBI's experience with UCBs. It was also argued that over a longer time period, the objective should be the financial inclusion of all persons through the banking system, and not to have two separate institutions, micro for the poor and banks for the rest. Finally, the RBI felt that any separate regulatory framework for micro-finance institutions (MFIs) should ideally be at the state level, and should not involve the RBI. In any case, the plea was for pursuing the policies of financial inclusion through banks, and in parallel micro-finance through banks, while considering an appropriate legal framework for dedicated MFIs, as contemplated by the government.

The micro-finance movement continues to thrive and has also spread to states which had been less exposed to them in the past. Furthermore, the use of the micro-finance route to administer government-approved and subsidised programmes reported significant debtor defaults, unlike others. In a few cases, micro-finance was expanded aggressively, resulting in one state government clamping down on the activities and discomfort among some others. There were cases of aggressive lending and use of recovery agents by the MFIs. The interest rates charged were considered excessive in many cases. In view of the emerging tensions between state governments and select MFIs, the RBI facilitated meetings between officials of state governments, the concerned bank and the relevant NGOs, and enabled the institution of some voluntary codes of conduct, thereby preserving the informality and flexibility of the micro-finance model while avoiding any formal and direct regulation. On a positive note, several innovative measures were undertaken by the RBI, NABARD and commercial banks to extend the reach of micro-finance, especially through the business correspondent model. The approach was broadly consistent with the global best practices.

In accordance with the announcement in the budget speech, a bill was introduced, but has not yet been approved by the Parliament. From all indications, five major issues were flagged during the discussions. First, there was a feeling that for-profit MFIs were no different from moneylenders, and should hence be brought under the moneylending legislations of the state governments concerned. Second, it was felt at the same time that there should be a ceiling on the interest rates charged to prevent moneylenders from using the micro-finance route to carry on their activities. Third, it was felt that if MFIs had any deposit-taking function, they should be brought under the regulation of the RBI. Fourth, opening up such MFIs for foreign equity and foreign commercial banks was viewed with discomfort, since MFIs were being accorded soft regulation only on the ground that they were in the nature of local, community-based organisations. Fifth, it was felt that formalising MFIs through legislations may amount to undermining the goal of inclusive banking, which was making impressive progress with the spread of new technologies. Finally, it was felt that mechanisms should be found to differentiate between the non-finance and finance functions of MFIs, in order to enlarge the regulatory scope, however soft, of such institutions.

The chapter 'Rural Banking: Review and Prospects' was based on a speech delivered on 16 December 2006 at Hyderabad in Andhra Pradesh, a state which, despite being reasonably prosperous in agriculture, found itself in the news after some farmers committed suicide. The issue of these suicides dominated public policy response and led to several measures, the impact of which, however, was limited. The government decided in 2006 that farmers should generally be charged an interest of 7 per cent per annum, although the government recognised that the solutions to the problem were more complex. The objective was to explain that rural banking had to be viewed in an overall context, especially with regard to the commercial viability of such activities and the management of risks. The context was that the RBI had been contributing to the successful achievement of the public policy goal to double the credit to agriculture within three years. The extension of credit at a uniform rate was not conducive to a sound credit culture. The government was fully aware of these issues, but had decided to show sensitivity to the deprivation prevalent within the farming community. Growth in agricultural output was a fraction of the pace at which manufacturing and services were growing in the economy. In deference to the stand taken by the RBI, the government had avoided placing the burden on the banking system by agreeing to reimburse the imputed losses the bank suffered on account of this decision. The RBI on its part agreed to actively assist the government to implement the decision and enhance the level of the transfer of profit to the government. The implication was that the amount of transfer of the RBI's profits to its reserves was less than what it would otherwise have been as per the agreed-upon policy. Against this background, it was considered necessary for the RBI to articulate that the issue of rural banking has to take into account several new realities in the Indian economy, especially in terms of the rural-urban continuum and the integration of the agrarian economy with the other vibrant elements of the economy.

There was a specific reference in the speech to the four deficits articulated by the prime minister at that time. The prime minister made a noteworthy observation in this regard—the need to bring moneylenders under some form of regulation. A reference in public policy to regulating moneylenders was pathbreaking, and in a way an endorsement of the initiatives already undertaken by the RBI at that time. The RBI constituted a committee chaired by a Deputy Governor to suggest a model legislation on regulating moneylending for the consideration of state governments, which was to replace the prevalent outdated, ineffective and diverse legislations. This initiative was in recognition of the fact that moneylenders continued to dominate, despite several policy initiatives to expand institutional credit.

As it turned out, none of the state governments adopted the recommended model legislation on moneylending; in fact, they did not even consider the subject. Furthermore, the subsidisation of agricultural lending by the government ceased to be temporary. The broader issues that need to be addressed to manage the problems of rural banking remain unaddressed. In fact, there have been further developments subsequent to this speech, in particular the waiver of most farmers outstanding debts. The usual intense dialogues between the RBI and the government did take place on the issues of waiver, and especially on the impact such generalised write-offs would have on credit culture. The government was well aware of the implications, but was also conscious of the fact that the fruits of high growth in recent years had not percolated to the farming community. The burden of tax concessions already granted to various non-farm activities was large on an annual basis, relative to the cost to the exchequer of the debt waiver as a one-time measure. It has been argued that waiving debts may not be the ideal method of demonstrating sensitivity to farmers' issues; however, it was difficult to find better ways to achieve the objectives in the short run. Furthermore, it was argued that the distortions induced by these debt waivers were insignificant relative to many other distortions in fiscal and credit dispensation to other sectors, which benefited fewer and comparatively more prosperous sections. The government, however, agreed to bear the cost of the debt waiver by fiscal transfer rather than by passing it on to the banking system, thus protecting the health of the latter. The RBI, for its part, undertook to implement the decision effectively, and also, as on a previous occasion, enhance the transfer of profits from the RBI to the government to meet the additional fiscal burden.

MONETARY POLICY IN A GLOBALISING WORLD

The speech on 'Monetary Policy: An Outline' was originally circulated as the presidential address at the annual conference of the Andhra Pradesh Economic Association on 12 February 2005. It was meant as a primer on the theory and practice of monetary policy, aimed at academics and market participants in view of the increasing role of monetary policy in the Indian economy, due to the economic reforms undertaken and the financial reforms underway. It was also considered timely, in view of the increasing linkages of the Indian economy with the global economy. The point made was that there was no single universally valid principle or practice in the conduct of monetary policy, but that there were common areas of interest and a similarity of tools. In particular, it was mentioned that after the financial crises of the 1990s in different parts of the world, concern for financial stability was an integral part of the central banks' activism. With regard to the Indian situation, it was stressed that the monetary policy had not only to be forward looking, but had also to grapple with an uncertain future related to the transition from a relatively closed to a progressively opening economy.

The objectives of monetary policy were interpreted by the RBI from time to time with the either explicit or implicit approval of the government. For instance, as part of the reform process, the RBI itself interpreted its objectives as price stability and the provision of adequate credit to productive sectors of the economy, the relative emphasis being dependent on the prevailing circumstances. In recent years, significantly, the maintenance of financial stability was added as an important consideration. Furthermore, in order to have some fix for influencing inflation expectations at a time when many central banks were inflation-targetters, the RBI elaborated its objective of price stability. The RBI indicated, in 2007, that in recognition of India's evolving integration with the global economy and societal preferences in that regard, the resolve while moving forward would be to condition inflation expectations in the range of 4.0 to 4.5 per cent, so that an inflation rate of around 3.0 per cent becomes a medium-term objective consistent with India's broader integration within the global economy. At the same time, the RBI recognised the role of public policy in managing supply shocks and the overall supply conditions in several areas, and hence articulated these aspects in its policy statements from time to time.

With regard to instruments of monetary policy, too, a very innovative approach was taken. By law, the RBI cannot issue its own bills. It proposed additional borrowing by the government as a means of sterilisation; however, such borrowings were not to be utilised as a budgetary resource, even though the government had to pay interest. The instruments were exactly similar to the normal treasury bills or bonds. The MSS was unique in the sense that it provided a new instrument with which to manage sterilisation operations, in addition to the Liquidity Adjustment Facility (LAF) with the RBI and the use of the CRR imposed on commercial banks. Together, the three provided a range of instruments that could distribute the burden of sterilisation between the government, the central bank and the banking system, and at the same time address sterilisation needs over different time horizons. These instruments enabled operations that could make unwinding smooth in the event of large capital outflows warranting a withdrawal of liquidity. Coupled with adequate forex reserves and freedom of operations in forex markets, the RBI had been fully equipped to manage possible excess volatilities in money and forex markets too, in addition to its capacity to operate in the secondary market in government securities. The instruments facilitate smooth management of excess volatilities in both directions.

The MSS arrangement, entered into in February 2004, involved a loss of some independence for the RBI since the issuance of MSS had to be approved by the government, but it enabled the government to be accountable for bearing the fiscal burden implicit in sterilisation operations. The government was farsighted enough to agree to this highly innovative arrangement during 2003-4, in anticipation of the huge capital inflows. The arrangements have since continued, and have undoubtedly served to manage volatility in capital flows, with the flexibility to build up or unwind the balances in MSS.

The speech 'Globalisation of Monetary Policy and the Indian Experience' was addressed to senior officials of central banks responsible for the formulation of monetary policy. It was presented at the eighth meeting of the Bank for International Settlements (BIS) Working Party on Monetary Policy in Asia on 8 June 2005. The address listed the forces at work that determine the globalisation of monetary policy and the challenges that were faced in the conduct of monetary policy as a result of such integration. A major part of the address was devoted to illustrating the importance of country-context by narrating the Indian experience. It provides an exhaustive list of the challenges faced and the means by which they were being addressed within the overall framework of the globalisation of monetary policy. In view of the complexities of and pressures on monetary policy, there was a specific mention of the judgements involved at different stages, calling for both knowledge and humility.

At the time of this presentation, there were three views put forward by influential sections with regard to the conduct of monetary policy in India. The first view stated that India has been globalised to the extent that it would be sensible for our policy to follow the systemically important economies in the world, in particular the US, in both style and substance. They pleaded recognition of the lack of autonomy of the monetary policy in India. The second view was that India is unique and its economy not sufficiently globalised, and hence an autonomous monetary policy should be followed, which should be squarely accountable for enabling growth and price stability. There was a third view, which took a more difficult and nuanced approach to the issue. This view desired the rapid opening up of the financial sector and the accelerated liberalisation of the regulatory framework. At the same time, they wished to continue with the heavy dependence on fiscal deficits, an administered interest rate regime, some amount of directed lending and significant interventions in several forms in financial markets. The objective of this presentation at the BIS meeting was to explain the constraints imposed simultaneously by the domestic public policy framework and the increasing global integration of the Indian economy. In practice, the RBI took the view that while domestic factors dominated the crafting of its policies, increasingly global factors had to be given importance as well, and the relative weights accorded to the two would depend on the evolving circumstances and the context.

In this regard, some broad illustrations of the dilemmas faced by the monetary policy during this period may be relevant. First, the public policy with regard to capital flows was generally in agreement in principle, with the RBI managing them effectively and containing external commercial borrowings. However, significantly, excessive capital inflows did take place during the period on several accounts, including external commercial borrowings, which are subject to controls. Second, there have been occasions when credit to some sectors were encouraged by the government in view of the developmental compulsions, although there has been substantial agreement on the overall need to avoid excesses in these sectors. Consequently, monetary and prudential policies and developmental priorities did not always converge. Third, some monetary measures like increasing the CRR and, in particular, the non-payment of interest on the deposits of banks held with the RBI were viewed with considerable discomfort in some circles, though it was made clear that the increases in reserve requirement were temporary, and that the medium-term objective was to bring it down. In fact, at one stage the RBI was compelled to compensate the commercial banks retrospectively with the interest on balances held with the RBI as per the directives under the CRR prescriptions. Fourth, legislative changes were brought about by an ordinance to facilitate a reduction in the statutory liquidatory ratio (SLR), signalling the availability of sufficient liquidity to financial markets while the Reserve Bank was tightening monetary policy. Fifth, there have been occasions when conflicting objectives—that of allowing flexibility in exchange rates and containing volatility—were signalled to markets in a way that was different from what the RBI was trying to communicate. These factors added to the complexities and dilemmas of the conduct of monetary policy, and the comment in the concluding part about the importance of blending the desirable with the feasible has to be viewed in the context of such realities.

The speech titled 'Monetary and Regulatory Policies: How to Get the Balance with Markets Right' was presented as the remarks of one of the panelists at the Annual General Meeting of the BIS on 29 June 2008. It was interesting that in this annual gathering of governors of central banks, there was an implicit recognition that the balance between the monetary and regulatory policies existing at the time was perhaps not entirely right. The subject chosen, therefore, displays the discomfort of central bankers at that point in time with regard to the balance between regulatory and monetary authorities vis-à-vis financial markets. There was widespread interest among central bankers in the unique way in which the Indian central bank attempted to manage the balance, viz., counter-cyclical in its approach to monetary and prudential policies and comprehensive in the application of regulatory policies. The remarks in the presentation explained that one cannot be judgemental about the balance across countries, but that one should assess the balance in a country-specific context. Of particular interest are statements where a distinction was made between addressing frictional issues as distinct from the underlying issues of levels of liquidity, and further, that exceptional or flexible arrangements were needed when out-of-the ordinary situations arise.

Some of the approaches of the RBI which were considered unorthodox in the past have been evaluated more objectively since the eruption of the global financial crisis in 2007–8. First, there is now greater agreement on the efficacy of taking account of bubbles in asset prices. Second, counter-cyclicality in the conduct of policy is better appreciated. Third, the use of prudential measures in conjunction with monetary policy is being commended. Fourth, there are serious reservations about the efficacy of a model of a single instrument and single objective of monetary policy, in contrast to a flexible model of multiple indicators, objectives and instruments adopted in India. Fifth, the focus on liquidity management—frictional, systemic and structural—is now considered essential to policy. Finally, in practice, several EMEs did take recourse to some form of managing what has been described as the impossible trinity.

It may be noted that the policy environment governing administered interest rates, the importance of ensuring the smooth conduct of large borrowings by the government, large exposure of banks to government securities, the dominating presence of public-sector banks in a bank-dominated economy and the statutory arrangements for governance in the RBI make it virtually impossible for the central bank to be effective unless it is in broad harmony with the government. Hence, intense consultations are always necessary, and almost all decisions relating to monetary policy are taken with the explicit or implicit consent of the government under all circumstances, with a degree of tolerance vis-à-vis the exercise of independence by the RBI. The RBI is in turn obliged to convince the government of the appropriateness of the measures contemplated. No doubt there have been differences in the weights to be accorded to the different considerations governing monetary policy, which are sometimes out in the open, but the RBI exercises its independence only within the space defined by the government. Against this background, the government's support to the exercise of some operational autonomy by the RBI during this period needs to be commended.

It may also be useful to recognise that the areas of difference in emphasis between the RBI and the government have been along predictable lines, consistent with theory and global practices. The weight to enabling growth is generally higher, and the early signs of over-heating are often ignored by governments while the manifestation of inflationary pressures results in calls for immediate stringent monetary actions, notwithstanding the importance of lagged effects. Similarly, large inflows of capital are welcomed by governments and some appreciation in exchange rate favoured due to the positive effects on corporate balance sheets, till the adverse impact of appreciation on the export sector becomes apparent. The financial markets, especially equity markets and financial institutions, have had significant roles in public policy in recent years, relative to participants in the real sector. For purposes of smoothening the effects of externally induced shocks, governments tended to rely on monetary policy initiatives, if it were convenient and feasible. India has not been immune to these dynamics between governments and central banks common to other countries, but it is undeniable that India is unique, in that, the few differences that prevailed during this period were often in the nature of creative tensions, with a notable beneficial impact on the economy.

ORGANISATION AND COMMUNICATION OF POLICIES OF RBI

The speech 'Central Bank Communications: Some Random Thoughts' was presented at the regional seminar on central bank communications sponsored by the International Monetary Fund (IMF), and held in Mumbai on 23 January 2006. It was addressed to the representatives of the central banks of Asian countries, but was also meant to respond to the market expectations of the RBI's communication strategies. There was a feeling among financial market participants that the RBI, in its policies, was resorting to surprise elements, and that the Bank should follow the example of other central banks, in particular the US, and accordingly provide financial markets with forward guidance. An attempt was therefore made to explain the approach of the RBI. First, the importance of communications should be viewed in the context of the responsibilities of central banks to maintain financial stability, which includes, but goes beyond, the conduct of monetary policy. Second, serious discomfort with forward guidance, resulting in the under-pricing of risks by the private sector, had to be flagged. In fact, it was mentioned that the so-called credibility bonus earned by the effective communication policy may be partly responsible for the upward movement of housing and equity prices becoming a global phenomenon. Third, the challenges for communication policy were more complex in EMEs, since they also have to respond to the policies enunciated by advanced economies like the US. Fourth, the central banks with their multiple functions had problems different from those banks with a single mandate and the exclusive function of dealing with the monetary policy. Finally, the communication of the central bank in influencing public policies is also important.

The speech 'What RBI means to the Common Person' is a translation (from Telugu) of a speech delivered in a village on 18 February 2007. This was part of the efforts made by the RBI to reach out to the common person. The RBI had set up websites in several languages. The purpose of the presentation was not only to inform people about the functioning of the RBI, but also to emphasise the criticality of coordination between state governments and the RBI while the latter performed its developmental function. The initiatives in coordination with state governments were many, and included a review of the functioning of the State Level Bankers' Committee, matters relating to debt management, banking and fiscal consolidation.

The presentation on the 'Organisation and Functioning of the RBI' was devoted to a description of governance arrangements, in particular the relationship with the government, and was delivered as a speech to the regional unit of the Indian Institute of Public Administration on 31 March 2008. There was a view taken in some circles that the RBI was governor-centric, and hence not consistent with the acceptable standards of governance. Another view stated that the RBI was unable to exercise sufficient independence from the government, in particular the Ministry of Finance, even though such autonomy was desirable. There were some doubts in select quarters, especially in the financial markets, about the level of professional skills in the RBI, although the RBI's credibility where the public at large was concerned was high. More importantly, the presentation explains the RBI's approach in bringing about changes in the domestic economy while responding to changes in the global economy, and simultaneously reorienting itself to manage the consequent emerging demands on its skills.

Apart from being informative, the presentation referred to the importance of coordination between the government and the RBI—which does not necessarily mean complete agreement—and that, in some cases, the RBI accepts responsibility for its decisions, even if those decisions had been taken in deference to the wishes of the government.

It is necessary to supplement the presentation with some examples of the complexities in the interface between the government and the RBI. The processes through which autonomy in operations was exercised and harmonisation in policies achieved by the RBI have been described earlier. The third and more crucial aspect of the relationship relates to the close coordination needed to bring about structural and systemic changes in the economy. One example relates to the impressive list of legislative amendments brought about in the RBI's areas of jurisdiction, payments systems, credit information companies, managing government securities at the Central and state levels, public-sector banking and securitisation, and all of these could be achieved through close consultation and coordination with the government. In fact, the government responded favourably to some revision of the RBI's original proposals with regard to some of these legislations.

The comment in the presentation about the RBI taking responsibility even if decisions had been taken in deference to the government's wishes is relevant both for the conduct of monetary policy and select actions on the regulatory front. Some examples would be in order. The RBI articulated a need for careful consideration of the monetary policy in response to high inflation, as explained in detail in the Governor's remarks on inflation in Pune on 23 June 2008. However, the RBI announced monetary measures on 24 June 2008. Both statements explained in detail the dilemmas and time-dimensions involved, and indicated the complexities in the conduct of monetary policy and communications with the financial markets. These statements illustrate that once expectations had been built in financial markets around the government's preferences, which is what happened vis-à-vis the events that led to the statements made above, the RBI had to fulfil those expectations as far as possible to avoid giving an impression of serious differences.

The speech 'The Virtues and Vices of Talking about Monetary Policy: Some Comments' was presented at a conference organised by the BIS on 26 June 2008 as part of an annual series, attended by eminent academics, including some nobel laureates and select central bankers. The Indian perspectives on communication policies, being somewhat unique, were presented in a candid fashion. The presentation included select issues relevant to EMEs, which faced greater complexities in communication. Some issues for debate in the context of the search for optimal communication policies of central banks were listed, and these seem most relevant to the global financial crisis of 2007–8. The concluding sentence on the issue refers to a potentially disturbing trend, whereby central banks may be seen to be focusing more on accountability to financial markets, by design or by necessity, rather than, say, to the government or the real sector or the public at large.

MANAGING CAPITAL ACCOUNT LIBERALISATION

The speech 'Foreign Exchange Reserves: New Realities and Options' was delivered at the annual meetings of the IMF and World Bank in Singapore on 18 September 2006. At that time, there was considerable concern with regard to the high level of forex reserves held mainly by the Asian countries, and it was felt that fiscal and other costs were very high. Both issues—that of the comfort level of reserves and of obtaining adequate reserves— became matters of debate. On the assumption that there were excess forex reserves which should be put to better use, several innovative suggestions were put forward. India also witnessed the beginnings of such a debate, and among the options suggested were encouraging outflows, utilising forex reserves for domestic currency expenditures in infrastructure and investing forex reserves in higher yielding instruments. The objective of the speech was to briefly review the situation and point out the acute limitations in taking such a simplistic view of forex reserves comfort or the use of such reserves. The importance of taking a balance sheet approach for each country, encompassing all external assets and liabilities of both the private and the public sector of a country, was particularly emphasised. The presentation provided a comprehensive analytical view of all the issues involved.

In retrospect, it has been noticed that the level of reserves has increased further in several countries. The downside of high reserves has not been as serious as had been feared by national authorities. The recent crisis and the state of the global financial architecture had added comfort to those with significant forex resources. In fact, countries with comfortable reserves have not seen the capital outflow from residents that had been observed in the previous crisis, although there might be other explanations for this. In particular, none of the innovative ideas have been actually adopted and implemented. Some countries have tried to augment returns by investing in riskier assets, and most of them seem to have paid a price for doing so, a price heavy for those who took recourse to sovereign wealth funds (SWFs). More recently, significant developments, such as the bilateral swap arrangements by the Federal Reserve in the US with several central banks and augmenting swap arrangements in Asia, seem to signify the value of the forex reserves of central banks in a world that is devoid of an appropriate global financial architecture to prevent or manage crises in currency markets.

The speech 'Management of the Capital Account in India: Some Perspectives' was delivered as the inaugural address at the Annual Conference of the Indian Econometric Society on 3 January 2008. The purpose of the presentation was to recognise the increasing pressures on monetary management in several EMEs in view of the strong capital inflows as well as the variety of measures being undertaken to manage capital flows. The government was also aware of some international experiences. There was, however, an influential viewpoint that fuller capital convertibility at a rapid pace and permitting appreciation of the exchange rate would be appropriate responses to the emerging issues. The thrust of the presentation was that mainstream academic thinking was changing in favour of active management of the capital account. While admitting that there were several dilemmas, trade-offs and judgements in the process of managing capital account, there was a detailed justification for adopting a pragmatic approach. A significant observation was that the RBI was equipped to manage a change in the direction of flows, hinting subtly at possible large capital outflows from India; however, this warning was largely ignored by market participants.

The unique features of the management of capital account in India may be recalled. First, there was an assumption that the country could not afford large current account deficits. Thus, the impression that India needed over the medium term US$ 400 billion of foreign investment for meeting infrastructure alone is untenable, since that implies a current account deficit rising to around 8 per cent of GDP. There was merit in directing the economy towards a manageable current account deficit and a reasonable level of capital flows consistent with macro-stability, the state of the financial markets, and the assurance from global financial architecture. Second, measures in terms of the reasonableness of amounts, and repatriation as well as surrender requirements of receipts on current account were required to ensure that capital transactions do not take place in the guise of current account. Third, both price-based and quantity-based measures were adopted to influence capital flows. Fourth, debt-flows, especially non-trade related short-term debt flows, were subjected to greater scrutiny and approval. Fifth, there was more rapid liberalisation of capital account transactions for households and corporates, but restrictions were in force with respect to the foreign currency exposures of financial intermediaries. The latter were also treated as part of prudential measures.

There were two implications of the above approach, namely that capital account management had been more effective in India than was assumed by many global analysts of capital controls; and that financial institutions as well as markets were the most vociferous in their impatience with these measures. In retrospect, active dialogues between the RBI and the government helped to moderate pressures to open the economy to large capital inflows, which were already in excess of the absorption capacity of the economy till the impact of the global financial crisis in 2008–9. Consequently, the movements in currency markets in India were considerably less volatile than, say, those in equity markets, although both markets were significantly influenced by portfolio flows in the short term.

The speech 'Government-owned Investment Vehicles and Capital Flows: An Indian Perspective' was delivered at an international round table on the subject in the US on 14 April 2008. The context was to respond to two important developments. First, the advanced economies were uncomfortable with the large-scale investments being made by some countries through SWFs. There was an attempt to monitor and, if possible, regulate the investments of such SWFs by the host countries. There was also pressure for greater accountability in the home countries. A voluntary code of conduct was also considered.

Second, there was a demand within India for a SWF in view of the comfortable level of reserves. The purpose of the speech was to suggest that a hasty view should not be taken with regard to regulating the inflow of investments of the SWFs of other countries. Similarly, caution was indicated with regard to the creation of SWFs, and in any case the main message was that forex reserves would be managed by the RBI as in the past; however, if a SWF was created, it should be entirely outside the RBI's balance sheet. In this regard, there was a reference to special arrangements vis-à-vis the use of forex reserves by India Infrastructure Finance Corporation Limited, whereby, under the government's directions, a part of the reserves was made available for Special Purpose Vehicle (SPV). A mention was also made that this SPV arrangement has a peculiar situation, whereby India is both the home country and the host country for a facility similar to a SWF.

GLOBAL FINANCIAL IMBALANCES AND CRISIS

The speech 'Implications of Global Financial Imbalances for EMEs', delivered on 4 November 2005, was presented at the round table discussion at an international symposium in Paris. The context was the serious concerns with regard to the growing global imbalances, and its possible impact on EMEs. The expectation at that point in time was that global imbalances would have to be corrected, but that the process may not be very smooth and may affect the EMEs adversely. The purpose of the presentation was to explain that different EMEs have different economic, financial and external-sector characteristics, and hence the impact would be different. It also provided a framework for analysing the impact in terms of the balance sheets of the government, the RBI, corporate entities, the banking sector and the real sector. It explained the monetary and prudential measures taken together to contain and manage downside risks in the event of a disruptive correction of imbalances. The concluding part emphasised the need for EMEs to strengthen their resilience through both sound macro-economic management and the adoption of appropriate prudential measures. It also pleaded, as early as in 2005, for coordinated efforts to cushion EMEs better against the risks of financial globalisation.

The growing global imbalances and possible risks to financial stability were articulated in detail in the policy statements of the RBI in a timely manner. As examples, two extracts from select policy statements are given here:

... However, world financial markets are known to be characterised by multiple equilibria where good state of markets could change into a bad state within a very short period. Abundant global liquidity and low short term interest rates over the past few years have also contributed to asset price rise and leveraging of corporate and household balance sheets in several parts of the world, covering both the emerging and the matured markets. Furthermore, considering that economic expansion may be at a very advanced stage of business cycle in some systemically important matured markets, it may be difficult to sustain the current high levels of corporate earnings. There is an even greater need now to keep a vigil on potential bubbles in the asset markets since real estate market valuations have, in the recent past, been supported by low-interest consumer debt. (Annual policy statement for 2005–6, RBI, 25 April 2005, paragraph 44)

Risks to global growth also emanate from the persisting macroeconomic imbalances and the resulting abundance of global liquidity which carries the potential of fuelling asset bubbles, excessive leveraging in financial markets and threats to global financial stability. The current configuration of good growth, low inflation, abundant liquidity, flat yield curves, lowering of credit risk premia and ever-expanding search for yields has also benefited many Emerging Market Economies which have strengthened their macro-fundamentals in an environment of low inflation, improved fiscal positions and balance of payments and substantial accumulation of foreign exchange reserves. On the downside, the same combination of factors has allowed the macro imbalances to widen and has resulted in a build-up of large volumes of debt, especially by the household sector. This has amplified the potential for sudden shifts in portfolios, investor preferences and currency alignments. The addition to global saving as a result of the increase in surpluses of oil exporters has enabled persistence of under-pricing of risks and a diffusion of risks across sectors. These factors have imparted an apparent disequilibrium that might require a larger adjustment at a later stage. In the light of these developments, available evidence indicates that global imbalances have not really unwound but on the contrary, have perhaps worsened and amplified the surrounding uncertainties and risks. (Mid-Term Review of Annual Policy Statements, RBI, 25 October 2005, paragraph 37)

The speech 'Global Imbalances: An Indian Perspective' was delivered as an address in the US on 1 May 2006. This presentation was also in response to the growing concern with imbalances, and their possible implications for emerging economies like India. The presentation provided unexceptional global perspectives on global imbalances in a summary fashion. The purpose, however, was to present India's perspectives and explain that India did not contribute to the global imbalances, but instead supported global stability. There were several observations which, in retrospect, appear very relevant in the context of the ongoing global financial crisis that emerged subsequent to this presentation. First, was there a dissonance between the perception of financial markets and that of policymakers with regard to global imbalances? The policymakers appeared to emit some signals of concern, but the response of financial markets was often out of alignment with those signals. Second, was there an advantage in assessing non-quantifiable factors to explain the persistence of what had been stated as a stable disequilibrium to describe the current status of the global economy? For example, the demand for the US dollar in terms of the confidence financial markets had in it as a lasting safe haven could be a factor, although the issue was whether it would be valid under all circumstances. The perception of continuing productivity gains in the US due to its proven flexibilities could be another.

The speech 'Globalisation, Money and Finance: Uncertainties and Dilemmas' was delivered on 28 September 2006 as valedictory address to a joint conference of industry and bank associations of India. The presentation was made in the context of widespread pressures to liberalise the financial sector, coupled with eagerness to spread financial innovations in India. Some of the observations made in 2006 are worth recalling in the context of the subsequent global financial crisis. First, public policy played an important role in managing the costs and benefits of globalisation. Second, in the context of globalised financial markets, monetary policy faced dilemmas in distinguishing news from noise. Third, financial stability considerations might require the use of both monetary and prudential measures. Fourth, there was an increasing tendency on the part of hedge funds to consolidate the clearing and settlement of their trades at a single firm called the prime broker. The prime brokerage posed some unique challenges for the management of counter-party and operational risks. Further concerns about hedge fund opacity and the possible liquidity risk have motivated a range of proposals for regulatory authorities to create and maintain a database of hedge fund positions. Fifth, there were uncertainties associated with the settling of trades in newer types of over-the-counter derivatives, particularly credit derivatives. Sixth, in view of the wide dispersion of risk, it was necessary to evolve mechanisms to ascertain the size and structure of risk components, the scale and direction of risk transfers and, therefore, the distribution of risk within the economy. Seventh, public policy ought to play a crucial role in ensuring a balanced reform in both the real and the financial sector. Eighth, was price stability an adequate goal for central banks? Finally, the presentation added, 'In the face of the consequent build-up of liquidity, elevated asset prices and soaring consumer indebtedness, is there a dark side to the future?'

The Epilogue to the book explores these in the context of the turbulence in the global economy in 2008–9, and its consequences for the Indian economy.

NOTES

1. There is no single acceptable definition of EMEs, although they are commonly referred to as economies with high growth prospects. The IMF, in its latest Global Financial Stability Report, has categorised the following countries as EMEs: Latin America—Argentina, Brazil, Chile, Colombia, Mexico, Peru, Venezuela; Asia—China, India, South Korea, Indonesia, Malaysia, Pakistan, the Philippines, Taiwan, Province of China and Thailand; Europe, Middle East and Africa—Czech Republic, Egypt, Hungary, Israel, Jordon, Morocco, Poland, Russia, South Africa and Turkey.

Indian Economy
Review and Prospects

1

India and the Global Economy*

In the first part of this chapter, as a background, there is a brief account of global economic integration and the role of public policy. This is followed by a review of India's policies with regard to the external sector. The third section mentions what appear to be the current challenges for the global economy as India integrates with it. The fourth section is in the nature of random thoughts on the public policy challenges facing India in its attempt to manage the integration smoothly. The fifth section elaborates on several issues with regard to financial integration, and includes the special characteristics of financial integration and public policy in this context, including that related to banks.

GLOBAL ECONOMIC INTEGRATION

The concept of globalisation, in the sense in which it is used now, can be traced to the phenomenon of nation-states. In the distant past, there were just human communities. For much of human history, most people remained confined to their communities, villages or local areas. With developments in communication and economic activity, it became progressively easier to move from the local to the regional, and then from the regional to the national

*Previously presented as address at the Lal Bahadur Shastri National Academy of Administration, Mussoorie, Uttaranchal, India, 17 July 2004.

level and finally across nations. Perhaps globalisation is a process that has been, in some sense, constrained by the authority of the nation-states, particularly in the twentieth century. It may be useful to touch upon the role of the public policy of nation-states in the context of globalisation. After the emergence of nation-states, each nation-state perceived that it was in its collective self-interest to promote or restrict involvement with citizens of other nation-states. While developments in technology enabled and accelerated the movements of goods, people and services, the policies of many nations tended to impose restrictions. A nation-state is presumed to restrict its citizens' involvement with other nation-states with only their collective self-interest in mind. It is, however, not easy to define what is in the collective self-interest of all its citizens or whether it is in the interest of only a few at the expense of others. In the context of public policy relating to globalisation, a critical issue is the trade-off between individual freedom and collective self-interest, and also whether the burden of proof lies with the individual or with the national authorities. It is difficult to resolve these issues, but they must be appreciated in the context of public policy.

At a conceptual level, a distinction can be made between technology-enabled (or induced) globalisation and public policy-induced restrictions or easing of restrictions. Globalisation has several dimensions, arising out of what may be called enhanced connectivity among people across national borders. Such enhanced connectivity is determined by three fundamental factors, viz., technology, individual taste and public policy. Cross-border integration can have several aspects: cultural, social, political and economic. For the purposes of this chapter, however, only economic integration is considered. Broadly speaking, economic integration occurs through three channels, viz., movement of people, of goods and of finance or capital.

First, with regard to the movement of people, the most notable achievement of recent globalisation is the freedom granted to many, if not all, from the tyranny of being restricted to a place and being denied the opportunity to move and connect freely. Second, with regard to trade in or movement of goods across national boundaries, two types of barriers are generally described, viz., natural barriers and artificial barriers. Of late, while multilateral trade agreements are encouraging reduction in such artificial barriers, developments in technology are also making it difficult for national authorities to enforce artificial barriers. The pace and nature of globalisation will naturally depend on the combined effect of technology and public policy, both at the national and international levels. The third dimension relates to capital movements, for which, too, the interplay between technology and public policy becomes relevant. There have been, however, some special characteristics of capital flows in recent years, led mainly by revolutionary changes in telecom and computing capabilities. These have highlighted the phenomenon of what is described as 'contagion', which implies the risk of a country being affected by developments totally outside of its policy ambit, although the domestic policy may, to some extent, influence the degree of its vulnerability to the contagion. In any case, cross-border flows of capital have wider macroeconomic implications, particularly in terms of the exchange rate, which directly affects the costs involved in the movement of people as well as goods and services, and also in terms of the conduct of monetary policy and the efficiency as well as stability of the financial system. Capital flows, by definition, generate further liabilities or assets, and could involve inter-generational equity issues. In this regard, it is useful to distinguish the extent of globalisation with respect to three different types of economic entities, viz., individuals or households, corporate entities and financial intermediaries. It has been noticed that financial intermediaries impinge on the contagion effects impacting financial stability in developing countries. The experience of Asia and Latin America has shown that the external liabilities of the private sector tend to devolve on national governments in the event of crises, and hence there is a role for public policy in trying to prevent crises and creating capacities to meet crises, if and when they arise.

In managing the process of economic integration that is driven by several forces, developing countries face challenges from a world order that is particularly burdensome to them. Yet, it is necessary for public policy to manage the process with a view to maximising benefits for its citizens while minimising the risks; however, the path of optimal integration is highly country-specific and contextual. On balance, there appears to be a greater advantage in achieving a well-managed and appropriate integration into the global process, which would imply more effective—but not necessarily intrusive or extensive—interventions by governments. In fact, while there are some infirmities in government interventions, markets do experience failures, and cannot exist without some externally imposed rules and public-policy prescriptions. As the poor, the vulnerable and the underprivileged continue to be the responsibility of national governments, national public policy continues to be relevant—particularly as it relates to global economic integration.

EXTERNAL SECTOR POLICIES: A REVIEW

It will be useful to outline the major developments in external-sector policies since independence to enable an appreciation of current and future challenges. During the first three decades of planned development, successive plans emphasised the need for financing development largely from resources mobilised domestically. First, Indian planners shared the export pessimism then pervading the developing world. Second, the existence of a large domestic market provided the scope for internalising forward and backward linkages. Third, development strategy hinged upon a programme of industrialisation to break through the vicious circle of backwardness. Fourth, the availability of foreign exchange was a major constraint, especially after the pound sterling balances were run down during the 1950s and 1960s. Export pessimism permeated the policy stance throughout the early decades of our planning. Accordingly, exports were regarded as residual, a vent-for-surplus on those occasions when such surpluses were available. Import substitution was the principal instrument of trade policy, and was regarded in the early years as not only the correct strategy, but also as inevitable in a continental economy like India.

It may be of interest to note that the objective of self-reliance did not find explicit commitment in the Second and Third Five-Year Plans, which were mainly concerned with generating the foreign exchange resources required for the plans. The third plan reflected the first signs of rethinking in policy strategy by dedicating itself to self-sustaining growth, which required domestic savings to progressively meet the demand of investment and for the balance of payments gap to be bridged over. The fourth plan contained an articulated approach to achieving self-reliance. While an export growth of 7 per cent per annum was considered an essential element of the strategy, it was envisaged that dependence on foreign aid would be halved during the course of the fourth plan (1969–74). It was in the fifth plan (1974–9) that self-reliance was recognised as an explicit objective. The sixth plan (1980–5) laid emphasis on strengthening the impulses of modernisation to achieve both economic and technological self-reliance. The seventh plan (1985–90) noted the conditions under which the concept of self-reliance had been defined earlier, particularly in the preceding plan. It conceptualised self-reliance not only in terms of reduced dependence on aid, but also in terms of building up domestic capabilities and reducing import dependence in strategic materials. The concept also encompassed the achievement of technological competence through liberal imports of technology. The Gulf Crisis and its impact on India provided several lessons, one of which was that a relatively closed economy does not provide immunity from a foreign exchange crisis. Incidentally, India excelled at managing the crisis, and emerged as one of the very few countries in the world, amongst both the developed and the developing, to have never substantially defaulted on its external obligations.

In the aftermath of the Gulf Crisis, policy actions were initiated as part of the overall macroeconomic management, well-coordinated to simultaneously achieve stabilisation and structural change. External-sector policies designed to progressively open up the Indian economy formed an integral part of the strategy for structural reforms. In this context, the *Report of the High Level Committee on Balance of Payments* (Dr Rangarajan Committee, 1993) recommended improvement in exports, related to both merchandise and invisibles; modulation of import demand on the basis of the availability of current receipts to ensure a level of current account deficit consistent with normal capital flows; enhancement of non-debt creating flows to limit the debt service burden; adoption of a market-determined exchange rate; building up the foreign exchange reserves to avoid liquidity crises and elimination of the dependence on short-term debt. It is evident that the external-sector policies of the 1990s, based on the report, paid rich dividends in terms of growth and resilience to a series of external and domestic shocks.

In the new millennium, however, there has been a dramatic shift in our approach to external-sector management, in tune with the changing circumstances. First, with the emergence of marginal current account surplus, it appears that the sustainability of current account deficit may not be a problem, although the deficit on trade account persists and has been increasing. Second, the main contributors to the positive outcome in current account are workers' remittances and export of software, both being a result of the process of global integration. Third, the exchange rate regime as well as external debt management has served us well, especially the avoidance of sovereign debt through commercial borrowings. The policy regime helped us withstand several global crises while maintaining a respectable growth. Fourth, the management of capital account, rather than the current account, has acquired primary focus. Fifth, a judicious integration with the global trade regime has imparted some competitive efficiency and confidence to the domestic industry, and perhaps even to commercial agriculture, though to a limited extent. Finally, it has become evident that the management of the external sector is closely linked to the domestic sector, and the major thrust of public policy now has to be managing integration. The integration of the Indian economy with the global economy and policies aimed thereat has to address domestic and external sectors in a holistic and harmonious way. In brief, we have moved from managing the external sector to implementing an optimal integration of the domestic and external sectors, and the global economy.

ADJUSTMENTS BY THE GLOBAL ECONOMY

The debate in India has customarily been on the contours of public policy in the context of increasing global economic integration. More recently, however, a debate in the rest of the world has become evident on the challenges likely to be faced by the global economy on account of the progressively increasing global integration of the Indian economy. The emphasis is of course on successful integration, which will no doubt depend on the appropriateness of our public policies and the private-sector responses. Hence, there is a need for an ongoing appreciation of the way the global economy is responding to the challenges of our integration, while we move forward with our own agenda of securing an optimal integration.

Currently, the major issue in the global economy appears to be the significant build-up of current account imbalances. The current account deficit of the US has been rising and is around 5 per cent of the GDP, while current account surpluses have been noticed in Asia and to some extent in Latin America and Russia. The external financing of the US deficit moved away from equity in the late 1990s to debt in recent years, possibly reflecting a perception of productivity growth in the former period and fiscal stress in the latter. Official reserves played a greater role than in the past in financing the US current account deficit in recent years. There is a perception that the US dollar is still relatively overvalued, warranting a correction. Simultaneously, the unique combination of easy monetary policy and lax fiscal policy in major industrialised countries is set to end, and financial markets are already in a state of uncertainty. Even assuming that the transition of monetary policies to a more neutral stance is managed well and that trade gets to be more evenly balanced, associated with some corrections in the US, the simultaneous emergence of China and India with significant competitive strengths in trade in goods as well as services will have to be accommodated by the global economy. Thus, the issue for the immediate future is that both correcting current global imbalances and integrating the two Asian giants may have to take place simultaneously in the global economy.

It is evident that China and India will have to place high priority on generating employment, and are poised for substantial increases in productivity. Consequently, the global economy will have to consider the implications of these developments on prices, exchange rates, wages and structures of employment in industrialised countries. Over the medium term, it is felt that outsourcing will grow in geometric progression, particularly to India, and may also cover high-end research and development. In manufacturing, China has emerged as a leader, and India is poised to join the race. Though agriculture is heavily subsidised in major industrialised countries, such subsidisation could be difficult to sustain from a fiscal point of view, since many of the countries concerned are poised to meet the mounting pension liabilities, not to mention the burgeoning healthcare costs involved in maintaining the changing demographics. One sector where industrialised economies continue to show considerable strength and dominance is the financial sector, which can be partly attributed to the confidence factor in financial markets that favours industrialised economies and traditional international financial centres. It is essential that we carefully monitor the developments in both real and financial sectors and modulate our policies in tandem with global developments so that global integration continues to be a positive sum game for all the countries.

RANDOM THOUGHTS ON OUR POLICIES

As mentioned, global economic integration is technology-induced and, simultaneously, policy-constrained or policy-restrained—in other words, policy-managed. While the economic integration of India with the global economy will continue to take place, a successful integration, with due regard to the interests of a vast majority, particularly the poor in our country, would be possible only through sound public policies that will need to be evolved and redesigned from time to time. The key phrases here are 'successful economic integration' and 'sound public policies'—both involving processes spread over time as well as interaction with global economies. If one were to make an informed guess at the prospects of such a successful integration of India, it may be said that upside and downside risks are evenly balanced, with a short-term bias towards upside risks—which would give us some time to work on mitigating the downside risks in the medium term. Indeed, the well-publicised BRIC report reflects considerable confidence in the future of the Indian economy, though it is necessary to read the fine print to realise that while India will be a superpower in 2050, 'if development proceeds successfully', the per capita income would still not be at a high-end. What needs to be recognised is that the report leans on the demographic strength that India derives from its huge workforce. In order to harness the demographic advantages, the quality of the labour force (in terms of the relevant skills that need to be sustained, reoriented and upgraded in a globally competitive era) and the physical health of the workforce become crucial. Education and health therefore provide the link between the supply and demand for labour through increases in productivity. Against this background, here are some random thoughts on the priorities for public policy to ensure the successful economic integration of India with the global economy.

First, pragmatic policies in the external sector, particularly in the management of the capital account and exchange rate, have served us well by contributing to growth, resilience to shocks and an overall stability. There is merit in continuing with a pragmatic, cautious and gradual approach in this regard, subject to improvements in the fiscal arena and the progress in strengthening the domestic financial sector.

Second, the management of the financial sector has been oriented towards gradual rebalancing between efficiency and stability, and the changing shares of public and private ownership. Enhanced competition among diverse players, including those from branches of foreign banks, has been encouraged. Considerable improvements have taken place in prudential governance, as well as in moving away from administrative measures to market-orientation. Improvements in efficiency and stability are palpable, and there is merit in continuing with such rebalancing while refocusing on consolidation, governance and moving towards Basel II—albeit gradually, as in the past.

Third, on the fiscal front, the ratio of public debt to GDP is high in our country, but the structure of public debt displays characteristics that make us less vulnerable than other countries with similar debt magnitudes. There is an advantage in continuing the progress in public-debt management, keeping structural aspects in view. As we proceed with fiscal consolidation, clearly focused on in the Union Budget 2004–5, there will be greater flexibility in the conduct of monetary policy and greater confidence in proceeding with financial-sector reforms. Furthermore, an effective and qualitative fiscal adjustment would enhance the scope for a more successful integration with the global economy.

Fourth, in matters relating to trade, a significant liberalisation of external trade has taken place smoothly, imparting competitive efficiency to the domestic sector. The apprehensions that existed till a few years ago about the adverse impact of such trade liberalisation have abated, and business confidence in the country has improved. While the gradual approach with a commitment to a liberalised trade regime has enabled productivity increases— almost up to the global best standards in many sectors—there are signs of pick up in investment activity that could catalyse the needed demand for credit and create employment. There is one significant incongruity, however, which should be corrected sooner rather than later, viz., the continuing trade restrictions within the country, even as there has been progress in liberalising external trade. There is incontrovertible—though generalised—evidence showing that persisting trade restrictions in a country are not in the public interest, and hence, as many distinguished economists plead, most of the exceptions to Article 301 of the Constitution, permitted on 'public interest' grounds, perhaps need to be done away with. (Article 301 reads: 'subject to other provisions of this part, trade, commerce, and intercourse throughout the territory of India shall be free'.) This may warrant the repeal of several legislations that restrict trade domestically in the 'public interest'. To alleviate any adverse impact on vulnerable sections, a straightforward subsidy could be considered in favour of the poor. There is another well-recognised distortion, vestiges of which still continue, in the form of reservation for small-scale industries. With the liberalisation of external trade, it is anomalous to persist with such distortions, even on a reduced scale. Thus, there is still an unfinished agenda on trade reforms, especially with regard to domestic trade, and a policy commitment to removing such distortions in a defined short timeframe would be ideal.

Fifth, it is interesting to note that the two sectors where India is globally most competitive, namely software and pharmaceuticals, are not power intensive and do not require bulky transportation. The competitiveness of the manufacturing industry is admittedly a function of the availability of reliable power supply at a reasonable cost. The budget of 2004–5 has rightly emphasised the importance of power, airports and seaports (apart from tourism, which has significant employment potential), but there is a need for implementation at a significantly faster pace than we have ever witnessed in any sector so far.

Sixth, there is universal recognition of the need to improve both productivity and output in agriculture and related activities to meet the objectives of growth and employment. Yet, despite best efforts and the excellent results achieved in that direction, there will have to be a massive shift in the workforce from agriculture to non-agricultural avocations. While it is difficult to estimate at this stage, we should be prepared for a large-scale migration of the workforce to the tune of ten million per year, from rural to semi-urban and urban areas. The quality of urban infrastructure, even in metropolitan cities, is not conducive to globally competitive economic activity. The inevitable large-scale redeployment of the migrating workforce would, therefore, need institutional arrangements, be they in the public or the private sector, to impart skills and skill upgradation. In these two matters relating to the workforce, some supply-led approaches appear to be in order, rather than waiting for the demand to be generated.

Seventh, improvements in institutional infrastructure in matters relating to administrative, judicial and other systems of governance are admittedly important. Needless to say, if we fail to record the rapid progress in these critical areas, we will fail in everything, especially in the economic arena.

Eighth, the quantity and quality of water, education and healthcare infrastructure are far from adequate, and are not even at the minimum level consistent with a modern society. These fall under the ambit of the delivery of public services, and the Prime Minister has already accorded a high priority to this issue. Any tangible reform in this area would require action on several fronts, that is, legislative, executive and judicial, and at several levels, Centre, state and local.

Ninth, there are regional inequalities in growth, and several analysts have tried to find the causes and suggest remedies. Recognising that the next phase of reforms in most of the physical, social and institutional infrastructure, especially in the area of delivery of services, would fall within the realm of the states, one should hope that the demonstration effect of a few high-performing states will spur the others, in the medium term, to compete for better governance and economic performance.

Finally, enhanced investment activity, particularly in the infrastructure area, would necessitate higher domestic savings, especially in the public sector, coupled with efficient financial intermediation. In addition, foreign savings need to be attracted and absorbed, with a strong preference for foreign direct investment (FDI), in all sectors, although in some sectors like banking, a calibrated approach may be warranted. At the same time, our enterprises should be enabled to attain a strong global presence in all sectors. In brief, our global integration has to be a two-way process, encompassing the movement of people with some caveats, trade in a free and equitable manner and financial integration on a specially sequenced basis. Hence, it is necessary to elaborate on financial integration.

FINANCIAL INTEGRATION

From a policy perspective, there are three fundamental issues with regard to financial integration, namely, 'how does financial globalisation help growth?', 'how does it impact macro-volatility?' and 'how can developing countries harness the benefits of globalisation?' These three issues have been addressed comprehensively in an IMF Occasional Paper (2003), and the following extracts from the summary of the paper do provide some answers:

> There is some evidence of a 'threshold effect' in the relationship between financial globalization and economic growth. The beneficial effects of financial globalization are more likely to be detected when the developing countries have a certain amount of absorptive capacity.... International financial integration should, in principle, also help countries to reduce macroeconomic volatility. The available evidence suggests that developing countries have not fully attained this potential benefit.... A type of threshold effect appears here as well—reductions in volatility are observed only after countries have attained a particular level of financial integration.... The evidence presented in this paper suggests that financial integration should be approached cautiously, with good institutions and macroeconomic frameworks viewed as important. The review of the available evidence does not, however, provide a clear road map for the optimal pace and sequencing of integration. Such questions can best be addressed only in the context of country-specific circumstances and institutional feature (p. ix).

The guidance provided for policymakers is perhaps clear from the above. Unlike in the case of trade integration, where benefits to all countries are demonstrable, in the case of financial integration, a 'threshold' is important for a country to get the full benefits. A judgemental view needs to be taken on whether and when a country has reached the 'threshold', and financial integration should be approached cautiously keeping in mind the country-specific context and institutional features. Fortunately, we in India have been adhering to a cautious and calibrated approach in our reforms so far, and there is merit in adopting a 'road map approach', building on the strengths that we have already developed.

One of the major concerns of developing countries in proceeding with financial integration appears to be financial stability. Hence, the role of cross-border linkages in this regard should not be ignored. It would be useful to draw upon the Introduction in an IMF Working Paper (2004) on the subject, which identifies four major trends in the financial economy of the past decades and mentions the following:

> Although these trends reflect important advances in finance that have contributed substantively to economic efficiency, they evidently have implications for the nature of financial risks and vulnerabilities and the way these affect the real economy, as well as for the role of policymakers in promoting financial stability. For instance, risk management and diversification techniques have, in principle, bolstered the resilience of the financial system, but the expansion of cross-sector and cross-border linkages implies more scope for contagion.

It is also necessary to recognise that financial integration complicates the conduct of monetary management. The growing cross-border integration of financial markets enables massive movements of capital, which quickly arbitrage interest rate differentials across national boundaries. This is reinforced by the ever-widening impact of the information technology revolution. Real long-term interest rates in industrialised countries have been converging since the late 1980s. Financial integration has also brought with it shocks common to several countries, since the 'confidence channel' transmits financial crises across countries swiftly. In a world of generalised uncertainty, monetary policy in several countries is faced with a progressive loss of discretion. For developing countries in particular, considerations relating to maximising output and employment weigh equally upon monetary authorities as does maintaining the price stability. In considering the pace of financial integration, the implications of a concurrent loss of a degree of autonomy in the conduct of the monetary policy of a country and the country context should not be lost sight of. The analytics presented in the *Report of the Committee on Capital Account Convertibility* (Tarapore Committee, 1997) are very relevant in this regard. In particular, they relate to what has been described as 'preconditions', such as fiscal consolidation and strength of the financial sector, and meeting such preconditions facilitates the conduct of monetary policy in a more open capital account regime.

It is also useful to recognise a close link between the extent of capital account liberalisation and the presence of foreign financial enterprises in a country. The nature of the link is best articulated in the following extracts from a recent book by Martin Wolf (2004):

> It is impossible for such tiny markets to support competition among self-standing national players with realistic aspirations to world-class performance. (p. 285)
>
> For all these reasons, a symbiosis exists between both current and capital account liberalization and the contribution made by the presence of foreign financial enterprises in the economy. This is a second reason for aspiring to capital account liberalization. (p. 286)
>
> For all these reasons, therefore, the elimination of controls on capital movement is a desirable objective. But it is one that also carries substantial risks. The right answer is not to avoid liberalizing for ever, but to carry it through in a carefully thought out and disciplined manner. In that way, it may be possible to achieve the objectives of integration without the crises that have, so often punctuated movement in that direction. (p. 288)

Thus, one of the important considerations for encouraging the presence of foreign financial enterprises is to ensure adequate and healthy competition. The compulsion to expand foreign enterprises would thus depend upon the quality of competition already existing in a country. In any case, the consensus appears to be that the process of liberalisation in the financial sector has to be carefully calibrated and sequenced.

BANKS AND FINANCIAL INTEGRATION

The major risks in financial integration faced by emerging economies relate to financial stability. In this regard, while the criticality of banks is generally acknowledged, it is worth reiterating, in the words of Martin Wolf (2004):

> Banks are the epicentres of financial fragility. The central role of banks in generating the financial feast and famine of the past three decades, particularly in relation to emerging market finance, is entirely predictable. If we are to manage a financially integrated world better than we have done so far, banks must be more effectively caged in the countries at the core of the financial system and those at the periphery. (p. 298)
>
> The fads and fancies of foolish bankers in the core countries have lain behind most of the financial crises of the past three decades. When elephants stampede, they trample down everything in the way. That is what happened to Latin America in the 1970s and 1980s and then East Asia in the 1990s. For this reason, Dobson and Hubauer have rightly argued that making the world safer requires changes at both the core and the periphery. They argue that not only the behaviour of the banks but even that of hedge funds is directly related to the frailty of banking. (p. 299)

It would be inappropriate to conclude from the above that capital market integration should not take place. From a policy perspective, the concluding remarks of Martin Wolf (2004) are very pertinent, and the extract reads as follows: 'But, for a host of reasons, EMEs should ultimately plan to integrate into the global capital markets, with emphasis on the words "ultimately" and "plan"' (p. 304).

FOREIGN BANKS AND FINANCIAL INTEGRATION

It will be useful to narrate the pros and cons of licensing foreign banks in emerging economies by drawing liberally from two recent publications. The pros relate to (*a*) increasing and diversifying available funds; (*b*) enhancing banking competition and efficiency; (*c*) developing financial markets and market infrastructure; (*d*) helping with recapitalisation and wider diversification of banks and (*e*) reducing the sensitivity of the host country banking system to local business cycles and changing financial market conditions. The arguments against foreign banks' entry encompass (*a*) weakening infant domestic banks; (*b*) servicing only the 'best' customers and neglect of small and medium enterprises (SMEs); (*c*) likelihood of bringing in instability; (*d*) concerns that the majority of banking assets will become foreign-owned and, above all, (*e*) challenges to financial supervisors in the emerging markets.

The challenges to emerging market banking supervisors have now come to the forefront of the research agenda. Policy concerns in recent years, with an increasingly large proportion of banking assets accounted for by foreign banks, have been well documented in the report on the BRICs (2003) and the IMF Working Paper (2004). The issues relate to (*a*) the licensing policy for foreign banks; (*b*) monitoring the local establishments of large international banks; (*c*) the sheer variety and complexity of new financial products, including derivatives; (*d*) familiarisation with and understanding of when, and to what extent, the overseas parent banking organisations will support their cross-border operations in times of difficulties or crises; (*e*) managing the systemic risks associated with cross-border banking; (*f*) the complications arising from the organisational positioning of foreign banks that are not necessarily stand-alone institutions, but rather are part of a holding company group, and the complexity of financial institutions active in a number of jurisdictions and (*g*) the possibility of increased operational risks due to integrated operations of consolidated financial institutions. While narrating the complexities, the IMF paper makes a reference to the broadening of supervisory concerns: 'This is a particular concern in the cases where foreign commercial banks expand their operations rapidly in the area of non-bank financial services, such as insurance, portfolio management, and investment banking' (p. 20). Hence, in the regulation and supervision of foreign banks with cross-border operations, the regulators will have to take into account all these fundamental realities.

On the basis of anecdotal evidence and perceptions of supervisors in emerging countries, some practical concerns need to be considered. First, there are occasions when the policy imperatives of regulators and supervisors do not fully align with the strategic business goals of banking-sector players. In such instances of conflict, it is likely that the interest of domestic banks would be more closely aligned with policy objectives than that of the foreign banks. Second, there may be instances when the relationship between a supervisor and the supervised foreign bank become the subject matter of inter-governmental concerns, which often puts emerging economies in a disadvantageous position. Third, the intimate knowledge that a national supervisor possesses with respect to the domestic ownership of a domestic bank is normally not available with regard to all foreign investors in any bank—domestic or foreign—with a presence in the host country. Fourth, there are concerns about the affiliations between banks and commercial firms, in terms of conflicts of interest and misallocation of credit. Similar concerns arise regarding affiliations between non-banking financial companies and banks, as also between non-financial companies and banks (for example, see Jorde 2003). Fifth, there are several policy issues with regard to liquidity management that may arise in the course of wider foreign participation in the financial markets. Premature exposure of weak domestic banks to international competitors in domestic markets has the potential to weaken the stability of the financial system as a whole.

There has been a recent development which impacts the level playing field between foreign banks present in EMSs and the domestic banks. During the annual meetings of the BIS on 26 June 2004, a formal announcement was made regarding the publication of the revised framework for capital adequacy, known as Basle II, as approved by the Group of Ten (G-10) countries. Studies on the quantitative impact of Basle II seem to indicate that foreign banks operating in emerging economies would require less regulatory capital and, by virtue of their lower capital servicing costs, could finely price their products and services to the detriment of domestic banks. However, it is too early to assess the advantage, if any.

Policymakers in emerging countries are fully aware of both the benefits and the risks arising out of the presence of foreign banks, and indeed foreign capital in banks, which leads them to impose a variety of restrictions, depending on the circumstances of each country. There are several ways in which restrictions are imposed on foreign ownership in the banking sector, whether through limiting foreign investment in domestic banks or the presence of foreign banks itself. The presence of a foreign bank is usually in one of three recognised forms (viz., a branch, subsidiary or a wholly owned subsidiary), and only a particular form of organisation may be permitted, usually with no choice given to the foreign bank. There are some restraints on the type of business permitted to a foreign bank (such as being restricted to foreign currency operations or non-acceptance of retail deposits or other specified operations) as well as stipulations with regard to the minimum capital requirement for a branch or a subsidiary of a foreign bank. There can also be practices amongst countries with regard to the aggregate foreign investment permitted in a local bank, as also on the maximum holdings by an individual or a corporate entity or an entity controlled by foreign financial institutions in a local bank. Similarly, regulations in some countries, consistent with the overall plan of financial integration, place an absolute limitation on the size of the total assets or capital of a foreign bank (which would indirectly restrict its total assets). It needs to be borne in mind that certain policies with regard to the entry of foreign investors or a foreign bank in a country may be triggered due to extraordinary circumstances, such as a financial crisis or as part of a structured crisis management package. There are instances where, as part of the response to banking crises, a higher level of initial foreign ownership have been permitted, but with stipulations for subsequent dilution. Furthermore, certain countries which, *ab initio*, had no private-sector banking, might welcome the presence of foreign banks. Similarly, expectations of joining a regional bloc, say the European Union (EU), might result in welcoming a larger presence of foreign banks.

The extent of foreign investment, the nature of such investment, the appropriate form of presence and the profile of the actual players in the banking sector are usually prescribed by the supervisors, taking into account the multiple challenges faced in a given country context, including the extent of financial integration sought to be achieved. In brief, each country picks up an appropriate package that is necessitated by the circumstances, which ensures the presence of foreign investors that fully satisfy the *'fit and proper'* criteria, and also that the presence of foreign banks is in the best national interest. It is noteworthy that our policy with regard to foreign banks is part of the planned strategy for rebalancing efficiency and stability in the financial system.

Against this background, what should be the policy considerations governing the presence of foreign banks? First, the issue is not one of being for or against foreign banks since financial integration necessitates their presence—be it in industrialised or developing countries. There are, however, special problems in the case of EMEs that have not reached the 'threshold' necessary to minimise the downside risks of the foreign banks' presence. These are key supervisory and regulatory issues, which arise as a result of greater foreign participation in the domestic financial system. Hence, policymakers, including the financial sector supervisors, have to carefully craft a road map to ultimately integrate the domestic financial sector globally, while also moving towards the 'threshold' based on perceptions of the international financial system and on domestic economic conditions. Second, it is quite often not a question of whether to have the presence of foreign banks, than to what extent, under what conditions, over what time horizon and in what form—with usually a particular form of presence being preferred. A more difficult question, especially with regard to foreign investors in local banks, is the identity and nature of investors—recognising that an absolute majority of portfolio flows originate in tax havens. The problem is, however, less complex in highly rated banks. Finally, there are pros and cons in any package of policy with regard to foreign banks. The weight to be attached to each of the pros and cons is country-specific, judgmental and evolving. Hence, a degree of transparency, a road map and considerable flexibility given to supervisors to exercise judgement on several aspects of the entry and presence of foreign banks appear to be the desirable components of an appropriate policy framework in this regard.

OUR APPROACH

India's approach to financial-sector reforms in general and to the management of the external sector in particular has served the country well, in terms of aiding growth, avoiding crises, enhancing efficiency and imparting resilience to the system. The development of financial markets has been, by and large, healthy. The basic features of the Indian approach are gradualism; coordination with other economic policies; pragmatism rather than ideology; relevance to the context; consultative processes; dynamism and good sequencing, so as to be able to meet the emerging domestic and international trends. In order to facilitate an understanding of the approach, a few illustrations would be in order. Convertibility on current account was announced in 1994 by the government and exchange control restrictions were removed over a period of time, emphasising the need for underlying real transactions and reasonableness of amounts. However, repatriation and surrender requirements still dominate the system, though some people aver that it is inconsistent with the concept of current account convertibility. The intention to move over to capital account convertibility was announced in 1997 and its achievement is still an ongoing process—which differentiates the roles of individuals, corporates and financial intermediaries. Likewise, with regard to Primary Dealers (PDs), initially, in 1996, only the PDs promoted by local banks or financial institutions were licensed. Foreign bank-sponsored PDs were licensed after about three years. In the banking system, diversified ownership of public-sector banks has been promoted over the years, and the performance of their listed stocks in the face of intense competition indicates improvements in the system. They do coexist with several old and new private-sector banks, and some of the new private-sector banks have proved to be of global standards. Recently, some private-sector banks promoted by domestic financial institutions have been permitted to conduct central and state government business supplementing the public-sector banks. In February 2004, transparent guidelines were issued by the RBI with regard to the prior acknowledgement needed from the RBI for any acquisition/ transfer of shares of a private-sector bank, which would take the aggregate shareholding of an individual or a group to the equivalent of 5 per cent or more of the paid-up capital of the bank. While this requirement already existed, transparency was imparted by the guidelines. On 2 July 2004, a comprehensive policy framework for ownership and governance in private-sector banks was placed in the public domain by the RBI in the form of draft guidelines for wider public debate. Based on the feedback received, a second draft of the guidelines would be prepared and put in the public domain for further discussion.

Foreign banks have been operating in India for decades, and a few of them have had operations in India for over a century. Quite a few foreign banks from diverse countries set up operations in India during the mid-1990s, following the liberalisation of the Indian economy. The number of foreign bank branches in India has increased significantly in recent years since a number of licences were issued by the RBI—well beyond the commitments made to the World Trade Organization (WTO). Although foreign banks can operate in India only by way of branch presence, some of them have established several subsidiaries in the form of either NBFCs or limited companies in the non-financial sector in India, which undertake diverse businesses such as dealing in securities, leasing and finance, information technology and so on.

The presence of foreign banks in India has benefited the financial system by enhancing competition, resulting in greater efficiency. There has also been a transfer of technology and specialised skills, which has had some 'demonstration effect' as Indian banks too have upgraded their skills, improved their scale of operations and diversified into other activities. At a time when access to foreign currency funds was a constraint for Indian companies, the presence of foreign banks in India enabled large Indian companies to access foreign currency resources from the overseas branches of these banks. Creating inter-bank markets in money and foreign exchange is a challenge in several developing countries. In India, however, the presence of foreign banks, as borrowers in the money market and their operations in the foreign exchange market, resulted in the creation and deepening, in terms of both volumes and products, of the inter-bank money market and forex market; although, by virtue of their skills and resources, the foreign banks tend to dominate in some financial markets. In the days ahead, the challenge for the supervisors would be to maximise the advantages and minimise the disadvantages of the foreign banks' local presence by synchronising the emerging dominance of their local operations with the progress in domestic financial markets as well as in the liberalisation of the capital account.

The RBI is currently examining various options for strengthening the financial sector in general and the banking sector in particular, concurrent with the well-calibrated de-regulation process already set in motion. The liberalisation measures would need to take into account several imperatives, such as the consolidation of the domestic banking sector; restructuring of development finance institutions (DFIs) and appropriate timing for the significant entry of foreign banks, so as to be co-terminus with the transition to greater capital account convertibility while being consistent with our continuing obligation under the WTO commitments. It is also necessary to examine several issues relating to foreign banks not in isolation, but as part of the overall reform paradigm of the banking sector. With respect to foreign banks, the issues include: choice of the mode of presence, acceptable transition path, according national treatment, addressing supervisory concerns, linkages between foreign banks and their presence in other (non-banking) financial services and the timing of various measures as per a road map to be drawn up. The RBI intends to formulate the guidelines through an ongoing process of consultation, as in the past. The proposed guidelines in this regard are expected to carry forward the process of financial integration of India in a carefully calibrated and transparent manner.

REFERENCES

Houben, A., Jan Kakes and Garry Schinasi. 2004. 'Towards a framework for safeguarding financial stability.' IMF Working Paper, No. WP/04/101, Washington D.C.

Jorde, Terry J. 2003. 'The future of banking: The structure and role of commercial affiliations.' Paper presented at the symposium hosted by the Federal Deposit Insurance Corporation, USA, 16 July.

Prasad, E., Kenneth Rogoff, Shang-Jin Wei and M. Ayhan Kose. 'Effects of financial globalisation on developing countries: Some empirical evidence.' IMF Occasional Paper, No. 220, Washington D.C.

Wilson, D. and Roopa Purushottaman. 2003. 'Dreaming with BRICs: The path to 2050.' Global Economics, Paper No. 99, New York: Goldman Sachs.

Wolf, M. 2004. *Why Globalization Works*. New Haven and London: Yale University Press.

2

Importance of Productivity in India*

It is well-known that economic growth, as a means of enhancing the welfare of people, depends both on the use of factors of production such as capital and labour, and the efficiency in resource use, often referred to as productivity. Recent developments indicate the growing importance of productivity, particularly for our economy at its present stage of development.

Trade integration amongst countries, which is driven more by technological developments than by public policy, has the overall effect of rewarding those with high and increasing productivity. In fact, recent experience shows that even in the industrialised economies, a public policy that attempts to protect less-than-competitive productive employment may not succeed, and even when it does to an extent, it is temporary and expensive in the face of rapid technological change. Such cross-border trade integration-induced pressures on productivity have some undeniable positive effects. For example, the price and quality of goods available to consumers are substantially determined by the most efficient producers in the world. Productivity gains that are transmitted through trade integration have positive effects on the standard of living as well as the quality of life.

The spread and thrust of ICT have provided unprecedented scope for productivity gains the world over in a very short span

*Previously presented as the inaugural address, Annual Conference of Indian Economic Association, Andhra University, Visakhapatnam, 27 December 2005.

of time. It is interesting to note that the deployment of ICT in India may contribute to productivity gains in the US but not necessarily to India if the public policy framework does not enable the adoption of modern ICT within India. Further, the changes in demography and their implications need to be viewed in a global perspective, rather than only in a national context. Thus, it is expected that India will contribute to the world a large young workforce in the first half of this century, when the rest of the world may be getting crowded with an elderly population. A large young workforce in India is often described as a 'demographic dividend', but we must recognise that the so-called demographic dividend may turn into a demographic nightmare if, in an increasingly globalised environment, adequate levels of productive employment is not ensured to our youth by an enabling public policy framework. Finally, before India enters the latter half of the twenty-first century with a large share of the elderly like the rest of the world, we will have to reckon with the need to provide for the increasingly ageing population. In other words, the current generation of young persons should grow rich well before they grow old, both on social and economic grounds, since they may not have a younger generation to take care of them. I hope I am not overstating the case for focusing on the growing importance of productivity.

The textbooks do provide simple definitions of productivity and techniques for measurement. Productivity may be defined as the ratio of the output of goods and services to the inputs— human as well as others—used in the production process. Labour productivity, the best known measure of factor productivity, reflects the influence of various factors (such as capital, quality of labour, technological change and organisation of production) that affect productivity. Based on inputs to production, labour productivity can be decomposed into two components: (a) productivity due to capital deepening (that is, improvements in physical capital available per labour unit) and (b) multifactor productivity (MFP) or total factor productivity (TFP). TFP is the contribution other than that emanating from the increased use of inputs (capital and labour). TFP thus measures the increase in efficiency with which resources are being used through innovations and improved management techniques to increase the output from a given combination of capital and labour. Although, conceptually, it is relatively easier to define productivity, its actual measurement is beset by a number of statistical issues such as accounting for quality adjustment and non-marketed output, such as public administration, in addition to the underground economy. In spite of the difficulties, an accurate measurement of productivity is an imperative, albeit with full awareness of the limitations of such an exercise. This is an area of fruitful research which the Andhra Pradesh Economic Association might like to consider.

As already mentioned, the main reason for the unprecedented productivity growth in the recent past has been the impressive technological progress. Robert Solow had emphasised the importance of technological change in long-term economic growth and productivity way back in the 1950s. However, the key issue— what determines technological progress—was left unanswered by assuming technological progress to be exogenous. Technological advance involves the creation of new ideas—partially non-rival and, therefore, having certain aspects of public goods—with increasing returns to scale. This, however, conflicts with the perfect-competition assumption. These weaknesses of the neo-classical model assuming exogenous technological progress were overcome with the development of the concept of endogenous growth propounded by Romer, and its subsequent refinements in the 1980s. In this approach, the long-run growth is determined within the model, with technological advance benefiting from research and development activity, supported by some monopoly power and increasing returns to scale.

Following the research report of the Centre for the Study of Living Standards (CSLS) in 1998, one can identify the following seven determinants of productivity growth: the rate of technological progress, investment in physical capital such as machinery and equipment and structures, the quality of the workforce, size and quality of the natural resource base, industrial structure and inter-sectoral shifts, the macroeconomic environment or aggregate demand conditions and the microeconomic policy environment. Similarly, Harris (1999), based on a review of the cross-country growth literature, has identified three proximate drivers (the Big Three) of productivity growth: investment in machinery and equipment; education, training and human capital and openness to trade and investment. While the proximate drivers may not be exhaustive, they do point to the critical elements of an enabling public policy for enhancing productivity and employment.

What is the role of ICT in enhancing productivity? ICT can have a positive impact on growth not only through a surge in ICT investment and strong productivity effects from the ICT-producing industries, but also through a more productive use of ICT in the rest of the economy. The ICT equipments enable new organisational models and other innovations in the production process, as well as the production of new goods and services. Thus, even if ICT investment goods are standard products, they enable firms to innovate and accumulate firm-specific capital with positive spillovers on production.

Ark and Inklaar (2005) posit that ICT investments may have a U-shaped effect on productivity. After some initial benefits from ICT investments ('hard savings'), the contribution may even become negative, since for reaping the full benefits of ICT, complementary investments in human and knowledge capital as well as in organisational innovations become necessary. Such complementary investments involve gestation lags and do not immediately result in an acceleration of productivity growth. It is only over time that the combination of ICT investment and intangible investments and innovations shows an effect on productivity ('soft savings'), reflected in the U-shaped relationship. The realisation of 'soft savings' involves more trial and error, and thus could benefit from an entrepreneurial environment and competitive labour and product markets.

There have been several empirical studies on productivity trends with special reference to the increased use of ICT and efficiency gains (see, for example, Ark and Inklaar 2005; Gorden 2004; Nordhaus 2005; Oliver and Sichel 2002). The major issues addressed relate to the acceleration of productivity since 1995 in the US but not in Europe; the role of ICT in productivity acceleration, with noticeable differences between the US and Europe; seeking explanations for the lagged or indirect effects of ICT and the differences in the impact of ICT on productivity in the manufacturing vis-à-vis the services sector. It is not my intention to go into the details of research, but only to highlight the importance of understanding the role of ICT in securing productivity gains, particularly since Andhra Pradesh has been one of the leading states in the area of ICT. Hopefully, the Andhra Pradesh Economic Association will consider exploring these issues relating to ICT.

It will be interesting to recall the empirical work done so far on trends in productivity in India. Most empirical studies on productivity in India have focussed on the growth in TFP in the manufacturing sector. These studies suggest a decline in the total factor productivity growth (TFPG) till the 1970s, with a turnaround taking place in the mid-1980s pursuant to the reoriented trade and industrial policies and improved infrastructure performance (Ahluwalia 1991; Balakrishnan and Pushpangadan 1994; Brahmananda 1982; Majumdar 1996; Pradhan and Barik 1999; Rao 1996a; Trivedi, et al. 2000). The proposition that the TFPG accelerated during the 1980s would be consistent with the recent contentious view associated with Rodrik and Subramanian (2004), who have argued that the transition to a high-growth phase occurred around 1980—a full decade before economic liberalisation—due to the pro-business policies that were beginning to be adopted during the 1980s. Various incremental reforms in the industrial sector during the 1980s appear to have had a positive impact on productivity during that decade. However, the pick up in productivity during the 1980s remains a matter of contention. Balakrishnan and Pushpangadan (1994), for instance, argue that the turnaround in productivity during the 1980s is the artefact of using the single-deflation method; there is no evidence of such a turnaround in cases where the double-deflation approach is adopted. (Under the single-deflation method, nominal value added is deflated by an index of the price of gross output. Under the double-deflation method, gross output and material input are deflated separately by output price index and input price index, respectively, and the difference is treated as real value added.)

Turning to the trends in productivity in the post-reform period, the evidence from empirical studies by researchers is ambiguous, although anecdotal evidence, especially of trends in recent years, shows significant increases in productivity. While studies by Unel (2003) and Tata Services Ltd. (2003) find an acceleration in the TFPG in the 1990s, Goldar (2004) and RBI (2004) find a deceleration in the TFPG. Notwithstanding the ambiguity regarding acceleration in TFPG, evidence suggests that trade liberalisation since 1991 has had a positive impact on the TFPG in India (Chand and Sen 2002; Das 2003; Krishna and Mitra 1998; Topalova 2004). At the sectoral level, there is evidence of improved TFPG for exporting sectors vis-à-vis the non-exporting ones (Dholakia and Kapur 2001; Unel 2003). More recently, Kato (2005) found that the smaller the market share of a firm, the higher its productivity growth.

One limitation of most studies in the Indian context is their focus on productivity in only the manufacturing sector. The share of the industrial sector in India's GDP is only 22 per cent, whereas the services sector has emerged as the predominant contributor to GDP with a share of 58 per cent. Since 1993-4, the services sector GDP has recorded an annual average growth of almost 8.0 per cent per annum, notably higher than the 6.7 per cent recorded by industry. Therefore, studies that focus on the manufacturing sector alone may not represent a true picture of the productivity of the economy as a whole. This is especially true in view of some evidence showing that productivity acceleration in the US during the second half of the 1990s was led by the services sector. For India, Virmani (2004) has recently attempted to measure the TFPG for the Indian economy as a whole. His estimates suggest that the TFPG has followed a V-shaped pattern since independence, with near flattening from the late 1980s. Growth in the TFP decelerated since the early 1950s, when it was about 2.5 per cent, till the mid-1970s, when it fell to less than 0.5 per cent. Subsequently, the TFPG recovered and peaked at about 2.6 per cent in 1988-9, and has broadly remained around these levels since then.

A second relevant factor in these empirical studies in India is that their focus is predominantly on the TFPG. In addition to TFPG, it is important to examine trends in labour productivity since it is a more proximate measure of the standard of living, which is especially relevant for countries with low living standards. Studies in this regard throw up some evidence of an increase in the growth rate of labour productivity during the 1990s (Balakrishnan and Babu 2003; RBI 2004). Thus, even if it is held that there has been no clear evidence of growth in the TFP, labour productivity growth could have been higher in the post-reforms period, although the evidence is not conclusive.

A third factor to be kept in mind is that many studies draw upon data up to 2000, while by all indications, significant gains in productivity have occurred in more recent years, particularly in manufacturing. Anecdotal evidence, in addition to relevant supporting data on trends in prices, and composition of our export basket and corporate balance sheets, indicates a significant acceleration in productivity gains in the economy. These are issues worth researching on a priority basis, including studies on capital productivity and the movement of the incremental capital-output ratio.

How does India fare in comparison with other countries? Cross-country evidence (Ark and Inklaar 2005) shows that labour productivity growth in India in recent years is better than that in Germany, the United Kingdom and the United States. Wage rates in India are much lower than in Thailand, Singapore, the Philippines, Malaysia and Korea. In terms of the unit labour cost, India has a competitive edge over Singapore, Korea and Malaysia. In the case of the iron and steel industry, India fares better than Hong Kong, Indonesia and Malaysia, both in terms of lower input costs and higher operating surplus. India leads in skill-based manufacturing activity, such as the ability to re-engineer equipment at lower capital costs, innovative process reengineering, availability of skilled technicians and quality mindset. On the other hand, the unit labour cost in India is higher in food products, electrical machinery and transport equipments, as compared to some other EMEs. Overall, the *Global Competitiveness Report*, 2004 (World

Economic Forum) has ranked India at the fifty-fifth position among 104 economies in terms of the Growth Competitiveness Index, and thirtieth in terms of the Business Competitiveness Index. Although labour productivity growth in India is higher than in advanced economies, it needs to be stressed that its level in India remains quite low in many sectors. Illustratively, productivity per worker in India is only 9 per cent of the US productivity, as compared with 14 per cent for China (Ark 2005).

An important issue for India is the relationship between productivity and employment. Does higher productivity lead to a reduction in employment? Prima facie, the evidence may appear to support such a proposition, but it might require deeper analysis. For instance, in the US productivity has rebounded in the last decade, while manufacturing employment has declined sharply. Such a simple positive correlation might be deceptive as it ignores productivity trends in competing economies. It could be the case that productivity in competitor countries might have exceeded that in the US. It is possible that the effects of rapid domestic productivity growth could have been more than offset by more rapid productivity growth and price declines arising from foreign competitors. Indeed, this appears to have been the case since, according to estimates by Nordhaus (2005), the relevant elasticities of employment with respect to productivity—about 0.25 to 0.5— indicate that faster productivity growth leads to increased rather than decreased employment in manufacturing. In brief, the implications of productivity trends on employment in our country depend not merely on what happens within India, but also on what happens in other countries contemporaneously, reaffirming the importance of tracking productivity both in India and in other countries in view of trade integration. I would flag this as another priority area for research by economists.

While a number of studies have examined the relationship between productivity and income on the one hand and between income and poverty on the other, the relationship between productivity and poverty is perhaps relatively less explored. A number of studies have found that productivity growth has a positive impact on income growth. Sustained and high growth is in turn found to reduce poverty levels in an economy. Thus, it is expected that productivity growth would also have the positive effect of reducing poverty in an economy, although the very short-run effect may be ambiguous, depending upon the effect of productivity growth on employment. While in the long run productivity growth enhances employment, the short-run effect could diminish employment if redeployment of labour is rendered difficult. Hence, a labour force supported by adequate human capital skills and robust governance institutions can help reap the benefits of productivity growth on employment more rapidly than otherwise. It must be noted that an inverse relationship between productivity growth and employment may in fact hold in the long run at a sectoral level (say, agriculture), but at the economy-wide levels, a positive relationship is expected as employment opportunities arise in newer industries and the services sector.

On the whole, productivity growth can have a positive impact on poverty reduction through two channels. First, an increase in productivity raises wages and incomes, and hence reduces poverty. Higher productivity-led wages and incomes can have a second-round impact on domestic demand, and, in turn, on employment and in further gains in poverty reduction. Second, productivity gains help to moderate the rate of increase in prices—as has been taking place in a number of countries. Lower inflation is equivalent to an increase in the purchasing power of current incomes. This indirect effect, operating through lower inflation, can also have a mitigating effect on poverty levels.

A detailed analysis of the relationship between productivity and poverty has recently been made by the International Labour Organisation in its *World Employment Report*, 2004–5 (WER). The cross-country empirical analysis contained in the report shows that poverty reduction is often, but not always, the mirror image of productivity gains. Productivity growth can and must go hand-in-hand with employment creation and poverty reduction, at least in the long run. But, as the report stresses, this does not occur automatically and in the same way for all regions. Economies may require a certain degree of productivity growth in order to improve labour market conditions and reap the beneficial effects of that growth. Major transitions or crises can have a negative impact on productivity growth, and labour markets need time to recover. A recent study (CSLS 2003) finds that productivity growth accounts for changes in poverty better than the more commonly used economic growth. According to the study, in countries with the lowest GINI indices, a 1 per cent rise in labour productivity is associated with a 1.02 per cent decline in the incidence of poverty. In countries with the highest GINI indices, the impact is less than half: a 1 per cent rise in labour productivity was associated with only a 0.45 per cent decline in the incidence of poverty. It appears that the effects of productivity growth on poverty depend inversely upon the income inequality levels: the higher the income inequality within a country, the more limited the impact of productivity growth on reducing poverty. On the other hand, the effect of productivity growth on poverty reduction is found to be stronger in countries with a relatively low income inequality. I will end this exploratory journey into the relationship between productivity growth and poverty reduction with an exhortation— that economic research in this area should be a priority in India since poverty alleviation is the biggest challenge, while increase in productivity is a necessary, though not a sufficient, condition for poverty eradication.

Before concluding this chapter, it is appropriate to present some illustrations of the manner in which the RBI has been contributing to enhancing productivity in our economy.

The first and foremost contribution is the lowering of inflation and, more importantly, inflation expectations. A growing consensus has emerged in recent times, both in academia and policy circles, that price stability—a low and stable inflation rate—provides substantial benefits to the economy. First, it prevents over-investment in the financial sector. Second, price stability lowers the uncertainty about relative prices and the future price level, making it easier for firms and individuals to take appropriate decisions, thereby increasing economic efficiency. Third, price stability also lowers the distortions from the interaction of the tax system and inflation. All these benefits of price stability suggest that by anchoring inflationary expectations, a stable inflation can increase the level of the resources productively employed in the economy. In the Indian context, the RBI exhibits a demonstrable commitment to price stability and growth, the relative emphasis being determined by the balance of domestic and global conditions. Measured in terms of the Wholesale Price Index (WPI), the annual rate of inflation halved from an average of around 11 per cent over a five-year period beginning from 1990–1, to around 5 per cent for the first five years of the current decade. This, as all would agree, has been an important factor enabling business to thrive and prosper, with positive spillovers on productivity improvements.

Second, the ease of credit availability is a crucial ingredient if business is to flourish. A growing economy needs access to credit on reasonable terms and conditions. To illustrate, the credit growth over the last five years has averaged 20 per cent, with the increase at around 25 per cent being particularly rapid during the last three years, riding on the back of broad-based credit demand across all sectors. In recognition of these facts, recent policies have placed explicit emphasis on streamlining credit delivery consistent with credit quality through a gamut of measures. Any discussion of productivity improvement needs to take on board the reach of the financial sector, particularly in rural and semi-urban areas. It is in this context that the recent policy statements of the RBI has rationalised the branch licensing policy and emphasised the need for the 'financial inclusion' of the vast segment of our population which has hitherto remained financially excluded. SHGs formed by NGOs and financed by banks represent an important constituent of this development process.

Third, the policy environment has been made conducive for Indian corporates to have a global presence, including global acquisitions. In particular, the corporates are free to leverage through external commercial borrowings, and Indian banks are enabled to fund such a presence. These initiatives help to exploit the synergies of the domestic and foreign operations of our corporates, thus enhancing the overall productivity.

Fourth, as regards the banking sector, Professor T.T. Ram Mohan (2005) has succinctly described the current status:

> There is the improved efficiency and stability of Indian banking. Banking has proved the soft underbelly of many an experiment in liberalisation. Not so in India. The decline in interest rates in recent years helped recapitalise the banking system. Now, the system is well placed to take advantage of this good fortune— both by garnering more savings and by delivering more credit. With financial markets having developed as well, the financial system is geared to meet the demands of growth.

Fifth, improvements in the communication policy of the RBI also have an indirect influence on productivity. For instance, the RBI has brought about changes in the institutional setting of the monetary policy by migrating from half-yearly announcements to a system of quarterly reviews from April 2005. The weight of evidence suggests that the increasing transparency and accountability reduce the uncertainty about monetary policy, interest rates and inflation. The consequent economic environment makes it conducive for businesses to flourish. The RBI has, therefore, been making pro-active efforts to improve transparency and the public availability of information. Such information dissemination leads to a minimisation of uncertainties about policy intentions, enhances market stability and has a long-run positive effect on productivity. The data available on the website of the RBI through the 'Database on Indian Economy' (available at https://reservebank.org.in) may be of particular interest in this context. The website is currently accessed extensively by market analysts and economic researchers from universities in the US and the UK.

Finally, the RBI has been interacting with market participants while remaining alert to global developments in order to ensure financial stability, since there is a clear global recognition of the disruptive effects of financial instability. India has been spared both currency and banking crises, unlike many other emerging countries. Further, amongst the major economies that do not contribute to current global imbalances, India and the Euro area are noteworthy. It is widely recognised that the financial-sector and external-sector reforms are amongst the most successful in India, which also reflects the enabling conditions ensured by the RBI for efficiency and stability. It must be recognised that stability has enabled the acceleration of growth rates, notwithstanding the significant borrowing requirements of the public sector, including the government and the infrastructural challenges.

From the perspective of the monetary policy formulation of the RBI, an understanding of the underlying trends in productivity is of critical importance in order to aim for low and stable inflation. Ultimately, inflation is determined by mismatches between demand and supply in the economy. Monetary authorities therefore ought to have a good fix on the movements in trends in the economy's productivity, since it is a key determinant of the potential growth of the economy. If the productivity of the economy is on an uptrend—that is, the potential growth of the economy has moved on to a higher trajectory—that would suggest, *ceteris paribus*, that the supply exceeds the demand in the economy, and hence provides monetary policy flexibility to pursue an accommodative monetary policy without stoking inflationary pressures. From the point of view of the conduct of the monetary policy, while it is important to have reliable estimates of the evolving productivity dynamics, it is critical to be able to form such assessments on a timely basis so as to avoid costly errors. Thus, for a central bank to deliver low and stable inflation while allowing employment and output close to their potential/natural levels, an analysis of productivity—on a real-time basis—remains a key input.

The RBI has a vital interest in the research and analysis of productivity trends in the Indian economy, which should take place on a continuing basis and in a timely manner, keeping in view similar developments in other major economies in the world.

REFERENCES

Ahluwalia, I.J. 1991. *Productivity and Growth in Indian Manufacturing.* New Delhi: Oxford University Press.

Ark, Bart van and Robert Inklaar. 2005. 'Catching up or getting stuck? Europe's troubles to exploit ICT's productivity potential.' Research Memorandum GD-79, Groningen Growth and Development Centre, September.

Ark, Bart van. 2005. 'Europe's productivity gap: Catching up or getting stuck?' Paper presented at International Symposium on Productivity, Competitiveness and Globalisation at Banque de France, Paris, 4 November.

Balakrishnan, Pulapre. 2004. 'Measuring Productivity in Manufacturing Sector.' *Economic and Political Weekly* 3, 10 April.

Balakrishnan, P. and K. Pushpangadan. 1994. 'Total factor productivity growth in manufacturing industry: A fresh look.' *Economic and Political Weekly* 29: 2028–35.

Balakrishnan, P. and M. Suresh Babu. 2003. 'Growth and distribution in Indian industry in the 1990s.' *Economic and Political Weekly* 37: 3997–4005.

Banga, Rashmi and Bishwanath Goldar. 2004. 'Contribution of services to output growth and productivity in Indian manufacturing: Pre and post reforms.' Working Paper No. 139. Indian Council for Research on International Economic Relations (ICRIER). July.

Barro, Robert J. and Xavier Sala-i-Martin. 1995. *Economic Growth.* New York: McGraw-Hill.

Belorgey, Nicolas, Remy Lecat and Tristan-Pierre Maury. 2004. 'Determinants of productivity per employee: An empirical estimation using panel data.' *Bulletin De La Banque De France Digest* 123. March.

Bosworth, Barry P. and Jack E. Triplett. 2003. Services Productivity in the United States: Griliches' Services Volume Revisited. Washington, D.C.: The Brookings Institution.

Brahmananda, P.R. 1982. *Productivity in the Indian Economy: Rising*

Inputs for Falling Outputs. Bombay: Himalaya Publishing House.

Centre for the Study of Living Standards (CSLS). 1998. 'Productivity: Key to Economic Success.' Report prepared by the CSLS for the Atlantic Canada Opportunities Agency, Ottawa (Ontario), Canada. March.

_____. 2003. 'Productivity Growth and Poverty Reduction in Developing Countries.' Research Report 2003–6. September.

Chand, S. and K. Sen. 2001. 'Trade liberalisation and productivity growth: Evidence from Indian manufacturing.' *Review of Development Economics* 6(1).

Das, D.K. 2003. 'Manufacturing productivity under varying trade regimes: India in the 1980s and 1990s.' Working Paper No. 107, ICRIER.

Dholakia, R.H. and D. Kapur. 2001. 'Economic reforms and trade performance: Private corporate sector in India.' *Economic and Political Weekly* 36(49).

Goldar, Bishwanath. 2004. 'Productivity trends in Indian manufacturing in the pre and post-reform periods.' Working Paper No. 137, ICRIER, June.

Gordon, Robert J. 'Exploding productivity growth: Context, causes and implications', Brookings Papers on Economic Activity (2), NW, Washington: Brookings Institution Press.

_____. 2004. 'Why was Europe left at the station when America's productivity locomotive departed.' NBER Working Paper 10661, National Bureau of Economic Research, Cambridge, MA 02138, August.

Griliches, Zvi, 1992. 'Output Measurement in the Service Sectors.' *Studies in Income and Wealth* 56, National Bureau of Economic Research, Chicago: University of Chicago Press.

Harris, Richard G. 1999. 'Determinants of Canadian productivity growth: Issues and prospects.' Discussion Paper No. 8, Industry Canada Research Publications Programme.

International Labour Organisation. 2005. *World Employment Report 2004–5: Employment, productivity and poverty reduction.* Geneva: ILO

Jorgenson, Dale W. and Kazu Motohasi. 2005. 'Information technology and the Japanese economy.' National Bureau of

Economic Research (NBER) Working Paper 11801, NBER, Cambridge MA, November.

Kato, Atsushi. 2005. 'Product market competition and productivity in Indian manufacturing industry.' Working Paper, Series No. E/263, Institute of Economic Growth, Delhi.

Krishna, P. and D. Mitra. 1998. 'Trade liberalisation, market discipline and productivity growth: New evidence from India.' *Journal of Development Economics*, 56(2): 447–62.

Lecat, Remy. 2004. 'Labour productivity in the major industrialised countries: The end of the catch-up process with the United States?' *Bulletin De La Banque De France Digest* 123 (March).

Majumdar, Sumit K. 1996. 'Fall and rise of productivity in Indian industry.' *Economic and Political Weekly* 31: M46–M53.

Maury, Tristan-Pierre and Bertrand Pluyaud. 2004. 'The breaks in per capita productivity trends in a number of industrial countries.' *Bulletin De La Banque De France Digest* 123 (March).

Nordhaus, William. 2005. 'The sources of the productivity rebound and the manufacturing employment puzzle.' Working Paper 11354, NBER, May.

Oliner, Stephen D. and Daniel E. Sichel. 2002. 'Information technology and productivity: Where are we now and where are we going?' *Federal Reserve Bank of Atlanta Economic Review*, Third Quarter.

Pradhan, G. and K. Barik. 1999. 'Total factor productivity growth in developing economies: A study of selected industries in India.' *Economic and Political Weekly* 34: M92–M105.

Ram Mohan, T.T. 2005. 'String of positives.' *The Economic Times*, 15 December.

Rao, J.M. 1996a. 'Manufacturing productivity growth: Method and measurement.' *Economic and Political Weekly* 31: 2927–36.

———. 1996b. 'Indices of industrial productivity growth: Disaggregation and interpretation', *Economic and Political Weekly* 32: 3177–88.

Reserve Bank of India. 2004. *Report on Currency and Finance, 2002–03*. New Delhi: RBI.

Rodrik, Dani and Arvind Subramanian. 2004. 'From hindu growth to productivity surve: The mystery of the Indian growth transition.' Working Paper No. 10376, NBER, March.

Romer, Paul M. 1986. 'Increasing returns and long run growth.' *Journal of Political Economy* 94: 1002–37.

Solow, R.M. 1957. 'Technical change and the aggregate production function.' *Review of Economics and Statistics* XXXIX: 312–20.

Tata Services Limited. 2003. *Reforms and Productivity Trends in Indian Manufacturing Sector*, Mumbai: Department of Economics and Statistics, Tata Services Limited.

Topalova, Petia. 2005. 'Trade liberalization and firm productivity: The case of India', Working Paper 11614, NBER, Cambridge, MA, September.

Triplett, Jack E. and Barry P. Bosworth. 2002. *Baumol's Disease Has Been Cured: IT and Multifactor Productivity in U.S. Services Industries*. Washington D.C.: Brookings Institution.

Trivedi, Pushpa, Anand Prakash and David Sinate. 2000. 'Productivity in major manufacturing industries in India: 1973–74 to 1997–98', Study No. 20, DRG, RBI, August.

Unel, Bulent. 2003. 'Productivity trends in India's manufacturing sectors in the last two decades', IMF Working Paper No. WP/03/22, International Monetary Fund, Washington D.C.

Virmani, Arvind. 2004. 'Sources of India's economic growth: Trends in total factor productivity', Working Paper No. 131, Indian Council for Research on International Economic Relations, New Delhi.

3

Reflections on India's
Economic Development*

This chapter provides some glimpses of the process of institution-building in India, which has enabled the progress we have made; analyses the current macroeconomic issues as identified by our recent monetary policy statements; assesses the outlook for the Indian economy by inviting attention to changing balances; illustrates the importance of balance and harmony with reference to reforms in the external and financial sectors and concludes with a discussion on some factors relevant to India's prospects in the global economy.

INSTITUTION-BUILDING

Among the institutions constituting strong pillars of current optimism on growth prospects over the long term are: a uniquely flexible federalism, democracy with universal adult suffrage and the coexistence of a public and a private sector. They deserve some elaboration.

At the time of independence, there were genuine apprehensions as to whether India would hold together. It is true that at that time, there were over 500 native or princely states, which had a

---

*Previously presented as an address to the Council on Foreign Relations at New York, 12 May 2006.

complex net of relationships with the colonial government in terms of paramountcy. They had to be integrated into the constitutional framework of a federation. The flexibility of the federal structure in the constitution assimilated divergent tendencies as they evolved through a process of political accommodation. For example, in 2000, three new states were carved out. We are a Union of States, but a number of states had to be created or re-created on several occasions, while boundaries were also altered in some cases. India, as per the constitution, started with Hindi as the official language of the union along with English as an alternate, for a defined period, which is again being extended. The constitution lists national languages, which numbered fourteen in 1950 and have now been expanded to twenty-two. Every currency note that we print has its denomination expressed in most of these national languages. In brief, India has worked hard to build itself into the viable and vibrant political entity that it is today in a short period, while encouraging democracy to take roots.

The constitution of the US or the developments in UK first established democracy, and then gradually conceded universal adult suffrage over the passage of a couple of centuries. India started with universal adult suffrage in 1950, and over the decades there has been democratic pressure for rapid and full inclusion of all sections in the mainstream. Other democracies started with equality and conceded affirmative action as a concession to realities. India asserted the goal of equality, but incorporated enabling affirmative actions in the constitution for a specific period—which has been extended from time to time by common consent. Thus, democracy has taken root in India essentially because of what Stephen Cohen calls the genius of Indian people for political accommodation and management.

The expansion of the public sector since independence in this milieu of socio-political transformation has been a major contributor to today's strengths. Expanded educational opportunities, coupled with nominal fees, led to an improvement in the quality of education. People could take advantage of the educational opportunities since the process was accompanied by expanding job opportunities in the public sector, based mainly on performance. Against this background, millions were convinced that they needed to work hard at education to be assured of vertical economic and social mobility. The vast public sector has also ensured the mobility of the middle class on a nation-wide basis, and has guaranteed a vibrant middle class. This in turn produced skilled workers and professionals, as well as a large consumer base and a potential entrepreneurial class. The large public sector has coexisted with a private sector, although the growth of the private sector was only sometimes enabled, and often constrained, by the public sector. The private sector, for its part, learnt to manage, survive and benefit from the public sector, while also being constrained by it. In brief, it is the combination of federalism, democracy and a mixed economy that produced a pan-Indian vibrant middle class of professionals and entrepreneurs.

Thus was built an inclusive democracy that virtually celebrates plurality and yet promotes a self-respecting nation proud of its unity in diversity. We believe that economic development needs to be viewed in this broader context. Prime Minister Manmohan Singh summed up the idea in this very forum—the Council on Foreign Relations—on 24 September 2004, at the Russel C. Leffingwell Lecture:

> This (impressive performance), of course is the result of sustained efforts, over the past 50 years to build those institutions that provide the underpinnings of economic development over the longer term, efforts that began early on as part of the vision of India's first prime-minister, Jawaharlal Nehru. It is also the result of economic reforms which have increased our competitiveness in recent years.

SELECT CURRENT ISSUES

Although there are several issues relevant to our economy, in the monetary policy statements of January 2006 as well as April 2006, the RBI flagged three issues as critical to maintaining the momentum of growth with stability, namely the physical infrastructure, fiscal deficit and agriculture.

First, the poor state of the physical infrastructure, both in terms of quantity and quality, has been rightly agitating the business class and policymakers. There is some reason to expect a satisfactory outcome, provided the improvement in the regulatory framework is sustained. The current investments are demand-led and are therefore likely to have a short gestation, coupled with a rapid payback on completion. Technological developments and rapid enhancement of domestic construction capabilities should aid the process of speedy and efficient implementation. Given the healthy fundamentals of the domestic financial sector and the enhanced interest of foreign investors, funding should not be a serious problem. When I mentioned my optimistic assessment along these lines in Basel, one of the comments was, 'with miserable infrastructure, India is already competitive in many areas. I should wonder what happens if the infrastructure really improves.'

Second, fiscal consolidation is taking place both at the Centre and in the states, and there is greater consensus now on the broad directions. The recent budget of the Central government brings the consolidation on track, targeting a fiscal deficit of 3 per cent by 2009 while eliminating revenue deficit. The recommendations of the Twelfth Finance Commission (Chairman, Dr C. Rangarajan) have reinforced the process to enable further fiscal consolidation at the state level. Our studies on state finances at the RBI provide grounds for optimism with regard to their fiscal health. From 2003–4, there has been a sharp correction both in the revenue and fiscal deficits and the process of correction is primarily due to buoyancy in revenue receipts, the states' own tax revenue, as well as transfer and devolution of resources from the Centre. It is noteworthy that for all the states together, the revenue deficit relative to the GDP is estimated to decline to 0.4 per cent in the current year from 1 per cent in the previous year and 2.7 per cent in 1990–2000. The corresponding picture for the gross fiscal deficit (GFD) relative to the GDP is 3.1 per cent compared to 3.7 per cent in the previous year and 4.7 per cent in 1990–2000. However, the issues of power subsidies and ensuring quality in the delivery of services, especially with regard to education and health, do need to be addressed.

Third, and perhaps the most difficult, is agriculture. A majority of the workforce is dependent on agriculture, while the GDP growth due to agriculture is marginally above the rate of growth of the population, in contrast to a strong growth rate in the non-agriculture sector. This has generated an understandably widespread feeling of absolute as well as relative deprivation among the farmers and the agricultural labour. While the scope for better terms in the global trading environment is still elusive, India has a large enough domestic market to facilitate a more rapid growth in agriculture. Yet, legislative, institutional, and attitudinal changes to supplement enhanced public and private investment may be needed. The RBI, for its part, is redoubling its efforts to revitalise the rural cooperative credit system, strengthen RRBs, provide incentives to commercial banks for investments in rural economy, and ensure an adequate and timely delivery of credit at an appropriate price. In fact, we are mounting a study of legislation and implementation of non-institutional moneylending, as it is the single largest source of credit for farmers.

OUTLOOK: CHANGING BALANCES

Progress in India is essentially one of shifting balances. These balances shift almost continuously, and often imperceptibly, and it is possible to hold that one way of assessing the outlook for the Indian economy is to appreciate these changing balances.

First, there is a changing balance in the debates on economic reforms. So far, the discussions have percolated from the English media to the vernacular (with the divide between the English media and the vernacular corresponding roughly to a socio-economic/urban-rural divide). It is interesting to note that while seventeen leading English newspapers have a combined circulation of 6.3 million and a readership of 17.9 million, fifty-four leading vernacular newspapers in India have a circulation of 21.4 million and a readership of 197.2 million. Important economic issues are more and more likely to be articulated and shaped by the vernacular media and distilled up to the English media, since it is the vernacular that predominantly represents the rising 200 million middle class.

Second, there are changes in the vertical balance between Central and provincial or state governments. The trend towards globalisation results in many of the discretionary powers of the Union government in the economic arena becoming aligned with bilateral or multilateral requirements, while critical areas in the economy where the government can play a role, like law and order, education, health, power, water and so on, remain substantively in the domain of the provinces. The fact that even a few years ago many in the world would not have heard of state chief ministers while they do so now points to an increasing decentralisation of economic reforms.

Third, the horizontal inter-provincial balance is also changing. States are now competing for private investments—the drivers of growth—whether domestic or foreign. Competition among states for Central government assistance on the basis of backwardness or need has been replaced with competition for private investments facilitating growth.

Fourth, within governments, both at the Union and provincial levels, regulatory agencies are expanding their role to reduce the discretionary authority of governments of the day.

Fifth, the most dynamic element of reform is the mix between public and private ownership of enterprises. The rebalancing of public enterprises is not dramatic, but the entry of, and threat posed by, the private sector and a diversified ownership of public enterprises through partial disinvestment have meant a change in both the operating environment and internal business culture of these enterprises—which, until recently, had employed and retained the largest pool of the best and the brightest. It is no wonder that equity markets in India have given a big 'thumbs up' to many public enterprises, including banks.

Sixth, the enormous and growing diversity in the funding and provision of essential services, such as health and education, is worth exploring. Enrolment in private schools or colleges, often funded through grants-in-aid, exceeds that in the public sector in many states. On the one hand, this is positive—since the fees are currently affordable—but on the other, it is a cause for concern since it implies that the public sector is being unable to deliver. In the short term, this is a waste of resources, and in the long term it has the potential to undermine India's greatest strength—a credible hope for millions, particularly the poor and the underprivileged—that of a better tomorrow through better education. Enhancement in the quality of education—primary, secondary and collegiate—in the large public sector is a most difficult yet crucial challenge. Some efforts are being made in this regard by many, such as Azim Premji—the chairman of one of the largest software companies in India—and the Tatas, one of the largest industrial houses in India. Ensuring access to quality education for the underprivileged in India is an issue that should be of greatest concern to all the thoughtful and concerned people of the world. Similar concerns can be raised with regard to the vital area of public health. Here, the private sector is an alternative, though it is often not an affordable one for most Indians.

Seventh, there is a dramatic—though not fully appreciated—rebalancing within the private sector in terms of what may be called the 'professionalisation' of industrial houses. A new, highly qualified and professional generation of leadership has replaced the older order in established industrial houses. At the same time, there has been an explosion of an entirely new set of industry leaders, particularly in newer fields such as software, pharmaceuticals, biotech and financial services. This professionalisation is also accompanied by the globalisation of operations of Indian industrial houses.

Eighth, it is sometimes argued that large size is absent in the Indian industry, but it is the wide spectrum of size and diversity that imparts dynamism and generates an entrepreneurial class as well as employment. In the recently held Davos summit, an Indian industrialist referred to two aspects of our business environment. He said that Indian business is often faced with chaos, and out of chaos comes creativity. He added that the cost per unit of output may often not be very low in India, but the cost per unit of innovation is!

Ninth, the relationship between labour and management is being gradually rebalanced. It has certainly improved since the 1991 reform. The recent data on strikes and the number of working days lost bear testimony to the maturity and wisdom of all concerned. Often, the labour market is cited as a problem, but many globally competitive Indian businesses do not seem to perceive it as an insurmountable one. Further, the implementation of provisions relating to the labour market under the Industrial Disputes Act, which is broadly in line with international standards, is becoming more pragmatic and less dogmatic in many progressive states. However, the need for greater labour flexibility with the attendant appropriate legislative changes, keeping in view the socio-economic conditions, is undeniable.

Tenth, there is often a concern about jobless growth, but in reality it is necessary to distinguish between lack-lustre growth in employment in the organised sector and expansion and intensification of employment in the unorganised sector. By way of illustration, thirty years ago 80 per cent of engineers or doctors moved into the organised sector, while now 60 to 70 per cent are self-employed. This implies a shift in the balance from what may be termed 'job orientation' to 'work orientation'. Despite these positive developments, the greatest challenge before the nation is the creation of productive work for the millions that are entering the market.

Finally, during the process of reform there is an initial tendency to be pro-business to obtain quick results, while for lasting impact, policy needs to be pro-market. The processes of decision-making, often considered painfully slow in India, are gradually emphasising an increasingly pro-market stance.

REFORMS IN EXTERNAL AND FINANCIAL SECTORS: BALANCE AND HARMONY

What are the dominant characteristics of reform in the external sector? On the trade account, the approach was to indicate the direction and encourage participants to equip themselves better, notwithstanding the risks of anticipatory actions in undermining the policy intent. In this context, a distinction needs to be made between promoting growth and enhancing efficiency in the context of economic reforms. Trade reforms in India were designed to enable domestic firms to restructure and spread the costs of adjustments over time—thus enabling enhanced efficiency through a gradual process. Growth is promoted on a longer-term basis in view of efficiency gains, which were made possible by the gradualist approach.

On the capital account, too, there has been a continuous resetting with a view to the gradual accelerating pace of liberalisation, depending on the domestic and global situation, but the direction has not been compromised. While there is full convertibility on the current account, and also for all authorised inflows as well as outflows on the capital account, the process of managing the capital account consists of operating two routes, namely automatic and non-automatic. As far as FDI is concerned, consistent rebalancing in the desired direction is done by expanding the automatic route, and by moving most of the prohibited transactions to the non-automatic but approval route and, at a later stage, to an automatic or deregulated regime. There is full convertibility for portfolio flows through foreign institutional investors (FIIs) as far as equity markets are concerned. A major area of managing the capital account relates to external debt, and the objective in this regard is, in a way, to ensure that short-term debt obligations conform to what is known as the Guidotti-Greenspan prescription for avoiding crisis in emerging economies. As regards residents, a distinction is made between resident individuals, the corporates and financial intermediaries—and a process of gradual liberalisation for each category, as appropriate, is the general approach. Currently, there is virtually full capital account convertibility for Indian corporates.

The emphasis on balance and gradual rebalancing, keeping in view the desired direction and the need to avoid any rollback, is thus evident with regard to the external sector, and is equally significant for progress in the financial sector. A few illustrations of gradualism may be in order.

First, the RBI was, till recently, *de facto* obliged to provide money to the government whenever needed, be it through overdrafts or through the private placement of government debt with the RBI, or through participation in primary issues. These have been eliminated with effect from April 2006, but the formal process was commenced in 1997, with an MoU with the government to eliminate automatic monetisation. More recently, private placement or participation was avoided. After being convinced that the new system works in practice, it has been possible to discharge the relevant mandate of the Fiscal Responsibility and Budget Management (FRBM) Act with effect from April 2006.

A second example relates to relaxations in foreign exchange regulations. The Foreign Exchange Regulations Act (FERA), 1973, prohibited most of the forex transactions unless exempted, and so the initial process of liberalisation involved enlarging the list of exemptions. This culminated in the above Act being replaced with the Foreign Exchange Management Act (FEMA) in June 2000, where all transactions are permitted unless prohibited or regulated.

A third example relates to competition and ownership of banks. Competition has been enhanced by gradually removing administered interest rate structures, permitting the entry of new private-sector banks and expanding the branch network of foreign banks. Unlike in most countries, a branch of a foreign bank in India can conduct any business that a bank incorporated in India may conduct. On ownership, while over 70 per cent of the banking business was in fully public sector-owned banks ten years ago, it is now less than 10 per cent, since there is a mix of public and private ownership in most public-sector banks. In fact, in many large public-sector banks, foreign ownership is close to the domestic private ownership. The two largest private-sector banks have foreign ownership of about 70 per cent. The shares of most domestic banks are quoted and traded in local stock exchanges, and if the stock market is any indication of the outlook, the prospects for public-sector banks are bright.

In this process of reform in the banking sector, the legacy problem of NPAs were managed by the public-sector banks themselves—with no banking crisis or *ex post* fiscal bail out. The government has actually benefited from the infusion of some capital in the public-sector banks, which was done to comply with the RBI's prudential regulations. By all accounts, the banking system as a whole has gradually improved in terms of efficiency and resilience, with the mix between public and private and domestic and foreign banks changing incrementally to enable a non-disruptive enhancement of competitive efficiency and stability.

Along with a continuous rebalancing within each sector, harmony in reforms across sectors is continuously sought. In a way, the complex tasks of timing and sequencing of reforms in India have been managed through continuous rebalancing within a broadly harmonised policy framework, often incrementally, and rarely in a dramatic fashion. For example, the progress in reforms in monetary management and financial sectors has been impressive, and in the external sector, *de facto*, very significant. Progress in the fiscal sector has not been as rapid, influencing the pace of reform in the financial and external sectors. Similarly, flexibilities in the real economy are necessary if the fruits of marketisation are to be obtained without the attendant risks. Several rigidities, especially in the regulatory environment and the agriculture sector, are being gradually removed, and reform in other sectors cannot be out of tune. Finally, clarity in property rights, enforcement, dispute resolution, etc., on an expeditious and reasonably predictable basis is also being pursued on several fronts, so that further progress can be made—say, in pricing of risks by banks—as efficiently as they are in developed economies.

Our experience with regard to the development and regulation of financial markets differs from that of developed economies. The latter experienced a co-development of markets, regulations and practices within the economies, and at a latter stage, through a process of evolution, integrated first domestically, and finally globally. In our case, non-existent or underdeveloped domestic market participants had to change their outlook rapidly. Regulators had to develop the requisite skills, and the self-regulatory organisations needed to be founded and strengthened. All these had to take place with narrower degrees of freedom and in a shorter time-span, in view of global developments and financial integration with its pre-disposed as well as preferred frameworks. The constant plea for the country context in reforms in the financial sector may be viewed in this analytical framework.

INDIA AND THE GLOBAL ECONOMY

There are several complex factors relating to the domestic economy that would influence the manner in which India will evolve in, and integrate with, the global economy in the long run. While it is beyond the scope of this chapter to attempt an analysis, it will discuss some of these domestic factors, namely trade-offs between efficiency and stability; the importance of political stability the process of empowerment of women; governance issues and demographic transition.

The balancing of efficiency considerations with stability will be critical to India's successful integration into the global economy. While several observers, especially in the financial sector, hold that India is risk-averse, there are others who assert that a risk-sensitive approach has paid rich dividends, both in terms of efficiency and stability. Two illustrations may suffice. At a macro level, India is investing around 30 per cent of GDP and recording a GDP growth rate in the range of 7 to 8 per cent—which reflects a high level of macro-efficiency relative to other high-growth performers in Asia. Second, at a micro level, there is evidence of increasing global competitiveness—particularly in the manufacturing industry, despite several handicaps such as the cost per unit of power in India, which is two to three times higher than that in other Asian countries. Also, the savings-investment balance is—and is perhaps likely to be—reasonable, at around 2 to 3 per cent of GDP as current account deficit. Going forward, India's risk-sensitive approach to management may ensure that it contributes to domestic growth and global stability.

Issues of political stability are closely related to those of economic stability—and the stability of the political system in India is noteworthy. The number of coalition partners in the government, the number of prime ministers and, indeed, of a series of elections to the Parliament and state assemblies in recent years may appear to indicate difficult political cycles. Yet the overall progress in economic and, indeed, social fronts in recent years, despite the apparently tortuous processes, demonstrates that economic policy cycles do not necessarily go with political cycles in India. There are grounds for optimism on the continued optimal balancing between socio-economic change and political system stability.

No doubt terrorism is a serious problem, but it is a localised problem, and the essential fairness of an open, multicultural society provides hope against any lasting adverse impact on stability. It is significant that there have been attacks on the iconic symbols of India—the Parliament, temples, mosques and the Indian Institute of Science. And in all these cases, evidence shows that it was driven by non-residents.

It is useful to recognise the importance of empowerment of women. Let me illustrate with some relevant facts from Andhra Pradesh. There is a reservation of one-third of the seats for women in medical colleges, but as of now, around half the students are women. Of the 92,000 students admitted to engineering colleges in Andhra Pradesh, over 30,000 were women. Similarly, in the political arena, women are well represented. In the local bodies, there are about 250,000 elected officials, ranging from a member of the gram panchayat to mayors of municipal corporations and chairpersons of zilla parishads, and of these, over 85,000 are women and the reservation for women has been operative since 1987. These developments, which are shared in different ways by other states, give a positive twist to the outlook for women's empowerment in the future.

The exploration of the future of India will not be complete without reference to a book by Dr Bimal Jalan, titled *Future of India: Politics, Economics and Governance*. In particular, he highlights issues relating to an enhancement in the quality of functioning of the Parliament, the bureaucracy and the judiciary. These are complex issues, but the continuation of good times in the economy is perhaps contingent upon the needed reforms in these areas— sooner rather than later.

India is expected to benefit from the demographic dividend in a global context. It is necessary to recognise that the bulge in the workforce, which is a source of strength, will be concentrated in the northern provinces of India. If education, skills, health and governance are improved, enabling a globally competitive labour force, there will be a demographic dividend. There is a greater advantage for India, relative to almost all other countries, in that the demographic transition in India will be stretched over a longer period, due to the sheer diversity in demographic profiles among different states. By 2016, in three states—Tamil Nadu, Kerala and Andhra Pradesh—the proportion of the elderly as a percentage of the total population will be in excess of 10 per cent. On the other hand, Uttar Pradesh and Bihar, the two most populous Indian states, are likely to have the lowest share, at 6.7 per cent and 7.1 per cent respectively. A preliminary observation based on migration data as per Census 2001 shows that Uttar Pradesh and Bihar are the two states with the highest number of people emigrating to other states in India. Employment appears to be the dominant factor behind migration, and this is a positive factor for us. In brief, the demographic profile of India may, in some ways, be mimicking the global profile.

It is interesting that the extreme diversities of the world, in terms of languages, religions, ideologies and traditions, are reflected in India. There is an overwhelming preference in Indian society and polity for coordination, cooperation and cooption, rather than confrontation. In sum, if there is one country that comes closest to a well-functioning, multicultural global village, it is India.

4

India
Development and Reform Experience, and Prospects*

Some hold the view that India was a poor country for the most part of human history, though there were pockets of prosperity and islands of riches. However, accounts of others, especially global travellers and those who invaded India, indicate that India was a prosperous country till at least the seventeenth century. According to an Organisation for Economic Co-operation and Development (OECD) publication, in AD 1700, broadly defined, India's GDP at US$ 90.8 billion was 24.4 per cent of the world GDP (Angus 2001). Lord Meghnad Desai, while delivering the first P.R. Brahmananda Memorial Lecture in Mumbai in September 2004, noted that the story of the nineteenth century for India is not one of gloom and doom. He added that during the second half of the nineteenth century, for which the data are best available, India was an open economy enjoying an export-led growth; however, there was a drain of the export surplus to pay Home Charges. During the forty-year period from 1860 to 1900, the per capita income growth was 0.5 to 1 per cent. According to Lord Desai, the first fifty years of the twentieth

*Previously presented as an address at the Bank of Mexico, Mexico City, 12 September 2007.

century were much less favourable for the Indian economy than the last forty years of the nineteenth century had been. Further, in a book titled *The National Income of India in the Twentieth Century*, Professor Sivasubramonian observed that in the first five decades of the twentieth century (1900–1 to 1946–7), before we got our independence in 1947, the per capita GDP in India was stagnant, as the trend growth in GDP during this period was 0.9 per cent with the population growing by 0.8 per cent (Sivasubramonian 2000).

As compared with near stagnant growth in the first fifty years of the twentieth century, the annual growth, averaging around 3.5 per cent during 1950 to 1980, was comparatively better, while the per capita growth broke out of the long period of inertia and averaged 1.1 per cent till around 1980. The average growth rate of around 6 per cent since the 1980s, while embarking on a higher average growth path of 8.6 per cent in the last four years, could be a paradigm shift.

The Indian experience clearly suggests that the mixed-economy model and planned development strategy in the first phase during the 1950s and 1960s improved the growth rate dramatically relative to previous decades, and also provided the essential building blocks and laid strong foundations for an indigenous industrial base, a vibrant entrepreneurial class and knowledge economy, with considerable improvement in vertical, social and economic mobility. However, the inward-looking import substitution strategy pursued during the initial decades of the planning period resulted in declining productivity and a high-cost economy. Realising this, significant changes in policy were initiated in the early 1980s, taking account of the oil shocks in the 1970s and early 1980s. These policy measures took India to a higher growth trajectory in the 1980s, but created some macroeconomic imbalances in its wake, leading to a crisis in 1991 that triggered more comprehensive and sustainable reforms. The policies since 1991 have provided ample opportunities to build on the strong foundations in the economic, political and social spheres, laid during the pre-reform period of planned development.

DEVELOPMENT EXPERIENCE: THE POST-REFORM PERIOD

Triggers of Reforms

While policy reforms in the 1980s provided the impetus for high growth and enhanced competitiveness, the growth process turned unsustainable. It was manifested in the growing macroeconomic imbalances over the decade in the form of high fiscal deficit, high levels of current account deficit and increasing levels of short-term external debt, besides a repressive and weakened financial system. The immediate provocation for the crisis in 1991 was also a combination of external events, which generated liquidity problems on the external front.

The gulf crisis of 1991 and the subsequently soaring oil prices not only affected India's oil imports, but also eroded export markets in West Asia and caused a setback to inward remittances and tourist earnings. The deterioration in exports on account of the break-up of the erstwhile USSR accentuated the crisis. At around the same time, India's credit rating was lowered, restricting its access to commercial borrowings, and there was unwillingness on the part of normal banking channels to renew short-term credit to Indian banks abroad. Exceptional financing measures became inevitable, and the overall deficit in 1990–1 was financed almost equally through recourse to IMF and drawdown of reserves. The severity of the balance of payments crisis in the early 1990s could be gauged from the fact that India's foreign currency assets depleted rapidly, from US$ 3.1 billion in August 1990 to US$ 975 million on 12 July 1991.

Reform Measures

During the crisis period, a conscious decision was taken to honour all debt obligations without seeking rescheduling, and several steps, including some unconventional ones, like pledging gold with international institutions, were resorted to to tide over the crisis. The immediate steps undertaken included, among others, a tightening of non-essential imports and availing credit from the IMF and other multilateral and bilateral donors. A macroeconomic structural and stabilisation programme encompassing trade, industry, foreign investment, exchange rate, public finance and the financial sector was put in place, creating an environment conducive to the expansion of trade and investment. It was recognised that trade policies, exchange rate policies and industrial policies would need to form part of an integrated policy framework if the aim was to improve the overall productivity, competitiveness and efficiency of the economic system in general, and the external sector in particular.

Features of Economic Reforms

Here, it may be interesting to enumerate some of the important features of the economic reform process undertaken by India since 1991.

First, the approach towards reforms in India has been cautious, with an appropriate sequencing of measures, complementary reforms across sectors (for example, the monetary, fiscal and external sectors) and development of financial institutions and markets. The objective has been to progress with some harmony across sectors.

Second, the pace and sequencing of liberalisation has been responsive to domestic developments, especially in the monetary and financial sectors, and the evolving international financial architecture. The reforms were debated intensely and designed essentially indigenously.

Third, the approach to reform was 'gradual but steady', rather than a 'big bang' approach. The reforms have generally been viewed as a process and not as an event. In this approach, the pace and sequencing of liberalisation could be tempered, keeping in view the degree of comfort in moving forward in a credible way.

Fourth, the major thrust driving the reform process was the quest for higher growth and efficiency, along with macroeconomic stability. At the same time, the reforms had to be 'inclusive', in the sense that the benefits of reforms were to be demonstrably shared by all sections, in particular the vulnerable ones. This has easily been a very significant electoral issue in both provincial and national elections.

SELECT ECONOMIC INDICATORS

GDP Growth

During 2003–7, the Indian economy entered a high-growth phase, with the GDP growth averaging 8.6 per cent per annum. The acceleration of growth during this period was accompanied by a significant moderation in volatility, especially in industry and services sectors. The structure of domestic output has distinctly shifted in favour of the services sector, while growth in industry is also accelerating. Indian industry appears to have responded well to global competition through restructuring and technological upgradation in recent years. India's growth is mainly driven by domestic consumption, which contributed, on an average, to almost two-thirds of the overall demand.

Saving and Investment Balances

A noteworthy feature of the ongoing structural transformation of the Indian economy is the significant increase in domestic saving and investment rates. The domestic investment rate increased from 24.3 per cent in 2000–1 to 33.8 per cent in 2005–6, and the domestic saving rate from 23.7 per cent in 2000–1 to 32.4 per cent during 2005–6. The household sector continued to be the major contributor to gross domestic saving with its saving rate placed at 22.3 per cent in 2005–6, while on account of the rise in profit, the saving rate of the private corporate sector rose to 8.1 per cent in 2005–6. The public sector, which started posting positive saving beginning 2003–4, recorded a saving rate of 2.0 per cent in 2005–6 on account of the continuing fiscal improvement, as against a negative saving rate of 1.7 per cent in 2000–1. It may be noted that over 95 per cent of investment is financed by domestic savings. Given the fact that Indian per capita income is increasing rapidly and policy efforts towards financial deepening to achieve a more inclusive growth are underway, the saving rate in India could even rise further in the medium to long term. The level of saving rate should help continue to finance the investment needs of the economy domestically, without undue dependence on foreign savings.

Productivity and Efficiency

In tandem with the acceleration in the rate of investment in the economy, there has been evidence of a pickup in the productivity and efficiency of capital use. Some of the recent studies relating to India have indicated an increase in TFP growth in recent years. For instance, Rodrick and Subramanian, in an IMF Working Paper of 2004, point out that India seems to have had a large amount of productivity growth from relatively modest reforms. A more recent paper by Barry Bosworth, Susan Collins and Arvind Virmani (2007) confirms this trend. They find that output per worker grew only 1.3 per cent annually during 1960–80, when GDP growth was also at a low of 3.4 per cent. The TFP growth was barely above zero, according to their calculations, indicating that growth in output was almost entirely driven by growth in inputs. In contrast, growth in output per worker nearly tripled to 3.8 per cent during 1980–2004, while TFP increased ten-fold to 2 per cent. Evidence of an increase in the growth of labour productivity is also available from other studies (Economic Intelligence Unit 2007). A study by Tata Services (2003) found that for the all-India manufacturing sector, labour productivity (output per unit of labour) has increased significantly during the post-reform period, compared with the pre-reform period.

Poverty and Employment

The sustained economic growth since the early 1990s has also been associated with some reduction in poverty. Based on uniform recall period consumption distribution, the proportion of people living below the poverty line declined from 36 per cent in 1993–4 to 27.8 per cent in 2004–5. There is also evidence of pick-up in employment growth from 1.57 per cent per annum (1993–4 to 1999–2000) to 2.48 per cent per annum (1999–2000 to 2004–5). According to some reports and other anecdotal evidence, the benefits of the recent surge in the growth rate of GDP are not just restricted to large cities, but have extended to people in other urban and semi-urban areas as well. There is also some evidence of reduction in underemployment and disguised unemployment in the informal sector.

Money, Prices and Credit

The high growth in GDP in recent years has been accompanied by some moderation in inflation to an average of 4.9 per cent during 2003–7. Historically, India has not seen very high inflation except temporary spikes on account of shocks like oil or drought. The headline inflation rate, in terms of the wholesale price index, has declined from an average of 8.2 per cent during 1980–1 to 1990–1, to 6.2 per cent during the post-crisis period, that is, 1992–3 to 2006–7, with a sharper moderation in the recent period.

During 2006–7, money supply (M3) increased by 21.3 per cent on a year-on-year basis, and was well above indicative projections for the year. It largely reflected the surge in capital flows in the country. Non-food credit extended by the scheduled commercial banks (SCBs) increased by 28.4 per cent during 2006–7, on top of the 31.8 per cent of the previous year. The growth in bank credit has favoured retail lending, particularly housing, real estate, trade, transport and professional services and NBFCs—sectors which hitherto were not significant in the credit market. These developments led to a lively debate on the signs of overheating in the economy, but the subsequent moderation in inflation has diffused the attention.

MONETARY POLICY AND REGULATORY FRAMEWORK

As regards the framework of monetary policy, the basic objectives of monetary policy, namely price stability and ensuring credit flow to support growth, have remained unchanged in India. Of late, considerations of macroeconomic and financial stability have assumed an added importance, in view of the increasing openness of the Indian economy.

In India, broad money (M3) emerged as an intermediate target from the mid-1980s, based on the premise of a stable relationship between money, output and prices. In the late 1990s, in view of the ongoing financial openness and increasing evidence of changes in the underlying transmission mechanism, with interest rates and exchange rates gaining in importance vis-à-vis quantity variables, the RBI adopted a multiple indicator approach in April 1998, whereby interest rates or rates of return in different financial markets, along with such data as on currency, credit, trade, capital flows, fiscal position, inflation, exchange rate, etc., are juxtaposed with the output data for drawing policy perspectives. The liquidity management in the system is carried out through open market operations (OMO) in the form of outright purchases/ sales of government securities and daily reverse repo and repo operations under the LAF, and this has emerged as the main instrument for interest rate signalling in the Indian economy. In the context of large capital flows and sterilisation, the availability of policy instruments to manage liquidity has been strengthened further with OMO through the MSS.

While the preferred instruments are indirect and varied, there has been no hesitation in taking recourse to direct instruments if circumstances warrant them. In fact, complex situations do warrant dynamics of different combinations of direct and indirect instruments, in multiple forms, to suit the conditions—especially the transmission mechanism.

Similarly, while there is considerable merit in maintaining a distinction between the monetary and prudential policies of the central bank, the RBI did not hesitate to enhance the provisioning requirements and risk weights for select categories of banking assets, namely real estate, housing, consumer finance and capital market exposures. There has also been close monitoring of off-balance sheet exposures of banks. Detailed guidelines have been issued for consultation, on product, accounting and prudential aspects of credit derivatives. A framework for governing banks' linkages with systemically important deposit-taking and non-deposit taking NBFCs has also been put in place.

More generally, the RBI's approach has been to recognise the positive contributions that financial innovations make to enhance the efficiency of financial intermediation. At the same time, the RBI considers, in a dynamic setting, appropriate safeguards to ensure stability, taking into account the prevailing governance standards, risk management systems and incentive frameworks in the foreign, public, private and cooperative banks, as also in the related non-banks. Overall, these progressive but cautious policies have contributed to both the efficiency and stability of the financial system, enabling current growth momentum in an environment of macro-stability.

Some of the important factors that shaped the changes in the monetary policy framework and operating procedures in India during the 1990s were the delinking of budget deficit from its automatic monetisation by the RBI, deregulation of interest rates and development of financial markets with reduced segmentation through better linkages and development of appropriate trading, payments and settlement systems along with technological infrastructure. With the enactment of the FRBM Act in 2003, the RBI has withdrawn from participating in the primary issues of Central government securities with effect from April 2006. The recent legislative amendments enable a flexible use of the cash reserve and statutory liquidity requirements for banks, without being constrained by a statutory floor or ceiling on the levels of such prescriptions by the RBI.

FISCAL POLICY REFORMS AND PUBLIC DEBT MANAGEMENT: CENTRE AND STATES

The fiscal system prevalent at the beginning of the 1990s was characterised by a sustained high fiscal deficit and mounting debt accumulation, which gave rise to inflation, financial repression and overall deterioration in the macroeconomic fundamentals of the economy. The average GFD of the Central government as per cent to GDP during the 1980s was 6.8 per cent, as against 3.8 per cent in the 1970s. A positive outcome in recent years is the marked improvement in the health of government finances with the adoption of the FRBM Act, 2003 by the Central government, and the Fiscal Responsibility Legislation (FRL) by several state governments.

RBI and States

Under India's federal system of government, the Constitution allocates the revenue powers and expenditure functions between the Central and state governments. In general, the functions required to maintain macroeconomic stability and international relations are assigned to the Centre, while the provision of public services such as law and order, internal security, public health, sanitation, water supply and agriculture is largely entrusted to the states. Both government layers share responsibility for education, health and infrastructure, though the states play a critical role.

In India, borrowing by state governments is subject to prior approval by the national government. This is embodied in Article 293 of the Indian Constitution, under which any state government that is indebted to the Central government requires prior approval for borrowings. Central approval is embedded in the procedure of sale of state government securities, and therefore cannot be violated. Furthermore, state governments are not permitted to borrow externally, unlike the Centre.

The RBI plays two crucial roles in relation to the Indian fiscal system, namely as banker to, and debt manager of, both the Central and state governments. The RBI Act allows the RBI, through agreement with a state government, to undertake its banking operations and the management of its public debt. While undertaking the role of banker for both the Central and state governments, the RBI also provides temporary support to tide over mismatches in their receipts and payments in the form of Ways and Means Advances (WMA).

The RBI has been organising a biannual Conference of State Finance Secretaries since November 1997. This Conference, right from its inception, has provided a very useful forum for interactiõn between all the stakeholders (state governments, the Central government and the RBI) on matters related to state finances, and for arriving at consensual solutions on issues of policy and operational significance. Among the areas that were deliberated, the more important ones relate to FRLs at state levels; standardisation of budgetary, accounting and transparency practices; cash management; management of the Consolidated Sinking Fund (CSF) and Natural Calamities Fund (NCF); evaluation of fiscal guarantees and so on. The RBI is proactive and responds from time to time to the needs of the states, as evident from two recent moves.

Faced with the accumulation of large surplus cash balances and a negative spread earned on the investment of such balances, some state governments had approached the RBI to arrange for the buy-back of their outstanding State Development Loans (SDLs). Accordingly, the RBI formulated a general scheme for the buy-back of SDLs, with the concurrence of the Government of India. Following the recommendations of the Twelfth Finance Commission, external loans would be passed on to the states (in rupee terms) on a back-to-back basis. Consequently, the state governments would now have to bear the foreign exchange risk in the context of such loans. Again, at the behest of state governments, the RBI recently organised a workshop on the management of foreign exchange risk, for the benefit of state government officials.

The RBI interacts with states on several other fronts, especially with regard to lending to agriculture, small industries, weaker sections, depositor protection, financial inclusion, financial literacy, responding to natural calamities, etc., mainly through the regional offices.

Management of Public Debt

The aggregate stock of public debt of the Centre and the states as a percentage of GDP is high, currently at around 75 per cent. There are, however, several unique features of the management of public debt in India, which are noteworthy. First, states have no direct exposure to external debt. Second, almost the whole of public debt is local currency denominated, and held almost wholly by residents. Third, public debt, of both the Centre and the states, is actively and prudently managed by the RBI, ensuring comfort to financial markets without any undue volatility. Fourth, the government securities market has developed significantly in recent years in terms of turnover, depth and participants, and significant further improvements are underway.

Fifth, contractual savings supplement marketable debt in financing deficits. Finally, direct monetary financing of primary issues of debt has been discontinued since April 2006. Hence, the high stock of public debt relative to GDP has not so far been a matter of concern as far as stability is concerned, while it is recognised that long-term sustainability would call for a gradual reduction to prudent levels.

EXTERNAL-SECTOR REFORMS

Benefiting from a calibrated and sequenced strategy of liberalisation, India's external sector has become more resilient. Exports have been growing at an average rate of around 25 per cent during the last three years, while imports have grown by around 35 per cent during the same period. The current account remained in surplus during 2001–2 to 2003–4, before turning into a modest deficit since then. There was a significant strengthening in the capital account, resulting in continued accretion to the foreign exchange reserves, which was around US$ 228.8 billion as on 31 August 2007. As could be seen from Table 2, there has been considerable improvement in liquidity and sustainability indicators of external debt.

The exchange rate of the rupee became market determined from 1 March 1993, and by August 1994 India became current account convertible by accepting Article VIII of the Articles of Agreement of the IMF. There was simultaneously a significant rationalisation of the tariff structure in a gradual manner, providing an opportunity for domestic industry to equip itself to face global competition. For instance, the customs duty on non-agricultural products has come down from 150 per cent in 1991–92 to 10.0 per cent in 2007–8. A qualitative change was brought about in the legal framework for liberalisation by the enactment of FEMA in June 2000. With this, the objectives of regulation have been redefined as facilitating trade and payments, as well as the orderly development and functioning of the foreign exchange market in India.

The extent and timing of capital account liberalisation is properly sequenced with other concomitant developments such as strengthening of the banking sector, fiscal consolidation, market development and integration, trade liberalisation, and the changing domestic and external economic environments. It is also recognised that there may be links between the current and capital accounts, and hence procedures are in place to avoid capital flows in the guise of current account transactions. Further, a hierarchy has been established in the sources and types of capital flows. The priority has been to liberalise inflows relative to outflows, but all outflows associated with inflows have been totally freed. Among the types of inflows, FDI is preferred for stability, while excessive short-term external debt is eschewed. A differentiation is made between corporates, individuals and banks. Operationally, the process of managing the capital account consists of operating two routes, namely automatic and non-automatic. Consistent rebalancing in the desired direction is done by expanding the automatic route and by moving most of the prohibited transactions to the non-automatic but approval route, and, at a later stage, to an automatic or deregulated regime.

There has been a significant liberalisation of the policy framework with regard to capital outflows over the past few years. Each country has to design its policy regime for capital outflows keeping in view the specific country context, especially characteristics of the real sector, and not merely the contextual level of inflows and extant absorptive capacity of the economy. First, the current regime of outflows in India is characterised by a liberal, but not incentivised, framework for corporates to invest in the real economy outside India, including through the acquisition route. The regime has served the country well since Indian corporates are increasingly able to establish synergies with overseas units, to make up for the lack of scale that has been a legacy problem in India, and to quickly acquire domain knowledge through acquisition. Second, significant liberalisation of outflows by individual households has been implemented following the recommendation of the Committee on Fuller Capital Account Convertibility (Chairman: Shri S.S. Tarapore, 2006). Further liberalisation here would be done in the light of some international experience, which shows that resident individuals often precede overseas investors in initiating outflows when perceptions with regard to the domestic economy's performance or stability appear to turn adverse. Third, as regards the regime for outflows through financial intermediaries, the approach is characterised by caution and quantitative stipulations, whereby both prudential considerations and compulsions of management of capital account are relevant.

FINANCIAL-SECTOR REFORMS

Major policy measures in the financial sector relate to phased reductions in statutory pre-emption, like CRR and statutory liquidity requirements and deregulation of interest rates on deposits and lending, except for a select segment. The diversification of ownership of banking institutions is yet another feature that has enabled private shareholding in public-sector banks, through listing on the stock exchanges, arising from dilution of government ownership.

The banking-sector reform combines a comprehensive reorientation of competition, regulation and ownership in a non-disruptive and cost-effective manner. Indeed, our banking reform is a good illustration of the dynamism of the public sector in managing the overhang problems, and the pragmatism of public policy in enabling the domestic and foreign private sectors to compete and expand. The regulatory framework in

India, in addition to prescribing prudential guidelines and encouraging market discipline, is increasingly focusing on ensuring good governance through 'fit and proper' owners and directors of banks. The RBI has issued detailed guidelines on ownership and governance in private-sector banks, emphasising diversified ownership. The RBI has also provided a significant thrust to the implementation of information technology in the banking sector.

FDI in private-sector banks is now allowed up to 74 per cent, subject to the prescribed guidelines. Again, 100 per cent FDI is allowed in nineteen activities under the automatic route in NBFCs. There are minimum capitalisation norms for such investments. Besides, 100 per cent NBFC subsidiary can also be established subject to clearance by the Foreign Investments Promotion Board (FIPB), Government of India. There has been a noticeable increase in the interest of foreign entities to acquire stakes in NBFCs. Policy initiatives have been taken in the recent past to ensure that such NBFCs adhere to the regulatory prescriptions spelt out for them.

In the cooperative segment, the UCBs had been suffering from the problem of multiple supervisory/regulatory authorities, as also the challenge of reconciling the democratic character with financial discipline. Therefore, several structural, legislative and regulatory measures have been initiated in recent years for UCBs, with a view to evolving a policy framework oriented towards the revival and healthy growth of the sector. A vision document for their healthy growth has been formulated. Restructuring of the larger weak banks has commenced, and is well underway. Similarly, issues relating to rural cooperative banking structures and RRBs have been considered actively; comprehensive measures have been planned, and some of them are under implementation.

Financial Markets Reforms

Financial markets in India, in the period before the early 1990s, were marked by administered interest rates, quantitative ceilings, statutory pre-emptions, captive market for government securities, excessive reliance on central bank financing of fiscal deficit, pegged exchange rate, and current and capital account restrictions. A wide range of regulatory and institutional reforms were introduced in a planned manner over a period to improve the efficiency of financial markets. These included the development of market micro-structure, removal of structural bottlenecks, introduction/diversification of new players/instruments, free pricing of financial assets, relaxation of quantitative restrictions, better regulatory systems, the introduction of new technology, improvement in trading infrastructure, clearing and settlement practices, and greater transparency.

Reforms in financial markets were carefully sequenced, ensuring that they were in sync with the real sector. The reforms were also important to develop the environment for effective monetary policymaking and monetary transmission mechanisms. A noteworthy feature is that the government securities and corporate debt market is essentially domestically driven, since the FII and non-resident participation in these markets are limited and subjected to ceilings.

The linkage between money, government securities and forex markets has been established, and is growing. The price discovery in the primary market is more credible than before and secondary markets have acquired greater depth and liquidity. The RBI has also initiated a number of steps—institutional, procedural and operational—for making the payment systems safe, secure and efficient. For efficiency enhancements and risk reduction, usage of the Real Time Gross Settlement (RTGS) System and other electronic payment mechanisms has been encouraged in a big way.

FINANCIAL INCLUSION AND CUSTOMER SERVICES

The RBI has undertaken a number of measures with the objective of attracting the financially excluded segment of the population into the structured financial system. The broad approach of the

RBI is aimed at 'connecting' people with the banking system. Measures relating to financial inclusion may be summarised as follows.

First, banks were advised to make available a basic banking 'no-frills' account with nil or minimum balances as well as other charges to ensure the outreach of such accounts to vast sections of the population. As there are many regional languages in India, banks are required to make available all printed material used by retail customers in the concerned regional language.

Second, banks have also been permitted to utilise the services of NGOs/SHGs, MFIs, and other civil society organisations as intermediaries in providing financial and banking services through the use of business facilitator and business correspondent (BC) models.

Third, banks are also entering into agreements with Indian Postal Authorities to use the large and well-spread network of post offices as BCs, thereby increasing their outreach and leveraging on the postman's intimate knowledge of the local population and the trust reposed in him. Similarly, banks, in association with insurance companies, are providing innovative insurance policies at affordable costs, covering life disability and health.

Fourth, the RBI has been encouraging the use of ICT solutions by banks to enhance their outreach with the help of their BCs. A multilingual website in thirteen Indian languages on all matters concerning banking and the common person has been launched by the RBI on 18 June 2007.

Several initiatives were also undertaken by the RBI to improve the delivery of customer services by banks.

First, the recommendations of the Standing Committee on Procedures and Performance Audit on Public Services, set up in November 2003, covering an individual customer's dealings with a bank in the areas of foreign exchange, currency and government transactions, including pensions, besides the main relationship as an account holder, are being implemented.

Second, in order to bring together all activities relating to customer service in banks and the RBI in a single department, the RBI constituted a new department called the 'Customer Service Department' on 1 July 2006. The new department has facilitated a sharper focus to customer service issues.

Third, the Banking Ombudsman Scheme, which was introduced in 1995 to provide an expeditious and inexpensive forum to bank customers for the resolution of their complaints relating to deficiency in banking services, was last revised in 2006. The scheme now has an enlarged scope, and is applicable to all commercial banks, RRBs and scheduled primary cooperative banks. The complainants can file their complaints in any form, including online.

Fourth, recognising an institutional gap in measuring the performance of banks against the codes and standards based on established best practices, the RBI set up the Banking Codes and Standards Board of India (BCSBI) in 2006. It is an autonomous and independent body, in the nature of a self-regulatory organisation. Banks register themselves with the Board as its members, and provide services as per the agreed standards and codes. The Board in turn monitors and assesses the compliance with the codes and standards that the banks have agreed to. The 'Code of Banks' Commitment to Customers' was released on 1 July 2006. The Code covers various aspects of individual transactions, such as deposit accounts, interest rates, fees and charges, remittances, settlement of claims with respect to deceased account holders, loan products, safety locker, credit cards, guarantees, collection of dues and complaints and grievance redressal. The RBI has also made it obligatory for banks to display and update, in their offices/branches as also on their websites, the details of various service charges in a prescribed format.

Fifth, as a lack of financial education on the part of bank customers contribute to the rising number of complaints, especially relating to credit card operations, the RBI is according top priority to financial education, which would ensure that the customers of banks take informed decisions. Individual banks have also started taking various steps in this regard, through, for instance, the 'financial education posters', 'short films' and websites, etc.

PROSPECTS, CHALLENGES AND STRENGTHS

Short-term Prospects

Medium-term Challenges

For a large and diverse economy with low per capita income, yet one that is undergoing structural transformation in a highly uncertain global environment, challenges for public policy are manifold. This section focuses on a few that the RBI considers crucial for enhancing medium-term prospects for equitable growth.

First, while over 60 per cent of the workforce is dependent on agriculture, the sector accounts for 20 per cent of the GDP. Further, the GDP growth generated from agriculture is only marginally above the rate of growth of the population, which is not adequate to ensure rapid poverty reduction. Not only does volatility in agricultural production have implications for overall growth, but, as the experience of 2006–7 amply demonstrated, also for maintaining a low and stable inflation. Enhanced growth of the agricultural sector is vital for ensuring food security, poverty alleviation, price stability, overall inclusive growth and sustainability of growth of the overall economy. Recently, our honourable Prime Minister announced a major scheme to double the growth rate of agriculture to 4.0 per cent over the Eleventh Plan period. A time-bound Food Security Mission was also announced to counter the rising prices of food products, and to ensure visible changes in their availability over three years.

Second, the manufacturing sector has recorded robust growth, despite several infrastructure deficiencies. The inadequate availability of modern infrastructure and shortage of skilled manpower are the most critical barriers to the growth of the manufacturing sector. It is essential to augment the existing infrastructure facilities, particularly the roads, ports and power, to provide an enabling environment for industry to prosper. The most important issues here are the regulatory framework and the overall investment climate, which are being addressed by the government. One other concern has been cost recovery, which is expected to improve with enlightened public-private partnership.

Third, a salient feature of the fiscal consolidation process in recent years, even after accounting for cyclical elements, has been the significant reduction in the key deficit indicators. Our studies on state finances in the RBI give us grounds for optimism with regard to their fiscal health. We recognise two important areas which, if addressed, would result in fiscal empowerment. One is the elimination of subsidies that are inappropriate and not directly targeted to the poor, and the other is the elimination of most tax exemptions, which are patently distortionary. Moreover, the delivery of essential public services such as education and health to a large section of our population is a major challenge.

Fourth, there is a growing recognition in India that governance reforms are critical to strengthening state capacity and enabling it to perform its core functions. The task of improving the institutions of economic governance comprise, among others, many organisations and actions essential for the good functioning of markets. It must be recognised that good governance can coexist only when the public sector functions fairly and efficiently, which can be achieved by improving and not undermining it. The business community therefore has a vital stake in improving and empowering public institutions. I would like to endorse what Professor Avinash K. Dixit, President-Elect, American Economic Association, said in the Second P.R. Brahmananda Memorial Lecture delivered by him in June 2007 in Mumbai:

> Finally, I think that the process of designing institutional reforms offers a good opportunity for fruitful collaboration between academic economists and businesspeople. Many academic economists used to dislike or disdain businesspeople and prefer a statist solution to economic problems. This is much less true in western countries these days, but the tendency may be more persistent in India. I hope even they will regard the task of improving the institutions of economic governance in a favorable light, seeing it as a way of constraining the opportunistic behavior of businesspeople. Many of them will also be attracted by the idea of a bottom-up rather than a top-down reform. There is a wealth of academic studies, theoretical and empirical, of the evolution,

performance, and limitations of such institutions. Businesspeople have a clear perception of the specific governance needs of their industries. The two can combine their brains and energies to adapt the lessons of these studies to the Indian situations, and contribute to creating a better environment for continued rapid economic progress of the country (Dixit 2007: 17–18).

Strengths

The Indian economy has some inherent strengths, both quantifiable and non-quantifiable, which would be of help in meeting the challenges ahead. Apart from the quantifiable strengths already described, there are certain 'not easily quantifiable strengths' that our economy possesses. First, a vast pool of science and technology graduates and the millions of people who are familiar with the English language are sources of strength. The familiarity with multiple languages in India prepares the people to adapt better to multicultural situations, making it easier for them to fit into international systems smoothly. Second, India also enjoys the distinction of being the biggest democracy of the world. The existence of a free press provides some insurance against excesses, and makes governments at all levels more accountable. Third, the initiatives of many states towards the empowerment of women have been impressive, and have helped to defend their rights and gain greater self-esteem and control over their own personal lives and social relationships. Fourth, the political climate is characterised by what may be termed political system stability, despite the coalition cabinets and periodic elections both at the Centre and in several states. Fifth, India will remain one of the youngest countries in the world over the next few decades. This 'demographic dividend' is seen as an inevitable advantage, provided pre-requisites such as skill-upgradation and sound governance to realise it are put in place. Sixth, in terms of the business environment, the impressive growth coupled with the market orientation of the economy has been a bottom-up exercise, with a very broad-based growing entrepreneurial class. These tendencies perhaps reflect a penchant for innovation among the already large and growing entrepreneurial class in India, which is imbued with professionalism and is seeking to be globally competitive.

REFERENCES

Angus, Maddison. 2001. 'The World Economy: A Millennium Perspective', OECD.

Bosworth, Barry, Susan M. Collins and Arvind Virmani. 2007. 'Sources of growth in the Indian economy.' NBER Working Paper No. W12901.

Dixit, Avinash K. 2007. 'Second P.R. Brahmananda memorial lecture.' RBI, Mumbai. June.

Rodrik, Dani and Arvind Subramanian. 2004. 'From "Hindu Growth" to productivity surge: The mystery of the Indian growth transition.' IMF Working Paper No. 4/77.

Sivasubramonian, S. 2000. *The National Income of India in the Twentieth Century*, New Delhi: Oxford University Press.

Tata Services Limited. 2003. *Reforms and Productivity Trends in Indian Manufacturing Sector*. Mumbai: Tata Services Limited, Department of Economics and Statistics.

II

Financial-Sector Reforms

5

Reforming India's Financial Sector
Changing Dimensions and Emerging Issues*

India embarked on a strategy of economic reforms in the wake of a balance-of-payments crisis in 1991; a central plank of these was reforms in the financial sector and, with banks being the mainstay of financial intermediation, the banking sector. At the same time, reforms were also undertaken in various segments of financial markets to enable the banking sector to perform its intermediation role in an efficient manner. The thrust of these reforms was to promote a diversified, efficient and competitive financial system, with the ultimate objective of improving the allocative efficiency of resources through operational flexibility, improved financial viability and institutional strengthening. The reform measures in the financial sector can be envisaged as having progressed along the following lines.

First, the reforms included the creation of a conducive policy environment—these were related to the lowering of the erstwhile high levels of statutory pre-emption in the form of reserve requirements, the gradual rationalisation of the administered interest rate structure to make it market-determined and streamlining the allocation of credit to certain sectors.

*Previously presented as an address at the International Centre for Monetary and Banking Studies, Geneva, 9 May 2006.

Second, the efficiency and productivity of the system has been improved by enhancing competition. Since the onset of reforms, clear and transparent guidelines were laid down for the establishment of new private banks, and foreign banks were allowed more liberal entry. A precondition for new banks was that the bank had to be fully computerised *ab initio*. This was done in order to infuse technological efficiency and productivity in the sector, and also to serve as a demonstration effect on existing banks. As many as ten new private banks are operating in India at present; foreign banks operating in India numbered over thirty by end-September 2005. Competition was encouraged among public-sector banks as well.

Third, the ownership base in domestic banks has been broad-based. The equity base of most public-sector banks was expanded by infusing private equity, although the government continued to retain majority shareholding. At present, public-sector banks with 100 per cent government ownership comprise around 10 per cent of commercial bank assets, compared to around 90 per cent at the beginning of reforms. The share of listed private banks—both old and new—in the total assets of private banks stood at over 90 per cent at end-March 2005.

Fourth, a set of micro-prudential measures were instituted to impart greater strength to the banking system, and also to ensure their safety and soundness with the objective of benchmarking against international best practices (risk-based capital standards, income recognition, asset classification and provisioning requirements for non-performing loans (NPLs) as well as provisioning for 'standard' loans, exposure limits for single and group borrowers, accounting rules, investment valuation norms). These norms have been tightened over the years in order to gradually converge towards international best practices.

Fifth, the process of regulation and supervision has also been strengthened. A strategy of on-site inspection and off-site surveillance mechanism, together with greater accountability of external audit, has been instituted. This has been complemented with a process of prompt corrective action mechanism.

Sixth, in tandem with improvements in prudential practices,

institutional arrangements to improve supervision and ensure the integrity of payment and settlement systems has been put in place. As early as 1994, a Board for Financial Supervision (BFS) was constituted, comprising select members of the RBI Board to pay undivided attention to supervision. The BFS ensures an integrated approach to the supervision of banks, NBFCs, UCBs, select development banks and PDs. As part of the process of ensuring a coordinated approach to supervision, a High Level Co-ordination Committee on Financial and Capital Markets was constituted in 1999 with the Governor, RBI, as chairman, and the chiefs of the securities market and insurance regulators, and the secretary of the Finance Ministry as members to iron out regulatory gaps and overlaps. To minimise settlement risks in the money, government securities, and forex markets, the Clearing Corporation of India Ltd (CCIL) was established in 2002. Acting as a central counterparty through novation, the CCIL provides guaranteed settlement, thereby limiting the problem of gridlock of settlements. A Board for Regulation and Supervision of Payment and Settlement Systems (BPSS) has also been recently constituted to prescribe policies relating to the oversight of the financial infrastructure relating to payment and settlement systems. Finally, to address the systemic risks arising from the growth of financial conglomerates, the RBI has put in place an oversight framework, which envisages periodic sharing of information among the concerned regulatory bodies.

Seventh, the legal environment for conducting banking business has also been strengthened. Debt recovery tribunals were introduced early into the reforms process, exclusively for the adjudication of delinquent loans with respect to banks. More recently, an Act to enforce securities and recover loans was enacted in 2003 to enhance the protection of lenders' rights. To combat the menace of crime-related money, the Prevention of Money Laundering Act was enacted in 2003 to provide the enabling legal framework. The Credit Information Companies (Regulation) Act, 2004 has recently been enacted by the Parliament, and is expected to enhance the quality of credit decision-making. The government is considering several major legal amendments to enhance the powers of the RBI. Major changes relate to the removal of restrictions on voting rights in banks, providing the legal basis for consolidated supervision, removal of the floor of 25 per cent with respect to SLR and empowering the RBI to supersede the board of a banking company.

Eighth, the reforms have focused on adopting appropriate processes in order to ensure the development of various segments of the markets. In the banking sector, the Indian Banks' Association (IBA) has emerged as an important self-regulatory body working for the growth of a healthy and forward-looking banking and financial services industry. In the debt market segment, the RBI interacts closely with the Fixed Income Money Market Dealers Association of India (FIMMDA) and the Primary Dealers Association of India (PDAI) for the overall improvement of government debt markets and the promotion of sound market practices. With regard to the payments system infrastructure, the introduction of the RTGS system since 2004 has made it possible for large value payments to be transacted in a faster, efficient and secure manner. In order to enhance the transparency of secondary market trades in government securities, a screen-based anonymous order matching system has been operationalised.

Ninth, the banking system has also witnessed greater levels of transparency and standards of disclosure with a greater volume of information being disclosed as 'Notes on Accounts' in their balance sheets. Salient among these are major profitability and financial ratios, details of capital structures, as well as movements in NPLs, movements in provisions and advances to sensitive sectors, to mention a few. The range of disclosures has gradually been expanded over the years to promote market discipline.

Tenth, corporate governance in banks has improved substantially over the years. A Consultative Group was constituted to explore the issue in all its facets in accordance with the best extant practices. Based on its recommendations, in June 2002 banks were advised to adopt and implement appropriate governance practices. As part of its efforts to promote sound corporate governance, the RBI has been focusing on ensuring 'fit and proper' owners and directors of the bank, and laying stress on diversified ownership. Banks have been advised to ensure that a nomination committee screens the nominated and elected directors to satisfy the 'fit and proper' criteria.

FEATURES OF REFORMS

The unique features of the progress in financial-sector reforms may be of some interest. First, financial-sector reforms were undertaken early in the reform cycle. Second, the reforms process was not driven by any banking crisis, nor was it the outcome of any external support package. Third, the design of the reforms was crafted through domestic expertise, taking on board the international experiences in this respect. Fourth, the reforms were carefully sequenced with respect to instruments and objectives. Thus, prudential norms and supervisory strengthening were introduced early in the reform cycle, followed by interest rate deregulation and the gradual lowering of statutory pre-emptions. The more complex aspects of legal and accounting measures were ushered in subsequently, when the basic tenets of reforms were already in place.

A unique feature of the reform of public-sector banks, which dominated the Indian banking sector, was the process of financial restructuring. Banks were recapitalised by the government to meet prudential norms through recapitalisation bonds. The mechanism of hiving off bad loans to a separate government asset management company was not considered appropriate in view of the moral hazard. The subsequent divestment of equity and offer to private shareholders was undertaken through a public offer, and not by sale to strategic investors. Consequently, all public-sector banks that issued shares to private shareholders have been listed on the exchanges and are subject to the same disclosure and market discipline standards as other listed entities. To address the problem of distressed assets, a mechanism has been developed to allow the sale of these assets to asset reconstruction companies (ARCs), which are in the private sector and operate as independent commercial entities.

In terms of the processes, too, certain interesting features of the reforms are in evidence. The first has been its gradualism, wherein reforms were undertaken only after a process of close and continuous consultation with all stakeholders. This participative process with wider involvement not only encouraged a more informed evaluation of the underlying content of policies, but also enhanced the credibility of policies and generated expectations among economic agents about the process being enduring in nature. The second has been a constant rebalancing of reform priorities predicated upon the domestic and global business environment, the institution of prudential practices, upgradation of the regulatory and supervisory framework, institution of appropriate institutional and legal reforms and the state of openness of the economy. The third important feature of the reforms has been its harmonisation with other policies, dictated by, among others, the state of preparedness of the financial sector and, above all, the underlying macroeconomic environment. Fourth, the reforms have progressed with emphasis on the common person, with the aim of developing a system that is responsive to the needs of all sections of society.

ASSESSMENT OF IMPACT

How useful has the financial liberalisation process in India been with regard to improving the functioning of markets and institutions? First, with the development of appropriate market regulation and associated payment and settlement systems, and the greater integration into global markets, the financial markets have witnessed a rapid growth and robustness. A range of instruments in domestic and foreign currency are traded in financial markets. In addition, the market in corporate bonds has been spurred with the increased use of external credit ratings. Further, derivative products covering forwards, swaps and options, as well as structured products, are transacted, enabling corporates and banks to manage their risk exposures. The market in securitised paper and both mortgage-backed and asset-backed securities has also grown significantly, supported by a well-developed credit rating industry. Second, liberalisation in the financial sector has led to the emergence of financial conglomerates, since banks have diversified their activities into insurance, asset management securities business, etc. Third, prudential regulation and supervision has improved; the combination of regulation, supervision and a better safety net has limited the impact of unforeseen shocks on the financial system. In addition, the role of market forces in enabling price discovery has been enhanced. The dismantling of the erstwhile administered interest rate structure has permitted financial intermediaries to pursue lending and deposit-taking based on commercial considerations and their asset-liability profiles. The financial liberalisation process has also enabled a reduction in the overhang of NPLs: this entailed both a 'stock' (restoration of net worth) and a 'flow' (improving future profitability) solution. The former was achieved through a carefully crafted capital infusion from the fisc, which aggregated, on a cumulative basis, to about 1 per cent of GDP; the flow solution, on the other hand, necessitated changes in the institutional and legal processes that were implemented over a period of time.

Moreover, financial entities have become increasingly conscious about risk management practices, and have instituted risk management models based on their product profiles, business philosophy and customer orientation. Additionally, access to credit has improved, through the newly-established domestic banks, foreign banks and bank-like intermediaries. Moreover, government debt markets have developed, enabling the RBI to undertake monetary policy more effectively, providing options to banks for liquidity management, and allowing less inflationary finance of fiscal deficits. The growth of government debt markets has also provided a benchmark for private debt markets to develop.

There have also been significant improvements in the information infrastructure. The accounting and auditing of intermediaries have been strengthened. The availability of information on borrowers has improved, which will help reduce information asymmetry among financial entities. The technological infrastructure has developed in tandem with modern-day requirements in information technology and communications networking. Moreover, the concept of finance has permeated various institutions, and a 'finance view' of all market transactions has emerged. Finally, the quality of human capital involved in the financial sector has typically been of the highest genre, facilitating a non-disruptive progress of the reforms process.

The improvements in the performance of the financial system over the decade-and-a-half of reforms are also reflected in the improvement in a number of indicators. Capital adequacy of the banking sector recorded a marked improvement and stood at 12.8 per cent at end-March 2005, comparable to 13 per cent for the US during the same period. Typically, the capital adequacy position of developed countries has remained range-bound within 10–14 per cent, and judged from that standpoint, our capital position compares favourably with those numbers.

On the asset quality front, notwithstanding the gradual tightening of prudential norms, NPLs to total loans of commercial banks, which was at a high of 15.7 per cent at end-March 1997, declined to 5.2 per cent at end-March 2005. These figures are broadly comparable to those prevailing in several leading European economies (like Italy, Germany and France), which typically ranged within 4–7 per cent of total loans, and lower than those in most Asian economies, although they were higher than those prevailing in countries such as the US, Canada and Australia. Net NPLs also witnessed a significant decline and stood at 2 per cent of net advances at end-March 2005, driven by the improvements in loan loss provisioning, which comprises over half the total provisions and contingencies.

Operating expenses of banks in India are also much more aligned to those prevailing internationally, hovering around 2.21 per cent during 2003–4 (2.16 per cent during 2004–5). In developed countries, in 2004, banks' operating expenses were 3.5 per cent in the US, 2.8 per cent in Canada and Italy, and 2.6 per cent in Australia, while they were in the range of 1.1 to 2 per cent in the banks of other developed countries such as Japan, Switzerland,

Germany and the UK. Bank profitability levels in India, as indicated by return on assets, have also shown an upward trend, and for most banks has been a little more than 1 per cent.

Incidentally, the turnaround in the financial performance of public-sector banks has resulted in the market valuation of government holdings far exceeding the recapitalisation cost. The Indian experience has shown that a strong regulatory framework that is non-discriminatory, market discipline through listing on stock exchanges and operational autonomy has had a positive impact on the functioning of public-sector banks.

WORK IN PROGRESS

Financial-sector reform is a continuous process that needs to be in tune with the emerging macroeconomic realities and the state of maturity of institutions and markets, mindful of financial stability. In this changing milieu, there are several areas that are being addressed now.

The first issue pertains to capital account convertibility. In view of the rapid changes that have taken place over the last few years and the growing integration of the Indian economy with the world economy, the RBI has recently set up a committee comprising eminent policymakers, financial-sector experts and members of the academia to suggest a roadmap for fuller capital account convertibility. The committee is required to, in this context, examine the implications of fuller capital account convertibility on monetary and exchange rate management, financial markets and the financial system.

The second issue relates to the fiscal area. The institution of the rule-based fiscal policy, as envisaged in the FRBM Act, 2003, has been on revenue-led fiscal consolidation, better expenditure outcomes and rationalisation of tax regimes, to remove distortions and improve the competitiveness of domestic goods and services in a globalised economic environment. In this context, the RBI has refrained from participating in the primary issues, except in exceptional circumstances. These *de facto* arrangements, which have been working satisfactorily for some time, have come into effect through legislative sanctions effective from 1 April 2006. While the Central government restated its commitment to fiscal consolidation as per the FRBM Act, several state governments have enacted legislation along similar lines, while some others are in the pipeline.

An important issue relating specifically to the banking sector is that of consolidation. Despite the liberalisation process, the structure of the Indian banking system has continued without much change, although DFIs were merged with banks. The consolidation process within the banking system in recent years has primarily been confined to a few mergers in the private-sector segment, induced by the financial position of the banks. Some mergers may take place in the future for compliance with minimum net worth requirement or norms on diversified ownership. The RBI has created an enabling environment by laying down guidelines on mergers and acquisitions. As the bottom lines of domestic banks come under increasing pressure and the options for organic growth exhaust themselves, banks will be exploring ways for inorganic expansion.

The fourth aspect is the role of foreign banks. In terms of assets, the share of foreign banks has roughly been around a quarter within the non-public sector banking category. They are dominant in certain segments, such as the forex market and the derivatives market, accounting for over half the off-balance sheet exposure of commercial banks. The RBI had, in February 2005, laid down clear and transparent guidelines, which provide a roadmap for the expansion of foreign banks. As it stands at present, foreign ownership in domestic banks is quite significant. In several new private banks this share is well over 50 per cent; these banks account for around half the total assets of domestic private banks. Even in several public-sector banks, the extent of foreign ownership within the private holding is close to that of the domestic private holding.

The fifth issue pertains to Basel II. Substantial progress has been made towards the implementation of Basel II in India, with foreign banks and Indian banks that have an operational presence outside India migrating to the Revised Framework with effect from 31 March 2008, while all other commercial banks, except RRBs and local area banks, are expected to migrate to these approaches no later than 31 March 2009. Banks are required to maintain a minimum capital to risk-weighted assets ratio (CRAR) of 9.0 per cent on an ongoing basis. As per the RBI guidelines, banks have adopted the Standardised Approach for credit risk and Basic Indicator Approach for operational risk. After having acquired adequate skills, banks would need to obtain prior approval of the RBI to migrate to the Internal Rating Based Approach for credit risk or the Advanced Measurement Approach for the operational risk. Under Basel II, the capital requirements of Indian banks are expected to go up as banks have to maintain capital for operational risk. The RBI has introduced capital instruments both in Tier I and Tier II, available in other jurisdictions. In addition, the RBI is involved in capacity building to ensure the regulator's ability to identify and permit eligible banks to adopt Internal Rating Based/Advanced Measurement approaches.

The sixth aspect is the role of capital in the case of RRBs and cooperative banks, which provide banking services primarily in the rural and semi-urban areas. The problems with regard to this segment have been widely documented: these include constraints on timely credit availability, its high cost, neglect of small farmers and the continued presence of informal lenders. It is argued that the greater part of the cooperative credit structure is multilayered, under-capitalised, over-staffed and under-skilled, often with a high level of delinquent loans. The RRBs also appear to share these problems, although there are several viable institutions in this category. These are being addressed on a priority basis. A national-level committee had recently made recommendations to revive and restructure the rural cooperative credit structure. These have been accepted by the government, which has set up a National Level Implementation and Monitoring Committee under the chairmanship of the Governor, RBI, for overall guidance in implementation. A process of revitalising the RRBs and UCBs in a medium-term framework is also underway.

Seventh, we are adopting a three-track approach with regard to capital adequacy rules. On the first track, the commercial banks are required to maintain capital for both credit and market risks as per the Basel I framework; cooperative banks on the second track are required to maintain capital for credit risk as per the Basel I framework and surrogates for market risk; RRBs on the third track which, though subject to prudential norms, do not have capital requirements on par with the Basel I framework. In other words, a major segment of systemic importance is under a full Basel I framework, a portion of the minor segment partly on Basel I framework and a smaller segment on a non-Basel framework. Even after commercial banks have begun implementing Basel II framework, banks, including UCBs and RRBs, continue to be on Basel I framework. This has not only ensured a greater outreach of the banking business, but also, in the present scenario of high growth, enable them to usefully lend to disadvantageous sections and successfully pierce the informal credit segment.

The eighth issue of relevance is that of financial inclusion. While the resource limitations experienced by low-income households will continue to constrain their access to and use of financial products, the challenge remains to develop appropriate policies, procedures, and products that can overcome this difficulty within the bounds of resource constraints. Apart from greater latitude in the range of identity documents that are acceptable to opening an account, there is also a need for independent information and advisory service. This needs to be supplemented by nurturing appropriate public-private partnerships. Some development to this effect is already evidenced in the significant growth and development of micro-finance activities. SHGs formed by NGOs and financed by banks represent an important constituent of this development process in India.

As part of its ongoing efforts to encourage greater financial inclusion, the Annual Policy Statement released in April 2006 pays particular attention to issues relating to farmers. A beginning has already been made to ensure greater outreach of banking facilities in rural areas through the appointment of reputed NGOs/post offices, etc., as banking facilitators and banking correspondents.

A working group has also been proposed to ensure greater outreach of banking facilities in rural areas, and to ensure the availability of bank finance at reasonable rates. A working group has also been proposed to suggest measures for assisting distressed farmers, including the provision of financial counselling services and the introduction of a specific Credit Guarantee Scheme under the Deposit Insurance and Credit Guarantee Corporation (DICGC) Act. The convenors of the State Level Bankers Committee in all states/union territories have been advised to identify at least one district in their area for achieving 100 per cent financial inclusion by providing a 'no-frills' account and a General Credit Card (GCC). A Technical Group has also been proposed to renew the existing legislative framework governing moneylending and its enforcement machinery so as to provide for greater credit penetration by the financial sector in rural areas at reasonable rates of interest.

The final area to have gained prominence in the recent past relates to customer service. The focus of attention is on the basic banking services provided to common persons, and the need for ensuring effective customer grievance redressal as well as a fair practice code. A banking ombudsman facility has been established, covering all states and union territories, for the redressal of grievances against deficient banking services. The recently constituted BCSBI is an important step in this regard, and this is expected to ensure that the banks formulate and adhere to their own comprehensive code of conduct for the fair treatment of customers. The Code of Banks' Commitment to Customers was released on 1 July 2006, and around sixty-seven banks have so far registered themselves with the BCSBI. Additionally, the constitution of a working group has been proposed in the latest policy to formulate a scheme for ensuring the reasonableness of the charges offered by banks on its various services.

It is widely acknowledged that India is the repository of the best human skills, especially in the financial sector. The technological competence of the Indian workforce is perhaps presently part of folklore. The present levels of growth optimism about the economy suggest that India is expected to remain one of the important growth drivers of the global economy in the near future. The financial infrastructure and regulatory framework in the country are broadly on par with those prevailing internationally. We are working towards evolving a globally competitive banking sector, stressing on the banking services relevant to our socio-economic conditions and contributing to both growth and stability.

6

Global Financial Turbulence and the Financial Sector in India
A Practitioner's Perspective*

This chapter will initially provide a broad overview of global developments, and then move on to briefly list the aspects of market and regulatory failures that characterised the recent developments. The contours of the financial-sector policies in India, with details of a few specific initiatives relevant to financial stability, provided in the concluding remarks at the end are in the nature of a few broad issues for further debate.

The trigger for the global developments in financial markets during the recent past was the rising default rates on sub-prime mortgages in the US; however, the source of the problem was perhaps not the macro-global imbalances, but the significant mispricing of risks in the financial system. Easy monetary policy in major financial centres, the globalisation of liquidity flows, widespread use of highly complex structured debt instruments and the inadequacy of banking supervision in coping with financial innovations contributed to the severity of the crisis. The persistent under-pricing of risks had been suspected by several central banks

---

*Previously presented as address, during the meeting of the Task Force on Financial Markets Regulation, organised by the Initiative for Policy Dialogue, Manchester, UK, 1 July 2008.

for quite some time, but it was felt by many that these risks were widely dispersed through financial innovation, and that they would not pose any serious problems to the banking system. When the sub-prime crisis did occur, however, it triggered a wide contagion, affecting many of the large global financial institutions. Banks in particular appear to have ceased to trust each other's creditworthiness, leading to difficulties in money markets in the US and European countries including the UK, resulting in the drying up of liquidity as each financial institution attempted to shore up its own liquidity to meet its obligations. The problems of a maturity mismatch in the conduits or structured investment vehicles (SIVs) created by banks for purposes of securitisation manifested themselves in a sudden spurt in banks' demand for liquidity to meet their liquidity support obligations to the SIVs or fund the assets of the SIVs that had been taken on to their balance sheets. It is now realised that the relevant banks had leveraged excessively and had either not fully recognised the risks or had seriously underpriced them, thus warranting a large capital infusion. There still remains uncertainty about the possible losses that are yet to be disclosed by several of them.

These developments have brought forward several new realities that pose severe challenges to macroeconomic management, in particular to monetary and regulatory policies globally. First, concerns relating to the US slowdown and its intensity have mounted in view of the potential spillover on to the global economy. Second, threats to the global economy are emanating from advanced economies in sharp contrast to earlier crises, which stemmed from the EMEs. Third, there are indications that protectionist tendencies have increased around the world, in anticipation of the growing possibilities of slower growth in advanced economies. Fourth, linkages between financial-sector developments and the real sector have become more worrisome than before, with apprehensions that the financial turmoil may spill over to the real sector, with adverse implications for employment and growth. With lending standards being tightened, the deterioration in asset quality and the deceleration in consumer loan demand, there are indications that events in the financial markets are beginning to have a long-term impact on the real economy as well. Fifth, higher and more volatile prices of food, energy and other commodities have compounded the problem, causing a significant upside bias to inflation and inflation expectations across the world, complicating the conduct of monetary policy at a time of severe financial stress. Further, while rising energy prices may come as an exogenous shock for several countries, for the global economy as a whole it is endogenous. Sixth, terms-of-trade losses due to soaring commodity prices not only reduce the capacity for a re-balancing in the world economy, but also impact several countries in different, but essentially adverse, ways. In fact, it is possible that new global economic imbalances have been emerging on account of the large movements in commodity prices, especially oil. Seventh, EMEs have been exhibiting resilience until now in the face of the global financial turmoil, reflecting relatively stronger macroeconomic frameworks and sustainable macroeconomic balances. However, it is uncertain as to how long and to what extent it will persist. On the other hand, inflationary pressures appear to be common to mature economies and EMEs, the latter, however, are under greater stress.

Depending on the evolving situations, the central banks in major countries have had to take recourse, in appropriate mix, to three instruments to avoid a serious spillover of these issues in money or credit markets in the wider economy: (*a*) adjustment of interest rates for borrowing and lending; (*b*) money market operations designed to inject special liquidity in order to avoid a breakdown in payment systems among banks and (*c*) to put in mechanisms for financial transactions among the largest of the financial intermediaries, which automatically impacts the second and third-rung intermediaries. Central banks in major industrialised economies by and large responded with injections of liquidity for a longer period than usual; they also resorted to a dilution in the quality of collateral required for liquidity support. Most of these operations have not been conducted at the penal rates expected in such situations. This is an unprecedented package which, some observers believe, is indicative of the seriousness of the underlying problems. In addition, there were some specific institution-oriented operations, for instance in the United States, Germany and the United Kingdom. While there have been inflationary pressures in most economies, the US has been faced with the threat of a serious slowdown in growth, warranting a series of cuts in policy rates in recent months.

In recent weeks, concerns over global inflationary pressures have taken centre-stage, even as there are no indications of whether threats to financial stability have been fully resolved, and whether the persistent threats of recession in the US have abated. Consequently, policy dilemmas have become more acute at the current juncture. The most urgent and short-term priority for central bankers at the moment seems to be to calm the nerves about inflation or anchor inflation expectations, with an implicit recognition that a somewhat elevated headline inflation in the short term may be difficult to avoid. Further, high inflation rates, when accompanied by a higher variability of inflation, gives rise to greater uncertainties. These acute policy dilemmas between growth and inflation have to be faced against the background of a financial turbulence that is yet to subside. There are also calls for a fundamental re-think on macroeconomic, monetary and financial-sector policies in order to meet the new challenges and realities, which perhaps represents a structural shift in the international financial architecture, demanding a potentially enhanced degree of coordination among monetary authorities and regulators. A review of the policies relating to financial regulation in a way needs to address both the acute policy dilemmas in the short run, and a fundamental re-think on the broader frameworks of financial and economic policies over the medium term.

Market Failures

What are some of the identifiable sources of the market failures that led to the current financial turbulence?

First, the prolonged benign macroeconomic conditions gave rise to complacency among many market participants and led to an erosion of sound practices, resulting in the adoption of poor credit risk appraisal standards.

Second, some of the standard risk management tools and models used by market participants were not equipped to estimate either the potential impact of adverse events for structured credit products or the high uncertainty around model estimates that largely missed the underlying combination of risks. Further, these risk models generally tended to induce market participants to adopt a unidirectional approach.

Third, many investors, including institutional ones, who had the capacity to carry out their own credit analysis, did not undertake a sufficient in-house examination of the risks in the assets underlying structured investments.

Fourth, the role of credit-rating agencies (CRAs) in the recent market developments has attracted attention.

Fifth, the distortions in incentive structures can be seen from various perspectives, namely incentives for originators, arrangers, distributors and managers in the originate-to-distribute model; the compensation schemes in financial institutions that do not distinguish between realised and unrealised profits; the encouragement of financial structures tailored to obtaining high ratings; etc.

Sixth, weaknesses in the public disclosures of financial institutions regarding the type and magnitude of the risks associated with their on- and off-balance sheet exposures are noticeable.

Seventh, large commercial banks and investment banks have assumed increasingly similar risk profiles, use similar models to assess and are subject to, the same risk-management challenges under the given circumstances.

Eighth, there is a new dimension to bank liquidity with the shifting emphasis to market-based wholesale or purchased liabilities. This makes banks increasingly dependent on the market for raising liquidity, while markets may have a tendency to shy away from providing liquidity when they are most needed.

Regulatory Shortcomings

While the foregoing brings out the failures of markets and market participants, some of the regulatory shortcomings identified are as follows.

First, the regulators recognised some of the underlying vulnerabilities in the financial sector but failed to take effective action, partly because they may have overestimated the strength and resilience of the financial system or assumed that the risks were well distributed among entities outside the banking system. Many analysts and policymakers had raised concerns about excessive risk-taking, loose underwriting standards and asset overvaluations, all of which have, in the absence of timely effective action, laid the seeds for crises.

Second, the limitations in regulatory arrangements, including the capital adequacy framework, contributed to the growth of unregulated exposures, excessive risk-taking and weak liquidity risk management.

Third, weaknesses in the application of accounting standards and the shortcomings associated with the valuation and financial reporting of structured products played a significant role in the current turbulence, through pro-cyclical valuations and the lack of full disclosure of banks' true risk profile through the cycle.

Fourth, the crisis revealed the need to adapt some of the central banks' tools and practices to manage system liquidity in the light of banks' cross-border operations. The recent experiences have highlighted the differences in the emergency liquidity frameworks of central banks on aspects such as range of collateral and range of eligible counterparties, and the differences in central bank practices.

Fifth, supervisors did not adequately address the deterioration in risk management standards in the regulated entities, which did not fully reckon the risks associated with new financial instruments. Besides, there were shortcomings in consolidated supervision as well.

Sixth, deficiencies in crisis management and bank resolution frameworks, including deposit insurance, have been observed, especially where central banks do not have a central supervisory role.

Seventh, the complex interrelationship between regulation, inappropriate accounting practices and regulators' excessive dependence on external ratings may have exacerbated the market turbulence.

Menu of Solutions

The above underlying factors clearly demonstrate a need to enhance the resilience of the global system and take into account some of the prescriptions that have been proffered for the consideration of policymakers. The recent developments in global financial markets have been closely followed by many. These include market participants, central bankers, supervisors, multilateral institutions, political leaders, analysts, academicians and also the layman. With so much attention focused on the ongoing turbulence by so many stakeholders, we have a wide menu of solutions and prescriptions. I will quickly run through some of these.

First, risk-management frameworks, including the governance arrangements in banks and financial institutions, need to be reviewed by the managements in light of the recent experiences.

Second, supervisors need to play a more active role in scrutinising the risk-management practices, including stress testing and governance arrangements, off-balance sheet entities and structured products. At the same time, it is crucial to recognise that risk management cannot be achieved solely by regulation. Consolidated supervision and prudential reporting should be applied to the off-balance sheet entities associated with financial institutions, and to loans sold with implicit or explicit recourse. There is a need to review the prudential norms linked to the external ratings assigned by the CRAs.

Third, supervisors should encourage institutions to develop more robust models that use more prudent and reliable assumptions and stress-testing methodologies, and monitor more closely the internal processes and controls for managing risk.

Fourth, there is a need to rationalise the regulatory and supervisory prescriptions with a view to reducing the scope for arbitraging. This also calls for a closer coordination of the relevant supervisors/supervisory arms.

Fifth, it is necessary to correct the imbalances in the incentive mechanisms at various levels.

Sixth, greater transparency is not only necessary to make markets more efficient and optimise the allocation of capital, but is also considered the best insurance policy against irrational herd behaviour and unjustified contagion in times of stress.

Seventh, there is a need to collectively review and resolve the element of pro-cyclicality in prudential regulations, accounting rules and the attitude of the authorities that tend to apply these.

Eighth, it is necessary for the CRAs to improve their governance and rating methodologies.

Ninth, it is arguably useful to re-visit the relevant accounting standards and explore the scope for applying fair value accounting through the cycle so as to mitigate pro-cyclicality.

Tenth, supervisors should have the clear authority to intervene at the first sign of weakness, preferably much before the institution's net worth turns negative.

Finally, deposit insurance systems should aim to limit the likelihood of retail depositor runs in troubled banks through adequate coverage, and have the capacity to pay depositors quickly.

INDIAN EXPERIENCE

Ensuring Financial Stability

In contrast to the above global scenario, India has by and large been spared global financial contagion due to the sub-prime turmoil for a variety of reasons. The credit derivatives market is in an embryonic stage; the originate-to-distribute model in India is not comparable to the ones prevailing in advanced markets; there are restrictions on investments by resident in such products issued abroad and regulatory guidelines on securitisation do not permit immediate profit recognition. Financial stability in India has been achieved through the perseverance of prudential policies which prevent institutions from excessive risk-taking, and financial markets from becoming extremely volatile and turbulent. As a result, while there are orderly conditions in financial markets, the financial institutions, especially banks, reflect strength and resilience. While supervision is exercised by a quasi-independent board carved out of the RBI Board, the interface between regulation and supervision is close with respect to banks and financial institutions, and on market regulation, a close coordination with other regulators exists. Let me recount this experience which, in some ways, reflects a policy that aimed to assure financial stability, while maintaining growth momentum at reasonable levels and according high priority to price stability.

Investment Portfolio

In 2000, the RBI conducted a stress test of the banks' investment portfolio in an increasing interest rate scenario, when the general trend was decreasing interest rates. At that time, banks in India were maintaining a surrogate capital charge for market risk, which was at variance with Basel norms. On the basis of the findings, in order to better position the banking system to meet the adverse impact of interest-rate risk, banks were advised in January 2002 to build up an Investment Fluctuation Reserve (IFR) within a period of five years. The prudential target for the IFR was 5 per cent of their investments in the 'Held for Trading' (HFT) and 'Available for Sale' (AFS) categories. Banks were encouraged to build up a higher percentage of IFR up to 10 per cent of their AFS and HFT investments. This counter-cyclical prudential requirement enabled banks to absorb some of the adverse impact when interest rates began moving in the opposite direction in late 2004. Banks have been maintaining a capital charge for market risk as envisaged under the Basel norms since end-March 2006.

Regulatory guidelines in India require banks to classify their investments into three categories, similar to international standards. The investments included in the Held to Maturity (HTM) category was capped at 25 per cent of the total investments, and banks are allowed to carry the investments in the HTM category at cost, subject amortisation of premium, if any. With the change in the direction of interest rates in 2004, the cap on the HTM category was reviewed in light of the statutory prescriptions (referred to as SLR in India), requiring banks to mandatorily invest up to 25 per cent of their Demand and Time Liabilities (DTL) in eligible government securities. In view of the statutory pre-emption and the long duration of government securities, banks were permitted to exceed the limit of 25 per cent of the total investments under the HTM category, provided the excess comprised only of SLR securities, and that the total SLR securities held in the HTM category was not more than 25 per cent of their DTL. Such shifting was allowed at acquisition cost or book value or market value on the date of transfer, whichever is the least, and the depreciation, if any, on such transfer was required to be fully provided for. The above transition is consistent with international standards that do not place any cap on the HTM category, and was considered advisable, taking into account the statutory nature of the SLR, while ensuring prudence and transparency in valuation on transfer to the HTM category. While the earlier prescription for this category was relatively more conservative, the changes in September 2004 recognised the dynamic interface with interest-rate cycles, and were counter-cyclical.

Capital Adequacy—Risk Weights

In view of the increase in the growth of advances to the real-estate sector, banks were advised to put in place a proper risk-management system to contain the risks involved. Banks were also advised to put in place a system to ensure the proper checking and documentation of related papers before sanctioning/disbursing such loans. In June 2005, the RBI advised banks to have a broad mandated policy with respect to their real-estate exposure, covering exposure limits, collaterals to be considered, margins to be kept, the sanctioning authority/level and the sector to be financed. In view of the rapid increase in loans to the real-estate sector, which raised concerns about asset quality and the potential systemic risks posed by such exposure, the risk weight on banks' exposure to commercial real estate was increased from 100 per cent to 125 per cent in July 2005, and further to 150 per cent in April 2006. The risk weights on the housing loans extended by banks to individuals against mortgage of housing properties and investments in mortgage-backed securities (MBS) of housing finance companies

(HFCs), recognised and supervised by the National Housing Bank (NHB), were increased from 50 to 75 per cent in December 2004. However, upon review, banks were advised to reduce the risk weight with respect to exposures arising out of housing loans up to Rs 30 lakh (US$ 75,000 approx) to individuals against the mortgage of residential housing properties from 75 to 50 per cent, in view of the lower perception of risks in these exposures.

In light of the strong growth in consumer credit and the volatility in capital markets, it was felt that the quality of lending could suffer during the phase of rapid expansion. Hence, as a counter-cyclical measure, we increased the risk weight for consumer credit and capital market exposures from 100 per cent to 125 per cent.

Provisions against Standard Assets

The prudential norms relating to income recognition, asset classification and provisioning, introduced during 1992–3, are being continuously monitored and refined to bring them on par with international best practices. In keeping with this, several measures were initiated in 2005–6. The provisions for standard assets were revised progressively in stages in November 2005, May 2006 and January 2007, in view of the continued high credit growth in the real-estate sector, personal loans, credit card receivables, and loans and advances qualifying as capital market exposure and a higher default rate with regard to personal loans and credit card receivables, which emerged as a matter of concern. The standard assets in the following categories of loans and advances attract a 2 per cent provisioning requirement: (*a*) personal loans (including credit card receivables); (*b*) loans and advances qualifying as capital market exposure; (*c*) real-estate loans (excluding residential housing loans) and (*d*) loans and advances to systemically important non-deposit accepting non-banking finance companies. In order to ensure continued and adequate availability of credit to the highly productive sectors of the economy, the provisioning requirement for all other loans and advances, classified as standard assets, was kept unchanged, viz., (a) direct advances to the agricultural and SME sectors at 0.25 per cent and (b) all other loans and advances at 0.4 per cent.

Exposure to Inter-Bank Liability

In order to reduce the extent of concentration of bank's liabilities, the RBI had issued guidelines to banks in March 2007 placing prudential limits on the extent of their Inter-Bank Liability (IBL) as a proportion of their networth (200 per cent). Those banks which had a higher capital adequacy ratio of 125 per cent of the regulatory minimum were allowed a higher limit of 300 per cent of networth. In addition, prudential limits have also been placed on the extent to which banks may access the inter-bank call money market, both as a lender and as a borrower.

Financial Regulation of Systemically Important NBFCs and Banks' Relationship with Them

The RBI has been strengthening the regulatory and supervisory framework for NBFCs since 1997 with the objective of making the NBFC sector vibrant and healthy. The focus was initially on deposit-taking NBFCs. These efforts were pursued further during 2006–7, when a major thrust was on strengthening the regulatory framework with regard to systemically important NBFCs so as to reduce the regulatory gaps. At that time, the regulatory focus was also widened to include systemically important non-deposit taking NBFCs, and prudential norms were specified for these entities. The application of different levels of regulations to the activities of banks and NBFCs, and even among different categories of NBFCs, had given rise to some issues relating to the uneven coverage of regulations. Based on the recommendations of an internal group and taking into consideration the feedback received thereon, a revised framework to address the issues pertaining to the overall regulation of systemically important NBFCs and the relationship between banks and NBFCs was put in place in December 2006.

Securitisation guidelines

The RBI issued guidelines on the securitisation of standard assets in February 2006. The guidelines are applicable to banks and financial institutions, including NBFCs. These guidelines provide for a conservative treatment of securitisation exposures for capital adequacy purposes, especially with regard to credit enhancement and liquidity facilities. The regulatory framework encourages greater participation by third parties with a view to ensuring better governance in the structuring of special purpose vehicles (SPVs), the products and the provision of support facilities. A unique feature of these guidelines, which may be at variance with the accounting standards, is that any profits on sale of assets to the SPV are not allowed to be recognised immediately on sale, but over the life of the pass through certificates issued by the SPV. We believe that these guidelines, as a package, have ensured an appropriate incentive mechanism for securitisation transactions.

Banks' Investment in Non-SLR Securities

The RBI had emphasised that banks should observe prudence in order to contain the risk arising out of their non-SLR (that is, non-government) investment portfolio, in particular through the private placement route. Detailed prudential guidelines on the subject were issued in June 2001, which were reviewed and revised in November 2003. These guidelines, *inter alia*, address aspects of coverage, regulatory requirements, listing and rating requirements, fixing of prudential limits, internal assessments, role of boards, disclosures and trading and settlement in debt securities. Banks were specifically advised to not be solely guided by the ratings assigned to these securities by the external rating agencies, but to do a detailed appraisal as in the case of direct lending.

Marking-to-market

The Indian accounting standards are generally aligned to the international financial reporting standards, although there are some differences. In India, we are yet to fully adopt the marking-to-market requirements, as available in the international standards. The Indian standards are relatively conservative and do not permit recognition of unrealised gains in the profit and loss account or equity, although unrealised losses are required to be accounted. Banks are required to mark-to-market the investments in the HFT and AFS categories at periodical intervals on a portfolio basis, and provide for the net losses and ignore the net gains. This has proved to be a stabilising factor, inasmuch as it has not induced an imbalance in the incentive structures and has also proved to be less pro-cyclical.

Moral Suasion and Supervisory Review

Moral suasion and the public articulation of concerns has helped to achieve a desired re-balancing of suspected excesses in risk-taking among banks. Some of the areas where moral suasion has been used are the need for banks to monitor the unhedged foreign currency exposures of their corporate clients, adoption of appropriate incentive mechanisms by banks for encouraging disclosures of derivative exposures by their corporate clients, banks' reliance on non-deposit resources to finance assets, their excessive reliance on wholesale deposits and uncomfortable loan-to-value (LTV) ratios with respect to housing loans, etc.

A supervisory review process (SRP) was initiated with select banks having significant exposure to sensitive sectors, including reliance on call money market, in order to ensure that effective risk mitigants and sound internal control systems were in place. In the first round, a framework was developed for monitoring the systemically important individual banks. The second round of SRP was directed to analyse banks' exposure to sensitive sectors and identify outliers. Based on the analyses of these outlier banks, guidelines were issued to all banks, indicating the need for better risk management systems in banks at operating levels.

In brief, in India the focus is on regulatory comfort, and goes beyond regulatory compliance. In a choice between emphasis of regulations on saving capital and protecting depositors' interests or reinforcing financial system stability, the latter have always prevailed.

INDIAN EXPERIENCE OF FINANCIAL-SECTOR LIBERALISATION AND DEVELOPMENT

It is necessary to clarify that while the measures mentioned above are aimed at fostering financial stability, in order to enhance efficiency several other initiatives have been taken to liberalise the macro-policy environment in which banks operate through a re-orientation of regulatory prescriptions by replacing micro-regulations with macro-prudential regulations, providing an enabling environment for universal banking, improved corporate governance in private-sector banks and enabling the consolidation of banks in the private sector. Some other important measures that promoted a vibrant and robust operating environment and framework for the banking system, along with promoting growth and business opportunities, include a reduction in pre-emption through reserve requirements; a shift to market-determined pricing for government securities; disbanding of some of the administered interest rates; auction-based repos-reverse repos for short-term liquidity management; facilitation of improved payments and settlement mechanism; setting up of the CCIL to act as central counter party for facilitating payments and a settlement system relating to fixed income securities, money market instruments, and foreign exchange transactions; setting up of the InfiNet as the communication backbone for the financial sector; introduction of the Negotiated Dealing System (NDS) for screen-based trading in government securities; introduction of the RTGS System; debt recovery tribunals, ARCs, settlement advisory committees, corporate debt restructuring mechanism, etc., for quicker recovery/ restructuring of stressed assets; promulgation of Securitisation and Reconstruction of Financial Assets and Enforcement of Securities Interest (SARFAESI) Act, 2002, and its subsequent amendment to ensure creditor rights; setting up of the Credit Information Bureau of India Limited (CIBIL) for information sharing on defaulters as well as other borrowers. These growth-oriented initiatives have appropriately complemented the stability-oriented ones.

Development Orientation

In the context of the rapidly evolving financial landscape, the RBI has also been suitably reorienting its regulatory and supervisory framework to meet the needs of the common man. The RBI has also endeavoured to improve the credit delivery and customer service of banks, and has simultaneously focused on financial inclusion and extension of banking services to the unbanked areas of the economy. The guidelines on lending to the priority sector included the improvement of credit delivery to those sectors of the economy that impact large segments of the population, the weaker section and the sectors that are employment-intensive, such as agriculture and tiny and small enterprises. In order to improve credit delivery to micro and small and medium enterprises, the RBI has urged banks to review their institutional arrangements for delivering credit to the SME sector, especially in identified clusters in various parts of the country, and to take measures to strengthen the expertise in, and systems at, branches located in or near such identified clusters with a view to providing adequate and timely credit. The RBI has taken several measures in recent years aimed at providing customer service at a reasonable cost. These measures include enhancing customer protection and disclosures, a code of ethics and grievance redressal, among others. The RBI's broad approach to financial inclusion aims at 'connecting people' with the banking system and not just credit dispensation; giving people access to the payments system and portraying financial inclusion as a viable business model and opportunity. The RBI has been initiating measures to improve the outreach of banks and their services, and promote financial inclusion in less developed states and union territories.

Monetary Policy

As part of the conduct of monetary policy, the RBI monitors, *inter alia*, monetary and credit aggregates. It uses both liquidity and interest rate instruments to achieve the monetary policy objectives. Pre-emptive actions have been taken since 2004 to withdraw monetary accommodation, which was reinforced with measures aimed at moderating early signs of over-heating. Further, appreciation of the possible permanent and temporary components with regard to oil prices has been articulated in the policies. While undertaking a nuanced approach to managing aggregate demand, recognising the elements of shock and the consequent impact on inflation expectations, the underlying demand conditions warranted several interest rate and liquidity measures in recent weeks.

While monetary policy influences aggregates, the reality is often dis-aggregated. Hence, the RBI uses prudential regulatory policies to complement the monetary policy measures and objectives. It is pertinent that the lender of the last resort function is not separate, either from monetary and liquidity management or from financial regulation. Thus, both monetary policy and prudential regulations are used as complementary tools to achieve the central bank objectives, and they both support and reinforce each other.

REMARKS ON BROADER ISSUES

The detailed account given above of developments in the global and the Indian financial sector would be incomplete without devoting some attention to the broader issues. These issues need to be reckoned and debated widely, lest the response to recent developments be construed as internal to the financial sector, warranting only such sector-specific solutions.

First, do the benefits of financial liberalisation and financial globalisation need to be re-evaluated? It is possible to argue that the liberalisation of trade in goods has contributed more to growth and price stability than financial-sector initiatives. In particular, it may be argued that the incentive frameworks for financial intermediaries appear disproportionate to their conceivable contribution to the economy. The arguments in favour of persevering with financial innovation and urging regulators to continue to prioritise facilitating innovations should be viewed in this context.

Second, have regulators placed greater emphasis on savings of capital in banks rather than on the interests of the depositors and on systemic stability? The recent compulsions to shore up capital on the part of some global financial institutions in advanced economies seem to suggest this. What induced the regulators to permit such excesses in leverage and savings of capital? Does this also involve issues pertaining to governance and accountability of regulators?

Third, is there a beginning of fiscalisation of the financial sector in view of the intensification of links between the two? For example, the recent episodes of participation of the sovereign wealth funds in the re-capitalisation of banks are tantamount to fiscal support. Further, large doses of liquidity support to financial markets by regulators against collateral may also involve quasi-fiscal costs, under some circumstances.

Fourth, is there what may be called a financialisation of the political economy? The attractiveness of financial intermediaries in terms of high profitability, significant growth—especially cross-border—the massive spread of investors and the inadequate scope for the application of principles of rules of origin in the financial sector could have resulted in an enhanced clout for these intermediaries in the political economy. Incidentally, Professor Jagdish Bhagwati's reference to Wall Street–Washington links is relevant in this context.

Fifth, has there been excessive financialisation of corporates, in the sense that large corporates take significant positions in the financial markets through their treasury operations? Increasingly, many of the positions of corporates in financial markets may not be related to their underlying business. Do we have an issue when such activities of corporates in financial markets, unrelated to their underlying business, are not regulated in the way similar activities of financial market intermediaries are?

To conclude, on the way forward, in order to exit the current financial turbulence and fortify ourselves against similar episodes in the future, we may need to look beyond reforms within the financial sector and address broader, related issues that impinge on the balance between the sovereign, the regulators, the financial institutions and the markets.

7

Rural Credit
Status and Agenda*

There are several concerns in relation to rural credit that are generally expressed in terms of inadequacy, constraints on timely availability, high cost, neglect of small and marginal farmers, low credit-deposit ratios in several states and the continued presence of informal markets. It is held that while commercial banks are more focused in improving efficiency and profitability, they have tended to give comparatively less priority to rural credit. RRBs and cooperatives appear to face serious problems of governance as well as operational efficiency. It is argued that the better part of the cooperative credit structure is multilayered, under-capitalized, over-staffed and under-skilled, often with mounting NPAs, and in a few cases has resulted in the erosion of public deposits as well. Several RRBs appear to share most of these problems, although there are some vibrant and viable institutions in this category. These problems relating to rural credit have been well-documented, and several policy approaches were made to rectify the situation. However, there is some element of dissatisfaction with the overall situation with regard to rural credit, which is not improving as desired despite such a series of actions. It is a matter of concern that cognisable

*Previously presented as a speech, delivered at the International Seminar in honour of Professor C.H. Hanumantha Rao, Administrative Staff College of India, Hyderabad, India, 16 November 2004.

success is eluding policymakers, at a time when the increasing commercialisation of agriculture and allied activities warrants a big thrust in institutional credit to agriculture. There is thus a discernible widespread intellectual recognition that while immediate measures are being undertaken to increase the flow of credit to agriculture, there is a need to review the policy of rural credit in a comprehensive and thorough manner.

The current strategy adopted by the RBI to increase the flow of credit may be summarised as follows. First, the coverage of rural credit is extended to include facilities such as storage as well as credit through NBFCs. Second, procedural and transactional bottlenecks are sought to be removed, including the elimination of the Service Area Approach (that is, earmarking identified areas to be serviced exclusively by a designated branch of a bank), reducing margins, redefining overdues to coincide with crop cycles, new debt restructuring policies, one-time settlement and relief measures for farmers indebted to non-institutional lenders, etc. Third, the Kisan Card Scheme (a credit card issued by a bank to a farmer to enable the purchase of fertilisers, seeds, pesticides, etc.) is being improved and widened in its coverage, while some banks are popularising GCCs, which are in the nature of clean overdrafts for multipurpose use, including consumption. Fourth, public and private-sector banks are being encouraged to enhance credit delivery, while strengthening disincentives for shortfall in priority sector lending (that is, shortfall in meeting the mandated share to sectors that are accorded a priority status, such as agriculture and small and medium industry). Fifth, banks are urged to price the credit to farmers based on an actual assessment of individual risk rather than on a flat rate depending on the category of borrower or end-use, while ensuring that the interest rates charged are justifiable as well as reasonable. In brief, the thrust is on enhancing credit delivery in a regime of reasonable credit prices within the existing legal and institutional constraints, and to this limited extent there has been a major change in the mindset.

Against this background, the agenda for the future consists of five parts. First, there is a need for legal and institutional changes relating to the governance, regulation, and functioning of the rural cooperative structure, and that of RRBs, which have to be critical instruments for rural credit in the future. In this regard, it is useful to note the nature of competition and accountability to shareholders governing the functioning of commercial banks, which would make their foray into rural credit predominantly subject to commercial considerations. The changes warranted in cooperatives as well as RRBs call for a deep commitment on the part of state governments and have a significant bearing on political economy. Thus, the current thrust to improve credit delivery may soon face limits unless the legal and institutional changes are agreed and acted upon in good faith in a timely fashion. It is the fervent hope of the RBI that a consensus on these fundamental changes, so essential for achieving the broad policy objectives, will develop soon.

Second, there are overhanging problems of NPLs and an erosion of deposits in both cooperatives and RRBs. There is some assessment of the magnitudes of losses and capital needs in RRBs, while in the case of cooperatives the data are not yet firm. It may not be appropriate to continue to permit institutions that are not solvent to seek and accept public deposits, and hence the RBI favours early restructuring and recapitalisation. There is an inevitable fiscal impact of any scheme of recapitalisation, which has to be transparent and has to bear all the costs of overhanging issues as well as capital adequacy to assure the continued solvency and safety of public deposits in the future. Such a one-time fiscal support is justifiable, urgent and essential for several reasons, including the fact that 'There Is No Alternative', and that a delayed response could end up being more expensive. The current acceleration in credit delivery can be sustained in the medium term if such fiscal support from the states and the Centre is firmly put in place soon, so as to revive or reorganise the rural cooperative structure and RRBs.

Third, there is a need to foster credit culture to make enhanced rural credit a lasting phenomenon. A benign credit culture is one which encourages appropriate credit price, credit delivery under transparent conditions of both lenders' and borrowers' liabilities and incentives for repayment rather than default. Measures that counter such a benign credit culture are often well-intended, but, as the experience has shown so far, they tend to be seriously counter-productive. There is a need for a consensus in this regard, so that the rural credit system in India can be compatible with our goals of higher growth and better equity. In this regard, it is necessary to recognise that the expansion of credit in some states that have a low credit-deposit ratio depends on a conducive credit culture, including factors relating to governance and commercial viability.

Fourth, on the critical issue of risk mitigation, it is held that experiments with crop or credit insurance in India have not been very satisfactory so far. In fact, many farmers argue that when compulsory insurance is resorted to, it increases the burden of borrowing from institutional sources, and once the transaction costs are added, the overall costs exceed the Prime Lending Rates significantly. There are several risks that a farmer faces, and of these future price and monsoon conditions are most severe, and almost entirely beyond the control of the farmer. While Minimum Support Price (that is, the price at which select public-sector institutions are obliged to purchase a commodity as an assurance for farmers) is a mechanism that has served us well, its cost effectiveness is subject to debate, and in any case the coverage is limited to cereals like rice and wheat and, in some areas, cotton. The farmer faces the risks of monsoon conditions and usually the adverse climatic conditions are widespread in a geographical area, with the result that severe limits are set on private insurance. Experts had flagged the issue of strategies to reduce risks as one of the four major areas of long-term planning as early as in 1993, but they covered only water conservation, venture capital and insurance promotion, wherever viable. Perhaps it is necessary to recognise that if some elements of insurance are *ab initio* not viable, extending credit becomes more risky and hence constrained.

Finally, in light of the above, there is merit in considering a comprehensive public policy on risk management in agriculture, as not only a means of relief for distressed farmers but also as an ingredient for more efficient commercialised agriculture. The components of such a policy have to be worked out in detail, but the public policy could, for instance, consider some of the elements described here.

First, establishing a well-articulated, objective and independent assessment of the impact of adverse monsoon conditions and appropriate relief to farmers on an assured basis.

Second, facilitating farmers to assure themselves of a price for all their products before harvesting or even sowing the seed, through a well-regulated network of forward, futures and options markets.

Third, establishing and implementing the liability of suppliers for any shortfall in quality or assured supply in vital inputs such as seeds, pesticides, power and water.

Fourth, gradually eliminating and replacing price subsidies with outlays on risk mitigation for farmers in the broadest sense.

Fifth, positioning flexibility in extending rural credit within a broad framework of such a comprehensive public policy on risk management in agriculture.

III

Banking-Sector Reforms

8

Banking-Sector Reforms in India
An Overview*

I t will be useful to briefly recall the nature of the Indian banking sector at the time of the initiation of financial-sector reforms in India in the early 1990s. The Indian financial system in the pre-reform period (that is, prior to the Gulf Crisis of 1991), essentially catered to the needs of planned development in a mixed-economy framework where the public sector played a dominant role in economic activity. The strategy of planned economic development required huge development expenditures, which were met through the government's dominance of bank ownership, automatic monetisation of fiscal deficit and subjecting the banking sector to large pre-emptions—both in terms of the statutory holding of government securities (SLR) and CRR. Besides, there was a complex structure of administered interest rates guided by social concerns, resulting in cross-subsidisation. These not only distorted the interest rate mechanism, but also adversely affected the viability and profitability of banks by the end of the 1980s. Banking, especially in EMEs, has traditionally been a highly protected industry with a regulated interest rate structure both for deposits and lending, and restrictions on foreign and domestic entry. It follows that the process of financial-sector reform in most emerging economies, while being specific to the circumstances

---

*Previously presented as address, Institute of Bankers of Pakistan, Karachi, 18 May 2005.

of each country, also has significant commonalities. A narration of the broad contours of reform in India would be helpful in appreciating both the commonalities and the differences in our paths of reforms.

CONTOURS OF BANKING REFORMS IN INDIA

First, reform measures were initiated and sequenced to create an enabling environment for banks to overcome external constraints— these were related to the administered structure of interest rates high levels of pre-emption in the form of reserve requirements, and credit allocation to certain sectors. Sequencing of interest rate deregulation has been an important component of the reform process and has imparted greater efficiency to resource allocation. The process has been gradual, and predicated upon the institution of prudential regulation for the banking system, market behaviour, financial opening and, above all, the underlying macroeconomic conditions. The interest rates in the banking system have been largely deregulated except for certain specific classes, namely savings deposit accounts, non-resident Indian (NRI) deposits, small loans up to Rs 2 lakh and export credit. The need for continuing with these prescriptions as well as those relating to priority-sector lending have been flagged for wider debate in the latest annual policy of the RBI. However, administered interest rates still prevail in small savings schemes of the government.

Second, as regards the policy environment of public ownership, it must be recognised that the lion's share of financial intermediation was accounted for by the public sector during the pre-reform period. As part of the reforms programme, there was an initial infusion of capital by the government in public-sector banks, which was followed by an expansion of the capital base with equity participation by private investors. The share of the public-sector banks in the aggregate assets of the banking sector has come down from 90 per cent in 1991 to around 75 per cent in 2004. The share of wholly government-owned public-sector banks (that is, where no diversification of ownership has taken place) sharply declined from about 90 per cent to 10 per cent of aggregate assets of all SCBs during the same period. Diversification of ownership has led to greater market accountability and improved efficiency. Since the initiation of reforms, infusion of funds by the government into public-sector banks for the purpose of recapitalisation amounted, on a cumulative basis, to less than 1 per cent of India's GDP, a figure much lower than that for many other countries. Even after accounting for the reduction in the government's shareholding on account of losses set off, the current market value of the share capital of the government in public-sector banks has increased manifold, and as such, what was perceived by the government as a bail-out of public-sector banks seems to be turning out to be a profitable investment where the government is concerned.

Third, one of the major objectives of banking-sector reforms has been to enhance efficiency and productivity through competition. Guidelines have been laid down for the establishment of new banks in the private sector and foreign banks have been allowed more liberal entry. Since 1993, twelve new private-sector banks have been set up. As already mentioned, an element of private shareholding in public-sector banks has been injected by enabling a reduction in government shareholding in public-sector banks to 51 per cent. As a major step towards enhancing competition in the banking sector, FDI in private-sector banks is now allowed up to 74 per cent, subject to conformity with the guidelines issued from time to time.

Fourth, consolidation in the banking sector has been another feature of the reform process. This also encompassed the DFIs, which have been providers of long-term finance, while the distinction between short-term and long-term finance providers has increasingly become blurred over time. The complexities involved in harmonising the role and operations of the DFIs were examined, and the RBI enabled the reverse-merger of a large DFI with its commercial banking subsidiary, which is a major initiative towards universal banking. Recently, another large term-lending institution has been converted into a bank. While guidelines for mergers between NBFCs and banks were issued sometime ago, guidelines for mergers between private-sector banks were issued on 11 May 2005. The principles underlying these guidelines would be applicable, where appropriate, to public-sector banks too, subject to the provisions of the relevant legislation.

Fifth, impressive institutional and legal reforms have been undertaken in relation to the banking sector. In 1994, BFS was constituted, comprising select members of the RBI Board with a variety of professional expertise to exercise 'undivided attention to supervision'. The BFS, which generally meets once a month, provides direction on a continuing basis on regulatory policies, including governance issues and supervisory practices. It also provides direction on supervisory action in specific cases. The BFS also ensures an integrated approach to the supervision of commercial banks, DFIs, NBFCs, UCBs and PDs. BPSS was also constituted in February 2005 to prescribe policies relating to the regulation and supervision of all types of payment and settlement systems, set standards for existing and future systems, authorise the payment and settlement systems and determine criteria for membership to these systems. The Credit Information Companies (Regulation) Bill, 2004 has been passed by both the houses of Parliament, while the Government Securities Bill, 2004 is being processed. Certain amendments are being considered by Parliament to enhance the RBI's regulatory and supervisory powers. Major amendments relate to the requirement of prior approval from the RBI in cases concerning the acquisition of 5 per cent or more shares of a banking company with a view to ensuring the 'fit and proper' status of significant shareholders, aligning voting rights with economic holding and empowering the RBI to supersede the Board of a banking company.

Sixth, there have been a number of measures to enhance the transparency and disclosures standards. For instance, with a view to enhancing transparency, all cases of penalty imposed by the RBI on banks, as well as directions issued on specific matters including those arising out of inspection, are to be placed in the public domain.

Seventh, while the regulatory framework and supervisory practices have almost converged with the best practices elsewhere in the world, two points are noteworthy. First, the CRAR has been kept at 9 per cent, that is, one percentage point above the international norm and second, banks are required to maintain a separate IFR out of profits towards interest rate risk at 5 per cent of their investment portfolio, under the categories HFT and AFS. This was prescribed at a time when interest rates were falling, and banks were realising large gains out of their treasury activities. Simultaneously, the conservative accounting norms did not allow banks to recognise the unrealised gains. Such unrealised gains, coupled with the creation of IFR, helped to cushion the valuation losses incurred due to the upward movement of interest rates in the longer tenors.

Eighth, of late, the regulatory framework in India, in addition to prescribing prudential guidelines and encouraging market discipline, is increasingly focusing on ensuring good governance through 'fit and proper' owners, directors and senior managers of banks. Transfer of shareholding of 5 per cent and above requires acknowledgement from the RBI, and such significant shareholders are put through a 'fit and proper' test. Banks have also been asked to ensure that the nominated and elected directors are screened by a nomination committee to satisfy the 'fit and proper' criteria. Directors are also required to sign a covenant indicating their roles and responsibilities. The RBI has recently issued detailed guidelines on ownership and governance in private-sector banks, emphasising diversified ownership. The listed banks are also required to comply with the governance principles laid down by the Securities and Exchange Board of India (SEBI)—the securities markets regulator.

PROCESSES OF BANKING REFORM

The processes adopted to bring about reforms in India may be of some interest in this context. It will be useful to recall some features of financial-sector reforms in India before narrating the processes. First, financial-sector reform was undertaken early in the reform cycle in India. Second, the financial sector was not driven by any crisis, and the reforms have not been an outcome of multilateral aid. Third, the design and detail of the reforms were evolved through domestic expertise, although international experience was always kept in mind. Fourth, the government preferred public-sector banks to manage the overhanging problems of the past rather than clean up the balance sheets with its support. Fifth, it was felt that there was enough room for growth and healthy competition for public and private-sector banks, as well as foreign and domestic banks. The twin governing principles are non-disruptive progress and consultative process.

In order to ensure timely and effective implementation of these measures, the RBI has been adopting a consultative approach before introducing policy measures. Suitable mechanisms have been instituted to deliberate upon various issues, so as to ensure that the benefits of financial efficiency and stability percolate to the common person and the services of the Indian financial system be benchmarked against international best standards in a transparent manner. Let me give a brief account of these mechanisms.

First, on all important issues, working groups are constituted or technical reports prepared, which generally encompass a review of the international best practices, options available and the way forward. Group membership may be internal or external to the RBI or mixed. Draft reports are often placed in the public domain, and final reports take account of inputs, in particular from industry associations and self-regulatory organisations. Reform measures emanate from such a series of reports, the pioneering ones being the *Report of the Committee on the Financial System* (Chairman: Shri M. Narasimham) in 1991; *Report of the High Level Committee on Balance of Payments* (Chairman: Dr C. Rangarajan) in 1992 and the *Report of the Committee on Banking Sector Reforms* (Chairman: Shri M. Narasimham) in 1998.

Second, Resource Management Discussion meetings are held by the RBI with select commercial banks, prior to the policy announcements. These meetings focus not only on the perception and outlook of bankers vis-à-vis the economy, liquidity conditions, credit flow, development of different markets and directions of interest rates, but also on issues relating to the developmental aspects of banking operations.

Third, we have formed a Technical Advisory Committee on Money, Foreign Exchange and Government Securities Markets (TAC). It has emerged as a key consultative mechanism amongst the regulators and various market players, including banks. The committee has been crystallising the synergies of experts across various fields of the financial market, and thereby acting as a facilitator for the RBI in steering reforms in money, government securities and foreign exchange markets.

Fourth, in order to strengthen the consultative process in the regulatory domain and place such a process on a continuing basis, the RBI has constituted a Standing Technical Advisory Committee on Financial Regulation along lines similar to that of the TAC. The committee consists of experts drawn from the academia, financial markets, banks, non-bank financial institutions (NBFIs), and CRAs. The committee examines the issues referred to it, and advises the RBI on desirable regulatory framework on an ongoing basis for banks, NBFIs and other market participants.

Fifth, to ensure periodic formal interaction amongst regulators, there is a High Level Coordination Committee on Financial and Capital Markets with the Governor, RBI, as chairman, and the heads of the securities market and insurance regulators, and the secretary of the Finance Ministry as members. This coordination committee has authorised the constitution of several standing committees to ensure coordination in regulatory frameworks at an operational level.

Sixth, the Standing Advisory Committee on UCBs has been playing an important role in providing suggestions on structural, regulatory and supervisory issues relating to UCBs, and facilitating the process of formulating future approaches for this sector. Similar mechanisms are being worked out for NBFCs.

Seventh, the RBI has also instituted a mechanism to place draft versions of important guidelines before the public for their comments before finalising the guidelines. To further this consultative process, and with the specific goal of making the regulatory guidelines more user-friendly, a Users' Consultative

Panel has been constituted, comprising the representatives of select banks and market participants. The panel provides feedback on regulatory instructions at the formulation stage to avoid any subsequent ambiguities and operational glitches.

Eighth, an extensive and transparent communication system has been evolved. The annual policy statements and their mid-term reviews communicate the RBI's stance on monetary policy for the immediate future of six months to one year. Over the years, the reports of various working groups and committees have emerged as another plank of the two-way communication from the RBI. An important feature of the RBI's communication policy is the almost real-time dissemination of information through its website. The auction results under the LAF of the day are posted on the website by 12.30 PM the same day, while by 2.30 PM the 'reference rates' of select foreign currencies are also uploaded. By the next morning, the press release on money market operations is issued. Every Saturday, by 12 PM, the weekly statistical supplement is placed on the website, which provides a fairly detailed, recent database on the RBI and the financial sector. All regulatory and administrative circulars of different departments of the RBI are placed on the website within half-an-hour of their finalisation.

Ninth, an important feature of the Indian financial-sector reforms is the authorities' intention to align the regulatory framework with international best practices, keeping in view the developmental needs of the country and various domestic factors. Towards this end, a Standing Committee on International Financial Standards and Codes was constituted in 1999. The Standing Committee had set up ten advisory groups in key areas of the financial sector, whose reports are available on the RBI website. The recommendations contained in these reports have either been implemented or are in the process of implementation. I would like to draw attention to two reports in particular that have a direct bearing on the banking system, viz., Advisory Group on Banking Supervision and Advisory Group on Corporate Governance. Subsequently, in 2004, we conducted a review of the recommendations of the advisory groups, and reported the progress and agenda ahead.

WHAT HAS BEEN THE IMPACT?

These reform measures have had a major impact on the overall efficiency and stability of the banking system in India. The present capital adequacy of Indian banks is comparable to those at the international level. There has been a marked improvement in the asset quality with the percentage of gross NPAs to gross advances for the banking system reduced from 14.4 per cent in 1998 to 7.2 per cent in 2004. The reform measures have also resulted in an improvement in the profitability of banks. The return on assets of banks rose from 0.4 per cent in 1991–2 to 1.2 per cent in 2003–4. Considering that, globally, the return on assets has been in the range of 0.9 to 1.5 per cent for 2004, Indian banks are well placed. The banking-sector reforms also emphasised the need to review the manpower resources and rationalise the requirements by drawing a realistic plan, so as to reduce the operating cost and improve profitability. Over the last few years, the business per employee for public-sector banks more than doubled to stand at around Rs 25 million in 2004.

CONTINUITY, CHANGE AND CONTEXT

We lay considerable emphasis on an appropriate mix between the elements of continuity and change in the process of reform; however, the dynamic elements in the mix are determined by the context. While there is usually a consensus on the broad direction, the relative emphasis on various elements of the process of reform keeps changing, depending on the evolving circumstances. Perhaps it will be useful to illustrate this approach to contextualising the mix of continuity and change.

The mid-term review in November 2003 reviewed the progress of implementation of various developmental as well as regulatory measures in the banking sector, and emphasised facilitating the ease of transactions made by the common person and strengthening credit delivery systems as a response to the pressing needs of the society and economy. The Annual Policy Statement of May 2004 carried this focus forward, but flagged major areas requiring urgent attention, especially in the areas of ownership, governance, conflicts of interest and customer protection. Some extracts of the policy statement are provided below:

First, it is necessary to articulate in a comprehensive and transparent manner the policy in regard to ownership and governance of both public and private sector banks keeping in view the special nature of banks. This will also facilitate the ongoing shift from external regulation to internal systems of controls and risk assessments. Second, from a systemic point of view, inter-relationships between activities of financial intermediaries and areas of conflict of interests need to be considered. Third, in order to protect the integrity of the financial system by reducing the likelihood of their becoming conduits for money laundering, terrorist financing and other unlawful activities and also to ensure audit trail, greater accent needs to be laid on the adoption of an effective consolidated know your customer (KYC) system, on both assets and liabilities, in all financial intermediaries regulated by RBI. At the same time, it is essential that banks do not seek intrusive details from their customers and do not resort to sharing of information regarding the customer except with the written consent of the customer. Fourth, while the stability and efficiency imparted to the large commercial banking system is universally recognised, there are some segments which warrant restructuring.

The Annual Policy Statement of May 2005 reiterates the concern for the common person, while enunciating a medium-term framework for the development of money, forex and government securities markets; enhancing credit flow to agriculture and small industry; action points in technology and payments systems; institutional reform in cooperative banking, NBFCs and RRBs, and for ensuring the availability of quality services to all sections of the population. The most distinguishing feature of the policy statement relates to the availability of banking services to the common person, especially depositors.

The statement reiterates that depositors' interests form the focal point of the regulatory framework for banking in India, and elaborates the theme as follows:

> A licence to do banking business provides the entity, the ability to accept deposits and access to deposit insurance for small depositors. Similarly, regulation and supervision by RBI enables these entities to access funds from a wider investor base and the payment and settlement systems provides efficient payments and funds transfer services. All these services, which are in the nature of public good, involve significant costs and are being made available only to ensure availability of banking and payment services to the entire population without discrimination.

The policy draws attention to the divergence in the treatment of depositors as compared to borrowers:

> ... while policies relating to credit allocation, credit pricing and credit restructuring should continue to receive attention, it is inappropriate to ignore the mandate relating to depositors' interests. Further, in our country, the socio-economic profile for a typical depositor who seeks safe avenues for his savings deserves special attention relative to other stakeholders in the banks.

Another significant area of concern has been the possible exclusion of a large section of the population from the provision of services, and the statement pleads for financial inclusion. It states:

> There has been expansion, greater competition and diversification of ownership of banks leading to both enhanced efficiency and systemic resilience in the banking sector. However, there are legitimate concerns in regard to the banking practices that tend to exclude rather than attract vast sections of population,

in particular pensioners, self-employed and those employed in unorganised sector. While commercial considerations are no doubt important, the banks have been bestowed with several privileges, especially of seeking public deposits on a highly leveraged basis, and consequently they should be obliged to provide banking services to all segments of the population, on equitable basis.

Operationally, it has been made clear that the RBI will implement policies to encourage those banks that provide extensive services, while disincentivising those that are not responsive to the banking needs of the community, including the underprivileged.

The quality of services rendered has also invited attention in the current policy. It states:

> Liberalisation and enhanced competition accord immense benefits, but experience has shown that consumers' interests are not necessarily accorded full protection and their grievances are not properly attended to. Several representations are being received in regard to recent trends of levying unreasonably high service/ user charges and enhancement of user charges without proper and prior intimation. Taking account of all these considerations, it has been decided by RBI to set up an independent Banking Codes and Standards Board of India on the model of the mechanism in the UK in order to ensure that comprehensive code of conduct for fair treatment of customers are evolved and adhered to.

BASEL II AND INDIA

It is essential to recognise that while these constitute contextually nuanced responses to changing circumstances within the country, the overwhelming compulsion to be in harmony with global developments is sought to be respected, and that essentially relates to Basel II.

Here, it will be appropriate to list some of the regulatory initiatives taken by the RBI that are relevant for Basel II. First, we have tried to ensure that the banks have a suitable risk management framework oriented towards their requirements, which are dictated by the size and complexity of business, risk philosophy, market perceptions and the expected level of capital. Second, Risk Based Supervision (RBS) in twenty-three banks has been introduced on a pilot basis. Third, we have been encouraging banks to formalise their capital adequacy assessment process (CAAP) in alignment with their business plan and performance budgeting system. This, together with the adoption of RBS, would aid in factoring the Pillar II requirements under Basel II. Fourth, we have been expanding the area of disclosures (Pillar III) so as to have greater transparency in the financial position and risk profile of banks. Finally, we have tried to build capacity for ensuring the regulator's ability to identify and permit eligible banks to adopt Internal Rating Based/Advanced Measurement approaches.

In the current scenario, banks are constantly pushing the frontiers of risk management. Compulsions arising out of increasing competition, as well as agency problems between management, owners, and other stakeholders are inducing banks to look at newer avenues to augment revenues, while trimming costs. While consolidation, competition and risk management are no doubt critical to the future of banking, I believe that governance and financial inclusion will also emerge as key issues for a country like India, at this stage of socio-economic development.

9

Micro-Finance
RBI's Approach*

REVIEW OF DEVELOPMENTS

The beginning of the micro-finance movement in India can be traced to the SHG-bank linkage programme, started as a pilot project in 1992 by the NABARD in consultation with the RBI. The RBI provided the policy support by advising banks to actively participate in the programme. In 1994, the RBI constituted a working group on NGOs and SHGs. On the group's recommendations, the RBI advised that the banks' financing of SHGs would be reckoned as part of their lending to weaker sections, and that such lending should be reviewed by banks as well as the State Level Bankers' Committee at regular intervals. As a follow-up to the recommendations of the NABARD Working Group, the RBI took a series of measures in April 1996 to give a thrust to micro-finance based lending, and these are worth recalling.

Banks were advised to consider lending to SHGs as part of their mainstream credit operations, to identify branches with the potential to link with SHGs, and provide the necessary support services to such branches, while including the SHG-lending within their Service Area Plan. The Service Area branches were in turn

---

*Previously presented as an address at the Micro-Finance Conference organised by the Centre for Analytical Finance, Indian School of Business, Hyderabad, India, 6 August 2005.

to fix their own programme for lending to SHGs, so as to enable them to benefit from the catalytic services of NGOs. The Service Area branch managers were asked to conduct an ongoing dialogue and establish a rapport with the NGOs and SHGs of the area in order to effect a linkage. Banks were also advised that SHGs, registered or unregistered, which engaged in promoting saving habits among their members, would be eligible to open savings bank accounts with banks, irrespective of whether they could avail of credit facilities from banks. It was also decided that the flexibility allowed to banks with respect to margins, security norms, etc., as part of the pilot project for savings-linked loans to SHGs, would continue. Further, it was decided that NABARD would continue to provide refinance to banks under the linkage project at the rates it had stipulated. Furthermore, subsequent to the Monetary and Credit Policy announcement for 1999–2000, banks were advised that interest rates applicable to loans given by banks to micro-credit organisations or by the micro-credit organisations to SHGs/ member beneficiaries would be left to their discretion. Also, the SHGs were to be free to decide on the interest rate to be charged their members, provided the rate of interest was not excessive.

While close coordination between the NABARD and the RBI characterised the growth of the micro-credit movement till 1999, the Government of India took an active interest in the subject, as evidenced by the successive announcements in the budget speeches of finance ministers since 1999. However, the announcements related essentially to the SHG programme, except in the budget speech of 2005, where there was a separate and distinct reference to MFIs with mention of a suitable legislation, although the thrust remains on linkage with the banks to provide financial intermediation. The budget speech states:

> At present, micro finance institutions (MFIs) obtain finance from banks according to guidelines issued by the RBI. MFIs seek to provide small scale credit and other financial services to low income households and small informal businesses. Government intends to promote MFIs in a big way. The way forward, I believe, is to identify MFIs, classify and rate such institutions and empower

them to intermediate between the lending banks and the beneficiaries. Commercial banks may appoint MFIs as 'banking correspondents' to provide transaction services on their behalf. Since MFIs require infusion of new capital, I propose to re-designate the existing Rs. 100 crore Micro Finance Development Fund as the 'Micro Finance Development and Equity Fund', and increase the corpus to Rs. 200 crore. The fund will be managed by a Board consisting of representatives of NABARD, commercial banks and professionals with domain knowledge. The Board will be asked to suggest suitable legislation, and I expect to introduce a draft Bill in the next fiscal year.

It must be recognised that the policy of expanding the thrust beyond micro-credit to the MFIs is not a reflection on the lack of progress in the provision of micro-credit, but a reiteration of its success and a possible approach to widen, deepen and strengthen the micro-finance movement as a whole. The evolution of the SHG-bank linkage programme can be viewed in terms of three distinct phases, viz., (a) pilot testing during 1992 to 1995; (b) mainstreaming during 1996 to 1998 and (c) expansion from 1998 onwards. The cumulative number of SHGs 'credit-linked' to banks showed a significant expansion, from 255 at end-March 1993 to 16.18 lakh at end-March 2005. Commensurate with an increase in the cumulative refinance support from NABARD from about Rs 0.3 crore at end-March 1993 to over Rs 3,092 crore by end-March 2005, the cumulative bank loans disbursed witnessed a sharp increase from about Rs 0.3 crore to around Rs 6,898 core during the period. This translates to an estimated 2.42 core poor families being brought within the fold of banking services. The loans per SHG increased to Rs 42,620 during 2004–5 from an average of Rs 36,179 in the previous year, reflecting the process of deepening credit access amongst the SHGs.

NEW PARADIGM

It is clear that the dominant theme so far has been one of extending micro-credit through SHG-bank linkages, with NABARD playing a leadership role and MFIs, mainly NGOs, playing a catalytic as well as an enabling role at the grassroots level. However, there is clearly an emerging new paradigm in the approach to micro-finance. It would be appropriate to recall that while the term 'micro-credit' has not been strictly defined at present, it usually refers to the credits of 'very small amounts'. However, for the purpose of exempting micro-finance companies registered under Section 25 of the Companies Act from the core regulatory provisions attracted by NBFCs, such companies are required by the RBI to be engaged solely in extending micro-finance up to Rs 50,000 for small businesses, and up to Rs 1.25 lakh for housing in rural areas. The term 'micro-finance' has been given a working definition by the Task Force on Supportive Policy and Regulatory Framework for Micro-Finance set up by NABARD in November 1998, which states: 'provision of thrift, credit and other financial services and products of very small amounts to the poor in rural, semi-urban and urban areas for enabling them to raise their income levels and improve living standards'. It is, however, understood that the MFIs provide other non-credit services as well, such as capacity building, training, marketing the products of the SHGs, micro-insurance, etc. Against this background, the following considerations are relevant:

First, micro-finance can be seen to be a broader concept than micro-credit, and the focus of discussion has now expanded beyond micro-credit to cover micro-finance.

Second, there is recognition in the *Annual Policy Statement* of the RBI for 2005–6 of the need to enhance financial inclusion, and banks were urged to review their existing practices so as to align them with the objective of financial inclusion with regard to banking services. This underlines the importance of the micro-finance movement in addressing the issue of financial exclusion.

Third, the increasing size and growth of MFIs seem to warrant a clearer policy framework to cover operations in financial services in addition to credit, with respect to both bank- and NABARD-led micro-finance through SHGs and MFIs.

Fourth, the delivery of non-credit financial services, such as insurance and mutual funds, by MFIs seems possible, but as a pre-condition, there is a need for a clear framework regulating the approach of different regulators to these non-bank financial services offered by MFIs. As currently there is no single regulator for this sector, banks and NBFCs fall under the regulatory purview of the RBI, while the other entities are covered by varying degrees of regulation under their respective state legislations.

Fifth, the organisational forms of MFIs appear varied, although the activities may in some cases include non-financial services. This makes them subject to differing legal frameworks as per the organisational form.

Sixth, different state governments take varying approaches to MFIs—including subsidising the interest rates. The nature and spread of the micro-finance movement also differ significantly across states.

Seventh, as per the information available, a significant part of the current micro-finance activity is related to credit, which can perhaps be attributed to both the felt credit needs and the absence of a conscious policy thrust with regard to non-credit related financial services.

Eighth, developments in technology seem to provide a window of opportunity to reduce transaction costs, and thus enable micro-finance to be a commercially viable and profitable activity.

Finally, the Finance Minister, in his budget speech for 2005-6, made a reference to the possibility of a suitable legislation in this regard.

A preliminary response to these developments has been on the following lines, though the issue needs to be revisited carefully in due course. Broadly, the RBI's approach has been to emphasise the informality of micro-finance and focus on the developmental aspects. The regulatory dispensation put in place by the RBI seeks to enable enhanced credit flow from banks through MFIs, and could be further refined by the RBI as necessary. With regard to the suggestion for bringing micro-finance entities under a system of regulation through a separate legislation, the RBI felt that the micro-finance movement across the country, involving the common people, has benefited immensely from its informality and flexibility. Hence, their organisation, structure and methods of working should be simple, and any regulation will be inconsistent with the core spirit of the movement. It was also felt that ideally, the NABARD or the banks should devise appropriate local safeguards in their relationship with the MFIs, taking into account the different organisational forms of such entities. In any case, if there is any statute for the regulation of MFIs contemplated, it may be at the state level, with no involvement of the RBI as banking regulator or for extending the deposit insurance.

ISSUES AND NEXT STEPS

In view of the new paradigm that was noticed with regard to microfinance, as exemplified by the statement of the Finance Minister in his budget speeches of 2005–6, the RBI decided to revisit the issue in a comprehensive manner. Accordingly, several initiatives were taken in recent months. First, consultations were arranged with several representatives of MFIs in select centres to obtain their views. Second, based on such consultations, a Technical Paper on policy relating to 'Development, Regulation and Supervision of Microfinance Services' was prepared, and discussed with the representatives of this sector on 18 July 2005. The recommendations of the paper were considered in consultation with the government. Third, and in parallel, an internal group of the RBI on Rural Credit and Micro-Finance Committee (also known as Khan Committee) had been set up to examine the issues relating to this sector, and the draft report of the group was placed in the public domain on 1 June 2005 for comments. The Report captures the experience of other countries and our requirements, both in terms of the development of micro-finance and of financial inclusion. The final version of the Khan Committee Report, dated 19 July 2005, has since been placed on the website of the RBI. The report considers (*a*) policy options and strategies for deepening and widening financial services; (*b*) the promotion, development and rating of MFIs and other outreach entities and (*c*) regulatory issues and concerns. The report will form the basis for evolving a policy framework in consultation with the government, NABARD and other stakeholders.

It is, however, necessary to recognise that there are several issues that have to be clarified as one proceeds with a response to what may be termed the new paradigm in micro-finance, described above. Importantly, the new paradigm seems to imply a process of formalising what has essentially been an informal mechanism of credit disbursal, occasionally coupled with other activities, and expanding its scope. It is worth recounting some of the major issues in this regard.

First, how do we distinguish MFIs from micro-credit institutions, and both of these from other financial institutions? Is it by the ceilings imposed on the size of deposits and lendings, and/or by other defining activities? What part or percentage of the activity could be non-financial while the institution continues to be an MFI? Is there merit in differentiating between not-for-profit MFIs and the profit-seeking ones?

Second, how do we identify, for regulatory purposes, micro-credit institutions as distinct from MFIs since the latter may need more varied skills and, in any case, warrant a policy view by more than one financial-sector regulator?

Third, should SHGs, which have no formal organisational structure, be brought within the ambit of the proposed formal framework for MFIs?

Fourth, there are currently five organisational forms of the MFIs, viz., trusts; societies; cooperative societies; not-for-profit companies and NBFCs. There are also instances of large corporates undertaking micro-credit activity as part of their operations. What are the merits and demerits of recognising one or more, or all, the organisational forms under a formalised regulatory framework for MFIs?

Fifth, there is also a need to recognise the large regional differences in the spread of SHGs and MFIs across the country. While the issue needs deeper analysis to identify the reasons for such variation and to promote a balanced growth of the MFIs, it, *prima facie*, appears that MFIs have flourished more in the states that have a well-developed banking infrastructure and outreach. Thus, MFIs in our country would seem to supplement, rather than substitute, a developed banking infrastructure.

Sixth, what should be the role of foreign capital and venture capital with regard to MFIs? Here, it may be necessary to recognise the orientation of micro-finance activity, given the limitations of size and skills in MFIs, and then the consistency with the risk-reward bias of such sources of commercial capital. As regards the external commercial borrowings, the imperatives of exchange rate risk and the capacity of MFIs to effectively assess and manage this risk would also need to be duly reckoned.

Seventh, what could be the scope and effectiveness of a self-regulatory organisation for the MFIs, and how does it dovetail with the possible formalised regulatory framework under contemplation?

Eighth, credit rating is usually assigned for the specific instruments issued or for a defined purpose, often on a continuing basis. There is merit in devising a rating system for MFIs, while recognising that such exercises are seldom for localised views amongst decentralised entities. It will be instructive to review our experience so far with regard to the utility and quality of the rating exercises of MFIs. How do we ensure that the rating exercise adds value to the localised operations of MFIs?

Ninth, what are the prospects for expanding the permission accorded by the RBI to the NBFCs for offering credit and other financial services to not-for-profit companies? What are the prospects for creating a separate category of NBFC-MFIs to be regulated by the RBI?

Finally, should all MFIs or only a select category of them be permitted to accept public deposits? While there is a view which states that only banks should be permitted to accept public deposits, currently NBFCs are also permitted to accept public deposits, but subject to the regulatory prescriptions of the RBI. Needless to say, it is the issue of accepting public deposits that poses major challenges, both legislative and, more importantly, that of moral hazard.

As the experience with cooperative banking shows, a soft regulatory regime relative to SCBs, be it in terms of governance or prudential aspects, tends to attract less than truly 'fit and proper' persons to capture such institutions. Indeed, it is possible to argue that our experience with bringing cooperative banks under the Banking Regulation Act, 1949 in 1966, coupled with their coverage under deposit insurance, compared with the health and reach of the cooperative sector before such regulations came into effect, would provide some lessons in this regard. In fact, the RBI, in its comments on the draft report of the Task Force on Revival of Cooperative Credit Institutions (Vaidyanathan Committee, February 2005), argued in favour of substituting the RBI's regulatory jurisdiction with a separate independent national or state-level regulatory body, broadly in line with what had been advocated by Dr Bimal Jalan in his policy statement in 2001 with regard to UCBs. Currently, it is proposed to examine the issue in detail in light of the recommendations of the Khan Committee, and keeping in mind the globally recognised Microfinance Consensus Guidelines issued in July 2003 by the Consultative Group to Assist the Poor (CGAP), incorporating the Guiding Principles on Regulation and Supervision of Microfinance, March 2002. These guiding principles highlight the globally recommended principles on the regulation and supervision of micro-finance, and need to be considered in the context of the conditions prevailing in our country.

Within the existing legal framework and institutional structures, there are several operational issues that could be addressed through the coordinated efforts of the Central government, state governments, regulators, banks and the NABARD. The RBI has an interest in pursuing the subject as part of its thrust towards financial inclusion. As the micro-credit approach yields place to a more encompassing micro-finance approach, coordinating mechanisms amongst financial-sector regulators and institutional regulators have to be considered. A view needs to be taken on whether to permit SCBs to participate in the equity of the MFIs. There may also be a need to establish processes for transition from one form of organisation to another, while remaining engaged in micro-finance activity. There are several tax measures, both at Central and state levels, from which MFIs have been seeking special dispensation, but a view is yet to be taken on many of them. Training and capacity-building is a high-priority area which, coupled with the widespread use of technology, could reduce transaction costs and improve overall effectiveness while imparting robustness to the movement. Some states like Andhra Pradesh intend to provide financial support for these purposes. There is considerable scope for increasing the tried and successful model of SHG-bank linkages, especially to the large tracts of the country that have not been adequately covered. The RBI is currently engaged in exploring a forum where these issues could be addressed on a continuing basis, through a participative and consultative process amongst all stakeholders.

In conclusion, it is necessary to recognise that we in India have to focus on extending financial services to both rural and urban areas to ensure the financial inclusion of all segments of the population. At the same time, one should avoid the temptation of creating one set of banking and financial institutions to cater to the poor or the unorganised, and another for the rest. The medium to long-term objective should be to ensure the inclusion of all segments in mainstream institutions while taking advantage of the flexibility of multiple models in delivering a wide range of financial services. In this light, a comprehensive framework to revive the cooperative credit system, revitalise the RRBs and reorient the commercial banking system needs to be given high priority while simultaneously encouraging and enabling the growth of the micro-finance movement in India, which has been very successful. We need to build on its strengths and extend it to vast areas that are inadequately covered by both banking and micro-credit entities. Micro-finance, broadly defined, needs to be explored in the light of the new paradigm described. The RBI and NABARD recognise the growing importance of micro-finance and are committed to enabling its healthy growth. However, several issues, both with regard to the regulation and development of MFIs, need to be considered, and must be comprehensively addressed. While the report of the Khan Committee provides a good starting point for taking a view on developmental aspects in particular, the CGAP's Guiding Principles on Regulation and

Supervision on Microfinance provide a valuable and globally relevant framework with regard to regulatory issues. The proposed forum for a consultative process on MFIs would also be useful in evolving an appropriate framework for the development of the MFI sector. No doubt a very well-crafted balance between regulation and growth objectives would be warranted in formulating our approach to a regulatory regime, keeping in view the big challenge—that of the financial inclusion of a large segment of the Indian population.

10

Rural Banking
Review and Prospects*

REVIEW OF EFFORTS

It will be useful to recall that rural banking in India was traditionally a monopoly of the moneylenders till the colonial government enacted the Co-operative Societies Act in 1904 with a view to making cooperatives the premier institutions for the disbursement of credit. The process of creating a three-tier structure commenced in 1915. The government would also provide agricultural loans, usually called Takkavi loans, which have since been discontinued. The RBI Act vested a unique responsibility for rural credit to the central bank. The *All India Rural Credit Survey* (1951) of the RBI opined that the cooperatives were an 'utter failure' in providing rural credit, but added that they played a vital role in agriculture credit. The Imperial Bank was nationalised as the State Bank of India (SBI), which was visualised as a vehicle for rural banking. A rural credit survey of 1966 also came to the conclusion that cooperatives were ineffective, but stressed how important it was that they succeed. Many state governments legislated the registration and regulation of moneylenders, but with little emphasis on implementation. The nationalisation of banks in

*Previously presented as the first Smarajit Ray Memorial Lecture organised by the Andhra Pradesh Mahila Abhivruddhi Society, Hyderabad, India, 16 December 2006.

1969 gave a boost to the expansion of banks and banking in rural areas. The RBI hived off a part of its role in agricultural credit to a separate national-level institution, viz., Agriculture Refinance and Development Corporation (ARDC) in 1975. Soon thereafter a legislation was enacted to create RRBs with participation from Central and state governments, and nationalised banks, which have their network spread almost all over the country. Subsequently, the ARDC was converted into the NABARD, which continued to receive lines of credit from the World Bank. The World Bank's lines of credit were, however, discontinued, on the grounds that the functioning of cooperatives had been less than acceptable. Simultaneously, the directed credit in the form of priority-sector lending continued, and the administered interest rate regime lasted.

During the reform period (that is, since 1991–2), capital was infused into the RRBs and the NABARD. While priority-sector lending continued, the administered interest rate regime was dismantled. To make up for the shortfall in priority-sector lending by banks, the Rural Infrastructure Development Fund (RIDF) was initiated to ensure the envisaged flow of bank resources to agriculture through the intermediation of the NABARD and the state governments. A Special Agricultural Credit Plan was also introduced. Innovations in the area of rural credit included the Kisan Credit Cards (a credit issued by a bank to a farmer to enable the purchase of fertiliser seeds, pesticides, etc.), and encouraging SHG-bank linkages. It may also be of interest to note that many district and state cooperative banks are yet to meet the applicable minimum capital requirements.

More recently, since 2004, vigorous efforts have been made to more than double the credit flow to agriculture. Emphasis has been laid on sound credit culture, effective credit delivery and appropriate credit pricing. New instruments for financial inclusion, such as GCCs and no-frills accounts, were initiated. The micro-finance programme was intensified and new guidelines for the business-facilitator model were issued. The use of technology for rural banking is being encouraged. Special Area Plans for banking in several states such as Uttaranchal, the northeastern states, Chhattisgarh, Bihar and Andaman-Nicobar have been formulated to suit local conditions. In terms of institutional development, consolidation of the RRBs, revamping of the UCBs as per the vision document, revival of the rural cooperative credit structure as per the Vaidyanathan Committee recommendations, a plan for restructuring long-term lending institutions for agriculture, and a revisit to prescriptions relating to priority-sector lending are underway. While a Working Group to review the legislations of various states with regard to moneylending has been formed, another Working Group is looking into relief measures for distressed farmers. Above all, as per the Government of India announcement in 2005, it has been decided to subsidise the commercial banks and NABARD to enable the provision of short-term credit at 7 per cent interest rate to the major segment of the farmers.

In brief, there have been vigorous and determined efforts towards the expansion of rural credit, especially through rural banking.

CURRENT PERCEPTION OF OUTCOMES

The litmus test of any effort is the outcome, and perhaps even more importantly, the perceptions of these outcomes. These can be summed up as follows.

First, the non-institutional credit still continues as far as rural areas and the agriculture sector are concerned.

Second, the credit-deposit ratio shows that despite the intermediation of banks, the ratio continues to be low in the rural area.

Third, the all-in costs of credit from banks, after factoring in timeliness, transaction-costs, access, etc., appears high for agriculture relative to the private corporate sector, even after accounting for the risks as reflected by the level of actual NPAs.

Fourth, the performance of some public-sector banks in rural and agricultural lending is also inadequate while that of most private and foreign banks is even lower, despite the considerable expansion of the scope of priority-sector lending.

Fifth, the credit system in rural areas finds it difficult to cope with the rising demands of commercialised agriculture, and in any case there are few credible risk-mitigation measures for borrowers, resulting in greater distress to farmers in areas with a significant presence of commercial crops.

Sixth, while there has been notable progress in micro-finance, it is mostly confined to the states with fairly well-developed banking systems. Further, the cost of credit at around 20 to 30 per cent also appears high.

Seventh, the cooperative credit system is in most parts dormant, and it has been commented that the three-tier structure helps finance the bureaucracy rather than benefit farmers. Similarly, in many parts of the country RRBs are less active, although in some others they have been expanding.

Eighth, while there has been significant growth in rural credit in recent years, its medium-term sustainability is contingent upon growth in agriculture and improvements in institutional settings.

In brief, the perceptions of the outcomes of vigorous and varied efforts to expand the reach of rural banking seem to be less than expected.

Perhaps it is time we ask ourselves some questions.

First, have our strategies, in terms of institutions and strategic directions, been flawed all along? Have we run out of ideas in this regard? Has our thinking on rural credit fallen behind the emerging realities in the economy? Is there a need to distinguish between the cause and the effect as also between the symptom and the disease? Is it the lack of credit availability or want of commercial viability of agriculture that is constraining the credit-flow or is it a complex combination of both? While we may not be able to answer many of these questions satisfactorily, I submit that we need to keep asking the right questions.

THE FOUR DEFICITS

In this regard, I would like to draw attention to the landmark observations made by the Prime Minister in his address at the Second Agriculture Summit held on 18 October 2006, wherein he developed the four deficits theme.

When we review our agricultural situation, it is clear that there are four deficits we need to bridge. These four deficits are (i) the public investment and credit deficit; (ii) the infrastructure deficit; (iii) the market economy deficit and (iv) the knowledge deficit. Taken together they are responsible for the development deficit in the agrarian and rural economy.

However, we need more thinking on the credit front. While the financial system should do more for the credit needs of farmers, we need to raise some questions. What do farmers need—a lower rate of interest or reliable access to credit at reasonable rates? Is our existing institutional framework adequate for meeting the requirements of our farmers who are a diverse lot? Do we need to create new institutional structures such as SHGs, micro finance institutions, etc, to provide improved and reliable access to credit? Or do we need to bring in money lenders under some form of regulation? It is necessary that we find answers to these questions in the near future.

NEW REALITIES

It is useful to recognise that there have been unprecedented structural changes in the fast growing domestic economy and the rapidly integrating global economy. These throw up what may be called new realities, but have to be met without losing sight of (a) the large population currently dependent on agriculture and (b) the medium-term trend towards a lower share of GDP generation in agriculture. Thus, while some short-term actions may be warranted in order to be sensitive to aspirations and expectations in rural areas, medium to longer-term strategies have to take into account what may be termed new realities, although some of them are old realities with greater relevance now and for the future. To elaborate on the theme:

First, there is a continuum of agricultural and non-agricultural activities, in terms of inputs, outputs, supply chains, etc., in an emerging, highly commercialised and globalising agriculture.

Second, there is a spectrum of financial services such as deposit-taking, lending, insurance, pension, mutual funds, etc., and there exist several financial intermediaries who need to complement and compete with each other even in rural areas. Banks and banking are a part of this emerging larger whole of financial institutions and their activities.

Third, there is a clear trend towards a rural-urban continuum in economic linkages, and the process of integration needs to be facilitated in the interests of growth and equity. Hence, segmentation of these through public policies or procedures should, at best, be an exception rather than the rule.

Fourth, the distinction between the productive and non-productive or consumption end becomes blurred, and in any case consumption smoothening is essential. Cash flow and risk management become more relevant relative to ensuring and monitoring the end use of funds.

Fifth, today's technology provides immense opportunities to financial intermediaries to reach a large section of the population, assess and price risks better, and minimise transaction costs. Naturally, this would need considerable business re-engineering.

Finally, there are dramatic changes in the demand for food and other articles and the supply of related inputs that need to constitute some of the basic elements of a new approach.

ISSUES

The new policy directions laid out by the Prime Minister clearly indicates how critical it is to improve the credit system, but rightly positions it as one of the four deficits that need to be addressed to manage the crisis of stagnation in Indian agriculture. Agriculture development has to be led by ensuring commercial viability, which has to be enabled by an appropriate credit system. In other words, credit can be a substitute for longer-term commercial viability only if a price is paid in both the financial and fiscal sectors. At the same time, a costly or inadequate credit system may constrain growth and commercial viability. The main issues in this regard, therefore, are related to what may be called policies complementary to credit or financial services for the upliftment of the rural economy. These are:

First, fiscal policy could play an enabling role in two ways, in terms of (*a*) targeting the poor for subsidy and (*b*) enhancing public investment while encouraging private investment that would benefit the rural economy. In order to make agriculture commercially viable, the costs and benefits of continuing with the existing allocation of resources for subsidising water, power and fertilisers may need to be assessed vis-à-vis bestowing focused attention on providing funds for risk mitigation, investments for enhancing supply, ensuring quality and rationalising availability.

Second, trade policy, both domestic and external, should facilitate the commercialising of agriculture, and thus enhance the scope for investments. Restrictions on trade within the country at a time when the economy is opening up may at times be less than optimal. As mentioned, savings in rural areas and agriculture are now transmitted by the banking system to urban areas and non-agriculture, often for want of commercially viable avenues in rural areas. Besides, banks have to improve their own risk assessment, pricing and credit disbursement procedures on an urgent basis.

Third, the major bottleneck lies in inadequate arrangements for risk mitigation, be it with regard to the quality or timeliness of inputs, especially seeds, fertilisers, water or power or the price of outputs. The risk mitigation for natural calamities or vagaries of weather is often discretionary, based on the assessment and response of public policy. Risk mitigation mechanisms will also make credit disbursal less risky.

Fourth, there are attitudinal aspects that need to be considered. It is often said that fiscal support to the manufacturing industry is called incentive, while similar support to agriculture is called subsidy. It may be worthwhile to consider the institutional arrangements and incentive framework that would facilitate attitudinal changes.

Fifth, the financial sector as a whole and the banking system in particular may have to consider a paradigm shift in strategies and processes consistent with the new thinking. The RBI and the entire banking system stand in readiness to serve this worthy cause of ensuring the development of the rural-agrarian economy by integrating it with the vibrant services and manufacturing sectors.

IV

Monetary Policy in a Globalising World

11

Monetary Policy
An Outline*

I n its conduct of monetary policy, the central bank responds
to the evolving economic activity within an articulated monetary
policy framework. This framework would normally have
three basic constituents, viz., (*a*) the objectives of monetary policy;
(*b*) the analytics of monetary policy focusing on the transmission
mechanism and (*c*) the operating procedure, focusing on operating
targets and instruments. For the sake of convenience, each of
these issues has been dealt with separately, and in this light, the
Indian experience has been touched upon briefly.

OBJECTIVES

Traditionally, central banks have pursued the twin objectives of
price stability and growth. Central banks have to keep in mind
the considerations of exchange rate stability and financial stability
in pursuing the basic objectives. Can we achieve these objectives
all at a time? As with most aspects of life, the objectives of
monetary policy are interrelated, and there are trade-offs as well.
For example, economists often talk of the Phillips curve, according
to which there is a short-run negative relation between inflation

*Previously presented as presidential address, Annual Conference of Andhra
Pradesh Economic Association, 12 February 2005, Visakhapatnam, India.

and unemployment. While there are various viewpoints on the Phillips curve, in a world where the Phillips curve is valid, a central bank can reduce inflation only at the cost of more unemployment. Similar trade-offs exist among the other objectives as well.

Faced with multiple objectives that are equally desirable, there remains the problem of assigning to each policy instrument the most appropriate objective. Accordingly, there is a broad consensus, both in academic and policy circles, that monetary policy is useful as an instrument in achieving the goal of price stability.

The adoption of price stability as the only objective of monetary policy is, however, by no means universal. While a number of prominent central banks, including the European Central Bank, the Bank of England and the Bank of Japan, have adopted price stability as the single objective of monetary policy, the Federal Reserve of the US continues to pursue multiple objectives of monetary policy, viz., (a) maximum employment; (b) stable prices and (c) moderate long-term interest rates. Central banks in several developing countries have taken up exchange rate management as another important policy objective. In recent years, particularly after the financial crises of 1990s, the concern for financial stability has become an integral part of the central bank's activism.

ANALYTICS OF MONETARY POLICY

The process through which changes in the monetary policy get transmitted to the ultimate objectives like inflation or growth has come to be known as the 'monetary transmission mechanism'. Interestingly, economists often refer to the channels of 'monetary transmission' as a black box—implying that while we know that monetary policy does influence output and inflation, we do not know for certain how precisely it does so. Nevertheless, in the literature, a number of transmission channels have been identified: (a) the quantum channel (for example, relating to money supply and credit); (b) the interest rate channel; (c) the exchange rate channel and (d) the asset price channel. How these channels function in a given economy depends on the stage of development of the economy and its underlying financial structure. For instance, in an open economy one would expect the exchange rate channel to be important; similarly, in an economy where banks are the major source of finance (as against the capital market), the credit channel seems to be a major conduit for monetary transmission. Besides, it needs to be noted that these channels are not mutually exclusive—in fact, there could be considerable feedback and interactions among them.

Central banks may not be in a position to directly achieve their ultimate objectives, and hence monetary policy is often formulated in terms of an intermediate target. For example, in a monetary targeting framework, a suitable monetary aggregate is considered an intermediate target based on the basic relationship between money, output and prices. The exchange rate as an intermediate target can be suitable for small open economies, setting it against a low-inflation anchor country. This may, however, entail a loss of independence in steering domestic interest rates.

In this context, it is necessary to touch upon what is known as the 'impossible trinity', or the 'trilemma' of monetary policy. This refers to the incompatibility between three policy choices, viz., (a) fixed exchange rate; (b) open capital account and (c) independent monetary policy. The basic message of the 'trilemma' is that a central bank can achieve any two of the above-mentioned parameters, but not all three. That is, if a country wants to have a fixed exchange rate and an independent monetary policy, it is difficult to maintain an open capital account.

Another important issue in monetary policy is the extent of transparency. Central bankers all over the world are not exactly known for clarity in their language. Nevertheless, the rational expectations school in macroeconomics holds that no policy can be successful over a period by 'fooling' the economic agents. In this context, one may differentiate between genuine uncertainties about the future vis-à-vis not revealing the expected outcome of the policy. In fact, since the 1990s, there has been a preference all over the world to improve the transparency of monetary policy.

In the context of improving transparency, the recent trend has been towards direct inflation targeting. The adoption of explicit inflation targeting as the final goal of monetary policy involves the preparation of an inflation forecast, which in a way serves the purpose of both an intermediate target and a final objective. The prerequisites for inflation targeting include a considerable degree of operational autonomy or independence for the central bank, flexible exchange rate conditions, well-developed financial markets and an absence of fiscal dominance.

In view of the growing complexities of macroeconomic management, several central banks, including the European Central Bank, have chosen to rely on a broad set of economic and leading indicators rather than focusing exclusively on an intermediate or a direct inflation target. The Federal Reserve has traditionally been following a more broad-based approach to the conduct of monetary policy in the US.

OPERATING PROCEDURES: INSTRUMENTS AND TARGETS

Operating procedures refer to the day-to-day implementation of monetary policy by central banks through various instruments. These instruments can be broadly classified as direct and indirect instruments. Typically, direct instruments include required cash and/or liquidity reserve ratios, directed credit and administered interest rates. The CRR determines the level of reserves (central bank money or cash) banks need to hold against their liabilities. Similarly, the liquidity reserve ratio requires banks to maintain a part of their liabilities in the form of liquid assets (for example, government securities). Credit and interest rate directives take the form of prescribed targets for the allocation of credit to preferred sectors/industries, and the prescription of deposit and lending rates.

The indirect instruments generally operate through price channels which cover repurchase (repos) and outright transactions in securities (OMO), standing facilities (refinance) and a market-based discount window. For example, if the central bank desires to inject liquidity for a short period, it could do so by providing funds to banks in exchange of securities at a desired interest rate, reversing the transaction at a pre-determined time. Similarly, if the central bank desires to influence liquidity on an enduring basis, it could resort to OMO, involving the outright purchase (or sale) of securities.

While OMO, including repo transactions, operate at the discretion of the central bank, standing facilities provide limited liquidity which could be accessed by eligible market participants (generally banks) at their discretion. Market-based discount windows make reserves available either through direct lending or through rediscounting or purchase of the financial assets held by banks.

In practice, the choice between direct and indirect instruments is not easy. While direct instruments are effective, they are considered inefficient in terms of their impact on the financial market. On the other hand, the use and efficacy of indirect instruments depend on the extent of the development of the supporting financial markets and institutions. These instruments are usually directed at attaining a prescribed value of the operating target. Central banks typically adopt either (*a*) bank reserves or (*b*) a very short-term interest rate (usually the overnight inter-bank rate) as the operating target.

The optimal choice between price and quantity targets would depend on the sources of disturbances in the goods and money markets. In reality, it often becomes difficult to trace the sources of instability. Hence, monetary policy is implemented by fixing, at least over some short interval of time, the value of an operating target. In a single-period context, the choice of the level of the target amounts to setting a rule for monetary policy. However, in a dynamic context, their connection is less straightforward. Indeed, there could be a deviation from a target, either intended or unintended, which may impart an inflationary bias when monetary policy is conducted with discretion. In order to address such problems of dynamic inconsistency, rule-based solutions are emphasised in the literature, for example, monetary rule (changes in money supply at a pre-determined rate) and Taylor-type rule (changes in interest rate based on a deviation of growth and inflation from their potential/desired levels). While a rule-based system imparts transparency, providing certainty about future policy response, it becomes ineffective in its response to unanticipated shocks, given its inflexibility. In practice, therefore, central banks follow an approach that has been best described as constrained discretion.

The operating procedures of the monetary policy of most central banks have largely converged to one of the following three variants: (*a*) estimate the demand for bank reserves and then carry out OMO to target short-term interest rates; (*b*) estimate market liquidity and carry out OMO to target the bank reserves, while allowing interest rates to adjust and (*c*) modulate monetary conditions in terms of both the quantum and price of liquidity through a mix of OMO, standing facilities and minimum reserve requirement, and changes in the policy rate with the objective of containing the overnight market interest rate within a narrow corridor of interest rate targets.

INDIAN SPECIFICS

Against this backdrop, let me now turn to the conduct of monetary policy in India.

What has been the objective of Indian monetary policy? The preamble to the Reserve Bank of India Act, 1934 sets out the objectives of the RBI thus: 'to regulate the issue of Bank notes and the keeping of reserves with a view to securing monetary stability in India and generally to operate the currency and credit system of the country to its advantage'. Although there is no explicit mandate for price stability, as is the current trend in many countries, the objectives of monetary policy in India have evolved into those of maintaining price stability and ensuring an adequate flow of credit to the productive sectors of the economy. In essence, monetary policy aims to maintain a judicious balance between price stability and economic growth. The relative emphasis between price stability and economic growth is governed by the prevailing circumstances of a particular time, and is spelt out from time to time in the policy announcements of the RBI.

Of late, considerations of financial stability have assumed greater importance in view of the increasing openness of the Indian economy and financial reforms. In the Indian context, financial stability could be interpreted to embrace three aspects, viz., (a) ensuring uninterrupted financial transactions; (b) maintaining a level of confidence in the financial system amongst all participants and stakeholders and (c) the absence of excess volatility that unduly and adversely affects real economic activity. The RBI endeavours to ensure all these aspects of financial stability.

As far as the conduct of monetary policy is concerned, it may be noted that the monetary policy in India used to be conducted, till 1997-8, with broad money (M3) as an intermediate target. The aim was to regulate money supply consistent with two parameters, viz., (a) the expected growth in real income and (b) a projected level of inflation. On the basis of the estimates of these two crucial parameters, the targeted monetary expansion could be set. In practice, the monetary targeting framework was used in a flexible manner with feedback from developments in the real sector. However, questions were raised about the appropriateness of such a framework vis-à-vis the changing interrelationship between money, output and prices in the wake of the financial-sector reforms and the opening up of the economy. The Working Group on Money Supply (1998) sought to address some of these issues. The most significant observation of the Group was regarding the changing nature of the transmission mechanism, as it highlighted that the interest rate channel was gaining in importance.

In line with this thinking, since 1998-9, the RBI has switched over to a multiple indicator approach. As per this approach, interest rates or rates of return in different markets (money, capital and government securities markets), along with data such as on currency, credit extended by banks and financial institutions, fiscal position, trade, capital flows, inflation rate, exchange rate, refinancing and transactions in foreign exchange available on a high-frequency basis, are juxtaposed with output to draw policy perspectives.

What is the operating procedure of monetary policy in India? In the current monetary policy framework, with the growing interlinkages in the financial market, reliance on direct instruments has been reduced and liquidity management in the system is carried out through OMO in the form of outright purchases/ sales of government securities and daily reverse repo and repo operations under the LAF. The LAF has enabled the RBI to modulate short-term liquidity under varied financial market conditions, including large capital inflows from abroad. In addition, it has enabled the RBI to set a corridor for short-term interest rates consistent with the policy objectives. This has also facilitated bringing down the CRR of banks without engendering liquidity pressure. These operations are supplemented by access to the RBI's standing facilities. In this new operating environment, changes in reverse repo and/or the bank rate have emerged as interest rate signals.

There is no explicit interest rate target envisaged in India. Nevertheless, a great deal of reliance has been placed in recent years on interest rates and exchange rates in the day-to-day conduct of monetary policy. In the context of the increasing openness of the economy and a market-determined exchange rate, the large capital inflows witnessed in recent years have posed major challenges to the conduct of monetary and exchange rate management. A critical issue in this regard is a view on whether the capital flows are temporary or permanent in nature. The recent episode of large capital flows prompted a debate in India on the need for exchange rate adjustment. In a scenario where monetary authorities are faced with uncertainty in determining whether inflows are temporary or permanent in nature, it is prudent to presume that such flows are temporary till they are firmly established as permanent.

The liquidity impact of large inflows was managed till 2003–04, largely through the day-to-day LAF and OMO. In the process, the stock of government securities available with the RBI declined progressively, and the burden of sterilisation fell increasingly on LAF operations. In order to address these issues, the RBI in March 2004 signed an MoU with the Government of India for the issuance of treasury bills and dated government securities under the MSS. The intention of the MSS is essentially to differentiate the liquidity absorption of a more enduring nature by way of sterilization from the day-to-day normal liquidity management operations. The ceiling on the outstanding obligations of the government under MSS has been initially indicated, but is subject to revision through mutual consultation. The issuances under the MSS are matched by an equivalent cash balance held by the government in a separate identifiable cash account, which is maintained and operated by the RBI. The operationalisation of MSS to absorb liquidity of a more enduring nature has considerably reduced the burden of sterilisation on the LAF window.

In its monetary operations, the RBI uses multiple instruments to ensure that appropriate liquidity is maintained in the system, so that all legitimate requirements of credit are met, consistent with the objective of price stability. Towards this end, the Bank pursues a policy of active management of liquidity through OMO, including LAF, MSS and CRR, and using the policy instruments at its disposal flexibly, as and when the situation warrants.

WAY AHEAD

The conduct of monetary policy is complex. It has not only to be forward-looking, but has to also grapple with an uncertain future. Additional complexities arise in the case of an emerging market like India, which is in transition from a relatively closed to a progressively open economy. In an environment of increasing capital flows, narrowing cross-border interest rate differentials and surplus liquidity conditions exchange rate movement tends to have linkages with interest rate movements. The challenge facing a monetary authority is to balance the various choices into a coherent whole and to formulate a policy as an art of the possible.

12

Globalisation of Monetary Policy and the Indian Experience*

This chapter draws attention to what may be termed the 'globalisation of the monetary policy' and the forces at work shaping it. Of course, each country has its own unique characteristics and the impact of globalisation on domestic policies is not the same for all countries. In this context, perhaps a review of the distinguishing features of the monetary policy in India and an assessment of how that policy has fared in India in the recent past would be appropriate.

THE GLOBALISATION OF MONETARY POLICY

The period since the 1990s has witnessed some convergence in the conduct of monetary policy worldwide. Currently, there are striking similarities in the tools that monetary authorities employ to assess macroeconomic developments and the formation of expectations. In the choice of instruments as well as in the operating procedures, there are common features. The institutional architectures have begun to display several commonalities.

Communication strategies, and thereby public accountability, are at the forefront in all central banks with the progressively

*Previously presented as inaugural address, Eighth Meeting of the BIS Working Party on Monetary Policy in Asia, RBI, Mumbai, 6–7 June 2005.

increasing globalisation of financial markets and emphasis on central bank autonomy. Finally, there is greater universal recognition of the trade-offs confronting monetary policy decisions.

While individual country experiences vary in tune with country-specific diversities, cross-country evidence highlights the fact that there are several common features driving this phenomenon.

First, cycles of economic activity have become increasingly synchronised across countries, irrespective of their levels/stages of development. Second, there is now widespread recognition of the adverse implications of high fiscal deficits on the conduct of monetary policy. Third, there have been significant shifts in instrument mix. Drastic reductions in statutory pre-emptions, greater reliance on indirect instruments, emphasis on the flexibility and timing of policy response and in general a greater market orientation, are all major elements of this shift. Fourth, there is greater activism in liquidity management and a focus on the short-end of the market spectrum; this has also been engendered by the growing integration of financial markets, both domestically and internationally. Fifth, at an operational level, there is greater transparency amongst monetary authorities as a strategic objective. This in turn has laid emphasis on information management—the quality and quantity of data dissemination represented by the release of adequate, timely and reliable information in a standardised form, and the dissemination of information on the dynamics of policy decisions. Sixth, there is greater coordination between central banks, fiscal authorities and the regulatory bodies governing financial markets. Seventh, there is a greater focus on the appropriate institutional structures that promote efficiency in the conduct of monetary policy. Eighth, in an environment of synchronised economic activity, international policy coordination has become extremely important. Finally, there is greater recognition of the fact that amidst the generalised uncertainty, monetary marksmanship is better adjudged in terms of ranges rather than in precise estimates.

These developments have been globally associated with a distinct lowering of inflation. In conjunction with more effective communication policies, this has earned for monetary authorities what has been described as a 'credibility bonus', which has helped in building a reputation for them in achieving the objectives of monetary policy. There is also greater sophistication in the conduct of monetary policy today, and central bankers are constantly engaged in refining their technical and managerial skills to deal with the complexities of financial markets.

On the downside, the challenges facing monetary authorities have become sharper. The heightened uncertainty surrounding the conduct of monetary policy has made the interpretation of macroeconomic and financial data difficult. Uncertainty is now more easily transmitted across the world through the 'confidence' channel, forcing monetary authorities to contend with the contagion from shocks. Since the 1990s, considerations of financial stability have assumed increasing importance in monetary policy across the globe.

It is useful to recognise some of the forces at work that indicate the pace of such globalisation of monetary policy. First, the increasing flow of goods and services across national borders leads to the networking of production systems and even standardisation in products, tastes and preferences. Second, financial integration powered by mobile capital flows leads to the merging of financial markets across national borders. Third, the explosion of communication technology helped in making the financial transactions faster and cheaper, thereby facilitating financial globalisation in a significant manner. Fourth, since the late 1980s, a factor driving the globalisation of the financial sector has been the setting of common standards in terms of prudential regulations, supervisory practices and disclosures. Under these conditions, monetary policy responses in various countries have tended to exhibit common characteristics. Undoubtedly, a complete congruence of national monetary policies is not feasible because of country-specific factors, but there are growing elements of globalisation in the sense that there are considerable similarities in the overall setting and conduct of monetary policy.

THE INDIAN EXPERIENCE

In reality, while there are growing tendencies towards globalisation, the conduct of monetary policy depends on a number of factors that are unique to a country and to the context. Given the policy goals, the contours of monetary policy are shaped by the macroeconomic structure of the economy and its institutional setting. Other important factors that play a decisive role are the degree of openness of the economy, the stage of development of financial markets, payment and settlement systems and the technological infrastructure. Against this backdrop, let me now turn to the specific features of the monetary policy in India.

First, while there is no explicit mandate for price stability, the conduct of monetary policy has evolved around the objectives of maintaining price stability and ensuring an adequate flow of credit to the productive sectors of the economy to sustain the overall economic growth. The relative emphasis on price stability and growth depends on the underlying macroeconomic conditions. In essence, monetary policy in India strives for a judicious balance between price stability and growth. The democratic processes in India work in favour of price stability, which in some ways amounts to an informal mandate to the central bank for maintaining an acceptable level of inflation.

Second, the monetary policy framework in India is guided by a 'multiple indicator' approach, wherein, besides monetary aggregates, information pertaining to a range of rates of return in different financial market segments along with the movements in currency, credit, the fiscal position, merchandise trade, capital flows, the inflation rate, the exchange rate, refinancing and transactions in foreign exchange—which are available on a high frequency basis—is juxtaposed with data on output and the real sector activity for drawing policy perspectives. The transition to a multiple indicator approach has been a logical outcome of monetary policy reforms. It has provided the RBI with the necessary flexibility to respond more effectively to changes in domestic and international economic and financial market conditions. From a medium to long-term perspective, however, the impact of money supply on inflation cannot be ignored, and for the purposes of policy, the RBI still continues to announce projections of money supply compatible with the outlook on GDP growth and expected inflation.

Third, liquidity management is carried out through OMO in the form of outright purchases/sales of government securities and reverse repo/repo operations, supplemented by the newly introduced MSS. The LAF, introduced in June 2000, enables the RBI to modulate short-term liquidity, of a temporary nature, under varied financial market conditions in order to ensure stable conditions in the overnight (call) money market. The LAF operates through reverse repo and repo auctions, thereby setting a corridor for a short-term interest rate consistent with policy objectives. The LAF operations, combined with strategic OMO consistent with market liquidity conditions, have evolved as the principal operating procedure of the monetary policy of the RBI.

Fourth, notwithstanding the concerted reforms undertaken since the 1990s, for example freeing monetary policy from the burden of automatic monetisation and a significant marketisation of the government's borrowing programme, monetary policy in India continues to be constrained by fiscal dominance. Debt-management considerations to ensure a smooth passage of the borrowing programme of the government, at minimum costs and roll-over risks, make the overall monetary management difficult when large and growing borrowing year after year puts pressure on the absorptive capacity of the market and on liquidity management. In this context, the FRBM, which envisages a vacation of primary financing of the fiscal deficit by the RBI from 2006–7, would enhance the flexibility of monetary management.

Fifth, the predominance of publicly-owned financial intermediaries has its implications for monetary policy. Cross-holdings and interrelationships in the financial sector emphasised in planned development were to achieve the social goals of the 'joint family' headed by the government. These are being gradually revamped, consistent with the needs of a market economy.

Sixth, a factor that further complicates the transmission mechanism of monetary policy is the limited size of the Indian financial system. Although India is essentially a bank-based economy, commercial credit penetration in the Indian economy is still relatively low. Concerns about credit to agriculture and SME usually relate to inadequacy, constraints on timely availability, high cost, neglect of small and marginal farmers, low credit-deposit ratios in several states and the continued presence of informal credit markets with high interest rates. It is in this context that the monetary policy in India continues to take cognisance of the need to ensure the financial inclusion of all segments of the population and the interests of depositors and the promotion of a conducive credit culture.

Seventh, the Indian financial system still shows some signs of stickiness in interest rates. Consequently, apart from the efforts to ensure a reduction in the existing high levels of revenue and fiscal deficits, rationalising the administered interest rates on contractual savings to impart efficiency and operational flexibility to the financial sector is one of the priorities of the policy.

Eighth, monetary management in India is somewhat constrained by the lack of comprehensive and timely information in some areas relative to the demands of a fast-growing and increasingly globalising economy. One lacuna is the absence of credible data on the labour market. Employment data essentially pertain to the organised sector, which constitutes less than 10 per cent of the total labour force. There is also considerable ambiguity about the very definition of 'employment', given the prevalence of under-employment and disguised unemployment. In the absence of data on the natural rate of unemployment, it is difficult to assess with a reasonable level of confidence the underlying conditions. Similarly, an assessment of the inflationary conditions in the economy is constrained by the lack of a comprehensive measure of consumer price inflation. The multiple consumer price indices, on the basis of occupational classification and residence (rural/urban), compound the problem, especially when differences in the weighting diagrams of the commodity baskets lead to differences in inflation numbers.

Ninth, the financial system in India has a relatively low vulnerability to asset bubbles. There is limited exposure of bank lending to the sensitive sectors, including real estate. While the demand for housing is strong, the overall exposure is moderated by assigning higher risk weights to housing loans than required under the Basel norm. The share of housing loans in the overall loan portfolio stood at about 10 per cent in March 2004, and the net NPAs were 1.4 per cent of the net outstanding loans as compared with 2.8 per cent of the aggregate portfolio.

AN ASSESSMENT

An assessment of the expectations vis-à-vis the outcomes suggests that monetary policy in India has performed reasonably well in terms of its objectives.

First, compared to many developing countries, India has been able to maintain a moderate level of inflation. Historically, inflation rates in India have rarely touched double digits, and when they did, it was the result of supply shocks from agricultural commodity prices or international oil prices.

Second, the monetary policy has been reasonably successful in dampening the volatility of output and imparting to the economy a growing resilience. The trend rate of GDP growth has risen steadily to around 6.0 per cent for about twenty-five years and India has emerged as one of the fastest growing economies in the world.

Third, the monetary policy has been successful in ensuring financial stability in India through a decade and a half when frequent financial crises led to debilitating losses in growth and welfare in large parts of the developing world. This period was also marked by pressures from within, such as geo-political tensions, drought and international sanctions. While we might have enjoyed an element of luck, we believe that we also benefited from the exercise of sound judgement and enhancement of skills at all levels. It is useful to note that the RBI has been engaged in the development of sound and efficient financial intermediaries and markets so as to provide solid foundations for the effective transmission of the monetary policy.

Fourth, success has been achieved in turning around and strengthening the external sector. Restrictions on imports have been virtually abolished and current account convertibility has been instituted since 1994. The capital account is virtually open to non-residents. An exchange rate policy of focusing on managing volatility with no fixed rate target while allowing the underlying demand and supply conditions to determine the exchange rate movements over a period in an orderly way has stood the test of time. India's external-sector management has been endorsed by the growing international investor confidence in the face of sub-investment grade sovereign ratings. Today, India holds the sixth largest stock of reserves in the world, sufficient to cover its entire external debt. Since 2002, India has turned creditor to the IMF, and is engaged in pre-paying bilateral and multilateral debt.

The conduct of monetary policy is becoming increasingly sophisticated and forward-looking, warranting a continuous upgradation of monitoring scan and technical skills. Flexibility and timeliness in policy response, coupled with transparency and accountability, hold the key to further enhancing credibility. Above all, the monetary authority has to address dilemmas, which exert conflicting pulls at every stage, and blend the desirable with the feasible. We have to recognise that judgements are involved at different stages which call for both knowledge and humility.

13

Monetary and Regulatory Policies
How to Get the Balance
with Markets Right*

I t is necessary to recognise the links and interactions between the monetary and regulatory policies, which may at times be reinforcing and at times conflicting. In this balance, the 'time dimension' is important. We know whether the balance is right or wrong only ex-post. For example, when prosperity prevails all around, everyone wants everything to be left to the markets; but when things go wrong, monetary and regulatory policies are invoked to save the situation. I will add that in maintaining the balance, public opinion is also important for ensuring the legitimacy and effectiveness of monetary policy. Public opinion goes beyond financial markets and institutions, but it is useful to remember that it also includes the government and the media.

The country context is important because institutional factors of governance, the state of market development and values are relevant in the context of 'balance'. Hence, we cannot be judgemental about the 'balance' across countries, but should assess the 'balance' only in a country-specific context. India's experience in recent years in viewing 'balance' is presented here.

First, with regard to monetary policies, we monitor the monetary and credit aggregates. We use both liquidity and interest

*Previously presented as remarks in the Annual General Meeting Panel of the Bank for International Settlements, Basel, Switzerland, 29 June 2008.

rate instruments. A dynamic balance is evident from the spread between the repo and reverse repo rates, which is enlarged during times of uncertainty. It has moved from 150 basis points to 100 basis points when times were good, and has now moved to 250 basis points, reflecting greater uncertainties. We believe that market participants should be willing to share some costs of uncertainties. Pre-emptive actions have been taken since 2004 to withdraw monetary accommodation, which were reinforced with measures aimed at moderating the early signs of over-heating. Further, a differentiated approach between the permanent and the temporary component with regard to oil prices has been articulated in the policies. We did not treat oil prices entirely as a shock and focus on what is described as core inflation. While undertaking a nuanced approach to managing aggregate demand, recognising the elements of shock and the consequent impact on inflation expectations, the underlying demand conditions warranted several interest rate and liquidity measures.

Second, while monetary policy influences aggregates, in reality the financial sector is often dis-aggregated. So we have used regulatory policies to supplement monetary measures. These relate mainly to risk weights and provisioning requirements with regard to exposure to NBFCs, capital markets, real estate, consumer credit, etc., sectoral caps and more recently, modulation of the exposure limits to oil companies.

Third, we do not take a view on asset prices, either in the real estate or the capital markets. Despite not taking a view, we wanted to protect the banking system from possible risks. In this regard, the nature of the markets is also important, for example, the housing markets in India are less than liquid. We also modified the overly conservative accounting norms that were earlier applicable to the HTM category in India.

Fourth, a SRP was initiated with select banks that have a significant exposure to sensitive sectors, including reliance on call money market, in order to ensure that effective risk mitigants and sound internal control systems were in place. In the first round, a framework was developed to monitor the systemically important individual banks. The second round of SRP was directed to analyse banks' exposure to sensitive sectors and identify outliers. Based on the analyses of these outlier banks, guidelines were issued to all banks indicating the need for better risk management systems at operating levels.

In brief, in India the focus is on regulatory comfort rather than on regulatory compliance. In a choice between emphasis of regulations on saving capital and protecting depositors' interests or reinforcing financial system stability, the latter has always prevailed.

Fifth, we regularly interact with the industry associations, namely the IBA, the Foreign Exchange Dealers Association of India, the PDAI, and the FIMMDA. Incidentally, the last two were promoted by the RBI. We have a three-stage participation in the process of formulating important regulations. This normally involves preliminary discussions with the representative bodies and select market participants; preparation of a technical report by working groups that often include the regulators and market participants and academia; and placing the report in the public domain for feedback. On the basis of the report and the initial feedback, draft guidelines are usually formulated, and again placed in the public domain for further feedback, on the basis of which these guidelines are finalised.

Sixth, our regulations and policies are focused on the common person. This is, for example, reflected in our approach to transparency by the industry, the ombudsman mechanism, the setting up of the BCSBI, guidelines on recovery agents, etc. This focus on the common person enhances the legitimacy of the RBI in the public eye vis-à-vis market intermediaries. Although the RBI issues micro-regulations at times, this is necessary to strike a better balance between financial institutions and public interest at a micro level, with reference to the common person.

Seventh, moral suasion and the public articulation of concerns have helped to achieve a desired re-balancing of suspected excesses in risk-taking among banks. Some of the areas where moral suasion has been used are the need for banks to monitor unhedged foreign currency exposures of their corporate clients, the adoption of appropriate incentive mechanisms by banks to encourage disclosures of derivative exposures by their corporate clients, banks' reliance on non-deposit resources to finance assets, their excessive reliance on wholesale deposits and uncomfortable LTV ratios with respect to housing loans, etc.

Eighth, the RBI has also focused on liquidity mechanisms and systems. Asset liability management is left to the banks, but regulatory limits on short-term buckets are prescribed. Further, in order to reduce the extent of concentration of a bank's liabilities, the RBI had issued guidelines to banks in March 2007 placing prudential limits on the extent of their IBL as a proportion of their networth (200 per cent). Those banks which had a higher capital adequacy ratio of 125 per cent of the regulatory minimum were allowed a higher limit of 300 per cent of networth. In addition, prudential limits have also been placed on the extent to which banks may access the inter-bank call money market, both as a lender and as a borrower.

Ninth, whenever situations that are out of the ordinary arise, exceptional or flexible arrangements are needed. Timely flexibility while reacting to the underlying balance is essential. This helps to avoid more serious problems relating to the balance over the medium-to-longer term. For example, recently oil imports had to be financed through off-market processes. Delayed adjustments to such sudden and unexpected cross-border exogenous developments at such times may impose a stress on liquidity. Hence, frictional issues of liquidity, as distinct from underlying issues of levels of liquidity, need to be addressed to look at the balance dynamics.

Organisation and Communication Policies of the RBI

14

Central Bank Communications
Some Random Thoughts*

In the past, central banking was shrouded in secrecy with some 'mystique' surrounding it. In recent years, however, there has been greater visibility, transparency and communication. What are the reasons for this? First, the increased independence of central banks, warranting publicly accountable conduct; second, the adoption of inflation targeting—whether through a legal sanction or otherwise; third, a mandate to the central banks, either explicit or implicit, for maintaining financial stability in a world where financial markets and their expectations matter. It is interesting to note that even in the UK, where there is a Financial Services Authority, it is the Bank of England which periodically publishes the Financial Stability Report.

What are the theoretical perspectives in this regard? The academic and policy literature recognises the role that communication plays in the effectiveness of monetary policy and focuses broadly on four aspects of policy, namely efficiency, time-consistency, optimality of communications and institutional-cum-decision-making processes. Efficiency issues centre around quality, elements of noise, formation of expectations and implementation lags. The time-consistency issues relate to the conditions for

*Previously presented as a speech, delivered at the Regional Seminar on Central Bank Communications sponsored by the International Monetary Fund, Hotel Taj Land End, Mumbai, India, 23 January 2006.

substitutability between communications and policy actions, and choices between the effectiveness of unanticipated policies relative to the elimination of uncertainty in private decision-making. The optimality issues address the dangers of disseminating information that could result in crowding out the formulation of independent beliefs by the private sector—a formulation that is critical to well-functioning markets. The institutional and decision-making processes of monetary policy refer to the recent trends towards autonomous group decision-making, like the Monetary Policy Committee of the UK, the composition of the groups, the periodicity of their meetings, the attributability of opinions, the transparency, etc. It should, therefore, be clear that even on the limited issue of communication policy with regard to monetary policy, the literature provides a framework, however, the practices tend to be diverse amongst countries. There is no universally valid international benchmark on the subject, but the framework, which is still evolving, is useful as a reference point for the exchange of information amongst different countries, which this Regional Seminar seeks to promote. While the framework for a country is useful, it is the judgement within the framework that really matters. In India, we are proceeding gradually towards a more open and participative process of monetary policy formulation.

The growing importance attached to communications by central banks is on account of their responsibility for maintaining financial stability—which includes but goes beyond the conduct of monetary policy. There is an assumption that well-informed market participants would enable, if not assure, an improved functioning of markets, and a central bank is in the best position to provide such useful information. However, whether the provision of information would result in shaping and managing expectations, and if so, whether it is desirable, are difficult issues. For example, since 1994, the US Federal Reserve appears to have been providing forward guidance, while the European Central Bank appears to prefer keeping the markets informed rather than guiding it. We in India have taken a middle path—that of sharing our analysis in addition to providing information, while in no way guiding the market participants. However, while doing so we have the benefit of two-way communication, of information as well as perceptions, between market participants and the RBI. The two-way process is enabled through formal structured meetings with industry associations, through standing advisory committees, informal/*ad hoc* committees, technical reports, working groups, etc.

At this stage, I must share one concern about the credibility bonus earned by the effective communications policy. Is it possible that such 'hands on' and 'very successful' communications by central banks in the world, 'aimed at' maintaining financial stability, have resulted in an under-pricing of risks by the private sector, or in a distinct lowering of the aversion to financial risks? Is it possible that this credibility bonus is partly responsible for the upward movement of housing and equity prices becoming a global phenomenon?

The issue of financial stability is of great significance and enormous complexity for central bankers in the EMEs. The EMEs vary considerably in their fiscal, current account, openness to the external sector and dependence on oil earnings or oil imports. Yet, analysts in the financial markets often treat them as a group, presumably because the EMEs are perceived to be high-risk and high-reward destinations for financial capital. That characteristic renders them vulnerable in capital flows, sometimes for reasons other than economic fundamentals in the country concerned. As the title implies, the EMEs are emerging from one state into another, namely from less market orientation to greater market orientation, and are thus in a state of transition. The central banks in the EMEs, in their pursuit of financial stability, face two additional challenges. First, to manage the transition in their own economies, which has socio-economic as well as political dimensions and second, to keep a watch on the sentiment of foreign capital flows—which could change for reasons other than domestic ones. While for a particular foreign investor it may be a small portfolio shift from an EME to an industrialised country, it may be one of large magnitude for the EME concerned. The challenges before communication policy are considerably more complex for central banks in the EMEs for another reason, namely the asymmetrical response of financial markets to the developments in the EMEs. For instance, the market reaction to an increase of, say, US$ 5 billion in the forex reserves of an EME would be comparatively subdued vis-à-vis the response to a decline in the reserves by a similar amount.

In India, several measures, monetary as well as administrative, were undertaken to meet the threats to financial stability, while complementary or parallel recourse was taken to communications. Some examples are: a speech in Goa in August 1997 to 'talk down the rupee'; reassuring statements on market developments in the context of the Asian crisis, combined with a package of measures, in tranches in 1997 and 1998; pre-emptive measures in mid-1998 in the context of the crisis in Russia; reassuring statements issued in the context of the Kargil war in 1999; a combination of liquidity injections and reassuring statements along with other measures in the context of 9/11; a combination of actions and measures at the time when Indian stock markets took a sharp downward turn on 17 May 2004, coinciding with the political transition at the national level and more recently, the attempt to explain the impact of redemption of the India Millennium Deposits to the extent of US$ 7 billion. There are several other instances of thoughtful inaction. For instance, the RBI decided to not take any measures or issue any statement when the US imposed sanctions on India. In brief, we have OMO and open mouth operations and open only eyes and ears operations in regard to threats to financial stability.

Many central banks perform a multitude of functions and their responsibilities are seldom restricted to monetary policy and financial stability. Hence, communication policies and strategies have to be tailored to meet the needs of the specific functions to be performed on the one hand, and on the other, to an overall consistent or common policy framework within which the central bank functions. For instance, the RBI is responsible for developing and regulating money, forex, and government securities markets, with some dilemmas that need to be resolved when the RBI is both a developer and a regulator. It is also a debt manager to the Central and the state governments. Thus, the communication policies, strategies, and contents, while dealing with market intermediaries, are different from those adopted while dealing with, say, state governments, for whom the RBI is also a banker and, as mentioned earlier, debt manager. The RBI is also a regulator, especially of banks, and serves distinct interests, namely those of depositors and consumers in general, as well as those relating to systemic efficiency and stability, and those of the banks themselves, whose health is critical to the financial sector. Communication policies are therefore tailored separately for each category of stakeholders. Finally, several services are rendered by a central bank, especially in matters relating to currency and coins, payments system, credit information and overall grievance redressals.

Communication strategies are designed keeping in mind the target audience. A central bank's communication is varied and includes the general public, financial market participants, media persons, entities that it regulates, academics, financial markets analysts, rating agencies, international or multilateral bodies, etc. Let me illustrate this point with a communication initiative that the RBI took recently. The Ombudsman Scheme for banks was revised recently and hence the objective was to inform the widest section of our population. A press release might not have fully served the purpose. So, a decision was taken to issue an advertisement—for which the content was indeed common, but the languages differed. It was interesting to note that while seventeen leading English newspapers have a combined circulation of 6.3 million and a readership of 17.9 million, the fifteen leading Hindi newspapers have a larger circulation at 8.1 million and a far larger readership at 87.0 million—that is, almost five times larger. In fact, fifty-four leading non-English newspapers in India have a circulation of 21.4 million and a readership of 197.2 million. This has been our target coverage for the latest effort in communication, recognising that most of the targeted 200 million middle-class people in India read vernacular newspapers.

Central banks face several dilemmas while designing an appropriate communications policy. What should be communicated and to what degree of disaggregation are one set of issues? The second set concerns the question: at what stage of evolution of internal thinking and debate should there be dissemination? The third set relates to the timing of communication with reference to its market impact. The fourth relates to the quality of information and the possible ways in which it could be perceived. Thus, alleged incoherence or an element of ambiguity on the part of central bankers in explaining policies is as much a reflection of the complexity of the issues as it is of the differing perceptions of the variety of audiences to which the communication is addressed.

In assessing the contribution of the media to the financial sector as a public good, I would distinguish among at least four types of effects. The first type may be characterised as the 'news effect', which would normally reflect factual or formal positions or events. In a sense, the media's reporting would be faithful and non-controversial. A second type can be identified as the 'rumour effect'. Rumours often have a destabilising effect, and in some cases, have the potential to degenerate into self-perpetuating or self-fulfilling events. The rumour effect often results in unintended losses or gains, and people may suspect the presence of some vested interest behind such rumours. Needless to say, the media's role will on the whole tend to be negative in this channel. The third type is marked by the 'survey effect'. It is not uncommon for the media to undertake opinion polls or surveys, and these could have methodological and other problems in terms of reflecting the true picture. These surveys have a tendency to influence the perception of markets, and sometimes that of the general public. In such a scenario, the media's contribution would depend on the scientific methodology adopted, the transparency of assumptions and objectivity in the presentation of the results. Adequate care is a precondition to ensure a positive effect through this channel. The fourth is the 'interpretation effect', where the media tries to interpret the stand taken by policymakers or markets or corporates. The interpretation effect may be positive or negative depending on the professional skills as well as commitment to objectives. Responsibility and accountability would be key to ensuring a positive effect through this channel. In brief, it is my submission that the media's responsibilities are not confined to its shareholders or its subscribers, but extend to the larger segment of the public. In this sense, the challenges and dilemmas before the media are perhaps no less than those before the central banks.

It is also fair and appropriate to recognise that the media itself faces several dilemmas. For example, there are pressures to be the first to report—a race to be the number one. There are incentives to be distinctive. They have several stakeholders to cater to. They may or may not have ideological predilections. However, as far as the RBI is concerned, the media has been very fair, and I find it a pleasure, an inspiration and educational to interact with the media. It is great fun to share my confusions and dilemmas with all types of media—which are amongst the best and the brightest in India.

Before concluding, it is essential to appreciate that communication policy is not merely about explaining or getting a feedback on policy, but may include elements that influence the policy direction itself. A central bank does this through several channels, including research publications and speeches. As Dr I.G. Patel, an eminent statesman-scholar and one of my distinguished predecessors, said in 2004:

> Communication is not just about transparency. It is also about education, guidance and steering things in the right direction. In this, the central bank can be an honest broker between the government and the public and even the parliament.

Perhaps it is possible to illustrate, with a certain lack of modesty, how this has been done through a quote from Mr S.S. Tarapore, my predecessor as deputy governor:

> While I have been assigned the task of talking about gold and capital account convertibility, before doing so I would, for a moment, like to refer to some developments prior to the setting up of the committee on Capital Account Convertibility (CAC). When the definitive history of India's policy on gold is written up, the speech by Dr Y.V. Reddy, Deputy Governor, Reserve Bank of India, at the World Gold Council Conference on 28 November 1996 will stand out as a watershed as it is perhaps the only speech by a senior Indian official which squarely takes on issues on gold policy and it will be appropriately recorded as a forerunner

of major policy change. It is by raising pertinent issues that Dr Reddy has paved the way for the committee to come up with specific recommendations on India's policy on gold.

An interesting question that arises concerns the role of the Governor of a central bank when important policy issues that impinge on central banking are involved. A quote from the late Dr I.G. Patel would perhaps be the best guide:

> But the point is, when such vital questions arise, the Governor can not just be inactive. He is a public servant with loyalty to the country and the constitution—not just to a government in transit. And yet, he can not behave as if every issue is of great import. He has to choose his ground and be discreet above all. Without offending the Government, he can start a debate and steer the argument in a certain direction. His ultimate defence is democracy and the tradition of free debate.

15

What RBI Means to the Common Person*

The RBI is above all a public institution serving the public interest. Though the word 'bank' is part of its name, profit is not its primary motive. Therefore, it is necessary for every common person to understand its role and functions in improving the welfare of the people at large.

The RBI is the 'central bank' of the country, and is uniquely placed to perform certain specific and challenging public responsibilities. It is the monetary authority of the country, and as everyone knows, the rupee is our currency unit in this country. The RBI broadly deals with the quantity of rupee resources that should ideally be available in the country to promote economic growth and smooth transactions in goods and services. A very large money supply could result in inflation or higher prices, which affect the common person the most. On the other hand, inadequate monetary resources can affect the growth and disrupt the payments system. The RBI tries to strike a proper balance through its policies.

Currency management is an important function. For example, the new currency notes are issued by the RBI, and old ones are withdrawn and destroyed. Their design, production and distribution are managed—to be spread over the entire country.

*Previously presented as a speech, delivered at Karamchedu Village, Ongole District, Andhra Pradesh, 18 February 2007. The speech was originally delivered in Telugu.

The RBI's currency note contains the words 'I promise to pay the bearer a sum of....' That is signed by the Governor. So the RBI has to ensure that the value of the rupee is maintained so that faith and trust of the people in the RBI is always present. To maintain the value of the rupee, the amount of goods and services that it can buy should not be eroded in such a way that confidence in the currency is lost. So the RBI's most important objective is to maintain price stability, contain inflation and anchor inflation expectations.

Incidentally, in the currency note the denomination is written in the two Central government official languages (English and Hindi) and fifteen national languages. It shows the diversity of our country and the RBI's commitment to reach out to one and all.

Speaking about the value of money, the RBI is concerned not only with the value of money in India, but with the related issue of the value of our rupee in relation to the currencies of other countries: that is, with maintaining the faith of people living outside our country in our currency. This work relates to exchange rate management. The rupee cannot be directly used in settling transactions with other countries, and international currencies like the US dollar have to be used. To ensure smooth international transactions, it is necessary to maintain the external stability of the rupee. Incidentally, confidence in the rupee outside our country also depends very much upon domestic price stability. Furthermore, the RBI also maintains and manages foreign exchange reserves to sustain this confidence.

People tend to borrow and lend money to each other for consumption and production purposes. Overall, the demand for and supply of such resources, in aggregate terms, need to be balanced by an appropriate level of interest rates, which provides incentives to savers as well as adequate returns to investors in industry, agriculture, etc. Such a balance is struck by the interest rate policies adopted by the RBI. I might be oversimplifying, but the idea is to strike a broad balance—both within our country and in relation to other countries.

The RBI has also been assigned several other responsibilities. Thus, it manages the public borrowings of the Central government and all state governments; is a banker to the Central and state governments and keeps their accounts; regulates payments and settlements systems and of some direct concern to many people is the fact that it regulates the banking system.

All information on matters such as these are placed in the public domain, through publications, press releases and speeches. Up-to-date information is available on the RBI website in both English and Hindi. Why do we explain our work and dilemmas in such detail? It is because the RBI is a public institution and RBI officials want the public to understand, appreciate, criticise and guide them. It is not a publicity drive, but is meant to enhance the RBI's efficiency and accountability to the public at large.

In this chapter I will elaborate some instances of how the RBI, as a public institution, is answerable to the government and, indeed, to the people at large, and the steps it has taken to get closer to the common person in recent years.

We have urged banks to be sensitive to the banking and financial needs of the common person and adopt a policy of financial inclusion, that is, to bring possibly every family—rich and poor, rural and urban—into the banking fold. 'No frills' accounts with perhaps a small overdraft facility should be the easiest option for financial inclusion. We are also looking at how technology can increase people's access to banking. GCC and Kisan Credit Cards can facilitate the disbursal of small credits to farmers without much paperwork each time they want to take loans or make transactions. We are also exploring alternatives such as satellite offices for banks, Automated Teller Machines (ATMs) and the use of post offices to extend banking facilities to rural areas. In urban areas, we are trying to provide efficient and quick service to bank customers by extending facilities such as mobile and internet banking and quick—almost minute by minute—and cost-effective transfer of funds from one account to another through the electronic funds transfer mechanism. We also encourage reliable, prompt and economical means of conducting day-to-day transactions, such as bill payments, receipts of salaries, dividends and pensions directly into the beneficiaries' bank accounts.

To ensure that people get good quality banking services at a reasonable cost, we have taken several measures. While banks can decide for themselves the services they will offer customers and at what cost, we have asked each bank to set for itself a measurable standard or benchmark for the quality of service it would provide its customers. An independent body set up by the RBI, called the BCSBI, will then assess the quality of services provided by that bank against the promises it has made. Any adverse remark by the BCSBI will give the RBI a reason for taking corrective steps. We have also asked banks to ensure that account holders have detailed information on the availability and cost of the various banking services offered to start a banking relationship. It is a customer's right to demand the services promised by the bank.

And if the customer does not receive the services promised by the bank, s/he can lodge a complaint against it—first to the higher authority of the bank concerned. If the complaint is not resolved within a reasonable time or to the customer's satisfaction, s/he can approach the Banking Ombudsman. The Banking Ombudsman is appointed by the RBI to provide an easy, hassle-free and less costly forum to bank customers to resolve their banking disputes. There is one Banking Ombudsman in virtually each state, who can be approached through mail or even through the Internet for resolution of complaints against the banks.

The RBI is also in the midst of improving its own processes so that its major direct customers, namely the governments and the banks, are provided with good service from the central bank. Two departments of the RBI are already ISO certified, which means that the processes in these departments are streamlined for better and quicker customer service and are constantly updated. We are in the process of obtaining this certificate for the other departments of the RBI that deal with the public.

We have consciously adopted a policy of reaching out to people so that they know what to expect, what choices they have, what rights and obligations they have in relation to banking services, etc. We already have several publications through which we reach out to researchers, students and other technical audiences. Our resolution for 2007–8 was to reach out to the common person through a special drive, for which we embarked on a financial education and financial literacy drive aimed at the common man. This was done both through banks and directly. A multilingual website has since been set up, and people are now able to read about us and our banking policies in their own mother tongues on the website. This information will also be made available through brochures, pamphlets, films, etc.

We in the RBI work as a family, and the RBI, as an equal opportunity employer, attracts the best talents to perform the challenging tasks. We have offices in most state capitals and a board of directors representing expertise in diversified fields. Our family journal has won several awards. We constantly strive to raise the morale among the people working at various levels of the RBI, and remain motivated to meet the challenges of serving the common person with every possible care and commitment.

Several aspects about the RBI have been mentioned so far, but something needs to be added about the RBI's relationship with the state of Andhra Pradesh. The RBI has always had excellent relations with the government of Andhra Pradesh and all the chief ministers. Both the RBI and the state have benefited from such meetings at several official levels. Let me highlight some recent developments in Andhra Pradesh about which the RBI is particularly pleased.

First, as banker to the state government, we are happy that since 2003–4 the state has never taken temporary advances from us to meet any day-to-day deficits between receipts and expenditure. This shows a prudent fiscal management.

Second, we find that the financial position of the state has been improving, and hence the government's borrowings for developmental purposes could be conducted by the RBI at a relatively lower cost. Financial markets continue to show increasing confidence in the state, year after year, particularly all through the new millennium.

Third, Andhra Pradesh is the first state in the country to sign an MoU with the RBI to consolidate and improve the UCB system, and the new scheme is working excellently in a spirit of cooperation and professionalism.

Fourth, the state has provided strong financial support to rural cooperatives, and is again the first state in the country among the few that have signed an MoU with the RBI to consolidate and develop the rural cooperative credit system. This scheme will revive and revitalise rural cooperatives with substantial financial support from the Government of India.

Fifth, the state has committed itself to revitalising and expanding rural credit. Last week, there was a meeting held between our deputy governor and Andhra Pradesh state government officials to work on a medium-term plan to expand financial inclusion through strengthening RRBs.

Sixth, the state has exceeded the national-level targets set with respect to the annual plan for rural credit, mainly for credit to agriculture, by doubling it between 2004–5.

Seventh, the state is amongst the pioneers in a programme of financial inclusion—that is, in ensuring bank accounts to all families that want it. This is the first step towards the goal of bank credit as a human right, advocated by Nobel Laureate Professor Mohammed Yunus on a recent visit to the RBI. One district, Srikakulam, is reported to have achieved 100 per cent financial inclusion. We agreed with the state government to have the progress evaluated by an expert body, so that we could learn about both its weaknesses and strengths while extending the programme to other districts as part of a mission. We have advised our banks to work vigorously towards this goal of universal financial inclusion, and the cooperation of state governments is critical for the success of these efforts.

Are these instances of cooperation between Andhra Pradesh and the RBI enough? Perhaps it is, but there are several areas where we, that is, the state government and the RBI, need to move closer, faster, deeper and into newer areas. The RBI has identified a few new areas for a vigorous drive in 2006–7, to which the government of Andhra Pradesh has assured its full support. These relate to financial literacy and credit counselling. Today, the common man is attracted to a lot of choices—some very risky ones—when he acquires surplus money. Where should one deposit the money, for what period and at what interest? How does one decide between mutual funds, bank deposits, life insurance, etc., against non-bank deposits and chit funds? How does one sustain and improve the financial status of the family and smoothen consumption even if incomes come in lump sums? People should be made aware so that they do not stand to lose by believing in the fake promises and propaganda of some greedy financial vultures. The RBI is in the process of preparing reading and visual material, and will fund the cost of making such material. However, literacy or education has to reach the masses, and for this mass financial-literacy drive, the Andhra Pradesh State Government has assured its full support to the RBI.

A second aspect that we want to attempt on a pilot basis and on a small scale to start with relates to credit counselling. Sometimes, people fall into debt out of ignorance or bad luck. They can be advised by some well-trained people on how to resolve the problem with minimal distress, by renegotiating, rescheduling of liabilities, etc. Such schemes exist in other countries and we have studied them. We are experimenting in this area in Maharashtra in a small way. We intend to launch pilot projects in other regions too, and the Andhra Pradesh State Government has expressed a strong interest in the programme. So, in credit counselling too, the Andhra government may be the first in the country to formally sign up for an initiative.

16

Organisation and Functioning of the RBI*

W hat has been the role of the RBI in the developments in the Indian economy? The RBI has, as part of public policy, made some contributions to the overall price stability and financial stability while enabling respectable growth in the recent period. Further, it is generally recognised that the financial sector and the external sector in India display considerable strength and resilience, although there are some areas that need attention. In India, most of the literature on public administration concentrates on the organisation and functioning of Central and state governments, statutory corporations, public enterprises and constitutional bodies. Perhaps there is merit in devoting the rest of the chapter to filling up this gap and discussing the organisation and functioning of the RBI in some detail.

The RBI was established on 1 April 1935 under the Reserve Bank of India Act, 1934. It was set up as a private shareholders' bank, but has been fully owned by the Government of India since its nationalisation in 1949.

---

*Previously presented as the Shri Yeshwantrao Chavan Memorial Lecture 2007–8, delivered at the Indian Institute of Public Administration, Maharashtra Branch, Mumbai, 31 March 2008. The original title was 'The Indian Economy and the Reserve Bank of India: Random Thoughts'. The parts relating to Indian economy have been deleted.

The Preamble to the RBI Act describes the basic objective of the constitution of the RBI thus: 'to regulate the issue of Bank notes and keeping of reserves with a view to securing monetary stability in India and generally, to operate the currency and credit system of the country to its advantage'. Thus, there is no explicit mandate for price stability or formal inflation targeting. Over the years, the twin objectives of monetary policy in India have evolved as maintaining price stability and ensuring an adequate flow of credit to facilitate the growth process. The relative emphasis between both objectives is modulated as per the prevailing circumstances and is articulated in the policy statements. A consideration of macroeconomic and financial stability is also subsumed in the articulation of policy.

The RBI is also entrusted with the management of foreign exchange reserves, which are reflected in its balance sheet. While the RBI is essentially a monetary authority, its founding statute mandates it to be the manager of the public debt of the Government of India, and the banker to the government.

While the RBI is the monetary authority of the country as per its founding statute, it has also been entrusted with work relating to banking regulation and supervision by a separate enactment in 1949, viz., the Banking Regulation Act. The RBI exercised a tight regime of exchange control, particularly under the Foreign Exchange Regulation Act (FERA), 1973; however, a qualitative change was brought about in the legal framework to enable liberalisation by the enactment of the FEMA in June 2000, which replaced the FERA. With this, the objectives of foreign exchange regulation have been redefined as the facilitating of external trade and payments, as well as the orderly development and functioning of the foreign exchange market in India.

It is significant to note that the RBI Act precludes the RBI from performing certain businesses such as trading; taking any direct interest in any commercial, industrial or other undertaking; purchasing shares or giving loans against the shares of any company; advancing money on the security of immovable property and the drawing or accepting of bills payable otherwise than on demand. These prohibitions are meant to protect the integrity of the institution.

GOVERNANCE ARRANGEMENTS

The 'general superintendence and direction of the affairs and business' of the RBI are 'entrusted to the Central Board of Directors'. The central board, nominated by the government, consists of fourteen eminent persons[1] drawn from different walks of life, who are the non-official directors. The secretary dealing with economic affairs in the Ministry of Finance is also a director on the central board, and has a voice but no vote. Further, the governor and the deputy governors are also appointed by the government as the chairman and non-voting directors of the board, respectively. The central board meets at least six times in a year and at least once a quarter.

The RBI General Regulations, 1949, mandate a Committee of the Central Board, which is in the nature of an executive board and meets once a week. The Committee of the Central Board quorum demands the presence of at least one non-official director. Currently, the normal attendance for the weekly meetings is three or four of the five non-official directors who reside in Mumbai. The weekly meetings review the economy and the financial market developments, and approve the weekly accounts of the RBI (which are placed on the RBI website every week, soon after their approval) and all other matters relating to the general conduct of the RBI's business. The Governor, and in his absence the senior-most deputy governor available, presides over these meetings.

The function of the supervision of the banking system, development of financial institutions, NBFCs, and the PDs is overseen by a separate BFS, which has been constituted by the government through separate regulations formulated under the RBI Act. The BFS has four non-official central board directors as its members and meets at least once a month, functioning virtually as an executive board in matters relating to regulation and supervision. While the Governor chairs the BFS, where all the deputy governors are members, one of the deputy governors is virtually its full-time vice-chairman. In addition to issue-based reviews and directions, the BFS reviews the functioning of individual banks, and with respect to select cases, there is also a monthly monitoring of individual banks. Thus, in a sense, the supervision function is handled somewhat independently, but within the RBI.

Yet another body recently constituted by the government through a separate regulation is the BPSS, which has two non-official central board directors as its members and meets at least once a quarter. The BPSS is now under re-constitution, consistent with the provisions of the recently enacted Payment and Settlement Systems Act, 2007.

In addition, the central board has three standing committees. The Inspection and Audit Sub-Committee comprises four non-official central board directors. The Building Sub-Committee and the Staff Sub-Committee have at least two non-official central board directors each, and intensely oversee the two important non-financial assets of the RBI.

There are also four local boards of the RBI for four regions of the country, each of which has five non-official members appointed by the Central government, and a chairman who is one of the directors of the central board. The local boards advise the central board on matters remitted to them and perform the duties delegated to them, currently by a resolution of the central board.

In recent years, the conduct of monetary policy has acquired complexity and significance in view of the greater integration of our economy with the global economy. Although there is no legal requirement for a Monetary Policy Committee to take appropriate decisions, it was internally decided in 2005 to constitute a Technical Advisory Committee on Monetary Policy. Currently, the Technical Advisory Committee on Monetary Policy consists of two non-official directors of the central board and five independent outside experts,[2] apart from the four deputy governors and the Governor. The Technical Advisory Committee on Monetary Policy usually meets once in a quarter, a week ahead of the announcement of the annual policy or the quarterly reviews of the monetary policy.

The RBI's accountability to the Parliament is essentially through the Ministry of Finance, though the Governor and the deputy governors appear, as called upon, before the parliamentary committees, especially before the Standing Committee on Finance.

Thus, the formal governance arrangements in the RBI are oriented towards a collegial approach to decision-making. Yet, as in the case of most of the central banks, the Governor holds a somewhat unique position in the organisation. The legal systems as well as tradition do bestow some authority on the Governor, meant to be commensurate with this unique position. As the Governor is the public face of the RBI in the eyes of the government and the public at large, the Governor is generally seen to be *de facto* accountable.

INDEPENDENCE OF THE RBI

On practical considerations, central bank independence may be broadly related to three areas, viz., managerial aspects, including personnel matters, financial aspects and policy aspects.

Managerial independence refers to the procedures for appointment, term of office and dismissal procedures for the top central bank officials and the governing body. It also includes the extent and nature of government representation in the governing body of the central bank, and the government's powers to issue directions.

Financial independence relates to the freedom of the central bank to decide the extent to which government expenditure will be either directly or indirectly financed via central bank credits. Direct or automatic access of the government to central bank credits would naturally imply that monetary policy is subordinated to fiscal policy.

Finally, policy independence relates to the flexibility given to the central bank in the formulation and execution of monetary policy under a given mandate.

While the Central government may give such directions to the RBI after consulting the Governor, as it may consider necessary in the public interest, the overall management of the RBI's affairs and business rests with the central board of directors. All directors of the central board, including the Governor and the deputy governors, are appointed by the government, and they could be superseded or removed.

The staffing pattern is left to the RBI, but rules governing their service conditions and compensation are currently not out of alignment with the public sector in general, and the banking sector in particular.

On the financial aspects of the RBI vis-à-vis the government, the phasing out of automatic monetisation of fiscal deficits by 1997 and the enactment of the FRBM legislation in 2003 are two important milestones with regard to providing safeguards to monetary policy from the consequences of an expansionary fiscal policy, and ensuring a degree of autonomy of the RBI. Consequently, barring emergencies, there are limits to the WMA by the RBI to the government, and the RBI is prohibited from participating in the primary issuance of all government securities.

The RBI has gradually withdrawn from the practice of providing concessional finance or refinance for specified sectors, although statutory provisions continue to enable it. The RBI advocates direct fiscal support to developmental activities so that the support is transparent, accountable and quantifiable, rather than through the monetary operations of the RBI, which would be tantamount to quasi-fiscal operations.

The RBI contributes to the exchequer by way of a transfer of balance of its annual profits, after making provisions and transfers to its reserves. The general principles regarding such transfers were rationalised as part of the reform process in 1997. The present arrangement is governed by the objective of strengthening the RBI balance sheet by achieving a stipulated level of reserves in the balance sheet over a period—although the time frame to achieve this level has been extended to accommodate immediate fiscal compulsions.

Harmonious relations between the government and the RBI have undoubtedly contributed to the successful policy outcomes thus far, but it would be inappropriate to conclude that there are no differences in analyses, approaches, judgements and instrumentalities. In the given legal and cultural context, while making every effort to offer its views, either informally or formally, but as unambiguously as possible, the RBI generally respects the wishes and final inclinations of the government. The RBI, however, has to accept the responsibility for all its decisions and actions, while being generally conscious of the impact its articulation and actions have on its credibility. The government, for its part, recognises the dilemmas before the RBI, and accords significant weight to the RBI's judgements.

In sum, *de jure,* the RBI has not been accorded autonomy on par with recent trends in some of the industrialised as well as emerging economies; but *de facto,* recent experience reflects a progressively higher degree of autonomy being enjoyed by the RBI. During the period of reform, since 1991, there has been a gradual and mutually agreed-upon progress towards greater autonomy in matters relating particularly to financial markets and the conduct of monetary policy.

RELATIONSHIP WITH THE MINISTRY OF FINANCE

In a way, I have answered this question when I mentioned that there is, in the Indian context, a greater *de facto* rather than *de jure* autonomy available to the RBI. It is necessary to recognise that *de facto* autonomy is possible only when the Central government, and in particular the Ministry of Finance, reposes confidence and trust in the RBI. In a way, it can be said that independence in abstract or absolute terms is not feasible in practice. An assessment of the extent of independence of a central bank or its autonomy vis-à-vis the government needs to reckon the independence with respect to which specific functions; with what objectives; in which context and through what instruments.

It is essential to avoid being dogmatic about the independence of a central bank, and to approach the subject with reference to fundamental objectives in a given context in a pragmatic fashion, within the legal framework. Perhaps, in the Indian context and at this juncture, it can be said that the RBI has considerable autonomy in monetary operations, but that it closely harmonises its policies with public policies in general, and coordinates actively with the government to bring about structural reforms in the economy.

Before concluding this section, it will be instructive to explore the explanations for what I may call globally prevalent noises with regard to relations between central banks and governments, especially the Ministry of Finance.

First, the very purpose behind creating a central bank is to have a slightly longer-term view of macroeconomic management. Hence, its perspectives are likely to be different from those of the government.

Second, the design of a central bank involves, among other things, a separation of the powers to spend money (which vests with the government) from the powers to create money (which vests with the monetary authority), with a view to avoiding inflationary financing of government spending. Hence, the focus and emphasis could be different due to the design itself.

Third, the distinctly apolitical identity of a central bank helps countries to mitigate some possible adverse consequences of spurts of political instability, by enabling the currency and the credit systems to operate as smoothly as possible at all times.

Fourth, the interests of the government, as a borrower in the financial market and also as a significant owner of entities regulated by the central bank, may not necessarily converge with those of the central bank.

Finally, if a central bank always concurs with the government, the former, as a distinct entity, becomes superfluous, while if it persists with constant disagreements, it becomes obnoxious. In reality, the relevant issue is how checks and balances work in a given context.

THE RBI: APPROACHES TO MANAGING REFORM

As a part of economic reforms, public policy in India has enabled changes in the domestic economy, and has been responding to changes in the global economy while reorienting public institutions to meet the consequent newly-emerging demands on them. The RBI is also a part of this process of managing reform. I would like to highlight some of the approaches adopted by the RBI in managing the reform process.

First, considerable attention is being paid to enhancing the knowledge base and skills within the institution. RBI officers are encouraged to upgrade their skills on a continuous basis. Select officers are trained, for about one year, in leading universities, including Harvard, Stanford, Oxford, Yale, LSE, etc., and these officers number around ninety so far. There are on our rolls, about sixty Ph.D.s and over 100 MBAs focusing on the financial sector. E-learning is facilitated through the Financial Stability Institute. There are incentives for the acquisition of academic qualifications on a full-time or part-time basis. Additionally, officers are sent to several training programmes, both in India and abroad.

Second, information on global best practices is obtained on a continuous basis. In many of the technical papers or reports of working groups that are placed on the RBI website, a reference to comparative country practices may be routine. In fact, a committee had assessed our standards and codes vis-à-vis the global standards on several aspects of the financial sector in 2001, and these have since been updated. Currently, an exercise of comprehensive self-assessment, using *inter alia* the IMF/World Bank Handbook on Financial Sector Assessment (2005) is underway under the chairmanship of Dr Rakesh Mohan, deputy governor, with Dr Subbarao, finance secretary, as the co-chairman. The process incorporates obtaining advice from about forty nationally and globally renowned experts.[3] The report on this self-assessment should be available soon in the public domain. Our senior officers are involved in several multilateral working groups, such as those of the Financial Stability Forum and the BIS, thus acquiring an in-depth knowledge of global practices. In fact, some of our professionals work on deputation in these multilateral institutions as well as some other central banks, thus bringing back a wealth of experience. Similarly, to facilitate wider exposure, officers are selectively enabled to work in NGOs or other financial institutions.

The annual conference of regional directors and heads of departments also provides an opportunity to learn from eminent personalities from diverse fields.[4]

Third, continuous efforts are made to benefit from outside expertise. Experts from outside the RBI, be they academics or market participants or representatives of industry associations, are associated usually as members and occasionally as special invitees with the working groups or committees constituted by the RBI. Their participation enhances the quality of work and the implementability of their recommendations in our situation. Several Standing Committees have the benefit of the advice of eminent professors from the IITs, IIMs, etc.[5] The Standing Committees exist for a wide range of activities, namely financial markets, technology, financial regulation, etc. The outside expertise adds value to the quality of decision-making and the credibility of the policy measures initiated.

Fourth, the procedures for decision-making and internal working are made more collegial and less hierarchical. The inter-departmental groups constituted with regard to various aspects of RBI functions include, for example, the Financial Markets Committee (which meets at least once a day, in the morning), the Deputy Governors' Committee (which meets once a week), the Regulated Institutions Group, the Monetary Policy Strategy Group, the Reserve Management Strategy Group (which meets once a month) and the Crisis Management Group (which meets whenever a crisis is anticipated or occurs). The process helps to enhance the quality of work and wide participation/commitment. For the purposes of coordination with the Central government, state governments and other regulators, we have several standing committees/groups—such as for cash and debt-management, financial conglomerates and technical groups with the Securities Exchange Board of India and the Insurance Regulatory and Development Authority. These are standard coordinating arrangements, but the RBI, in view of its responsibility towards financial stability, takes an active interest in these and benefits from them.

Fifth, considerable emphasis has been laid on innovative approaches to managing the reform process. For example, the urban cooperative banks faced severe problems due to the dual control of the RBI and the state governments. The RBI's efforts to divest its role altogether did not succeed. Hence, it was decided to make institutional arrangements to ensure coordination with state governments, whenever a state was willing. The Federation of Urban Cooperative Banks was also made a partner in the process. Consequently, task forces have been established in several states through an MoU. Yet another example of mutual understanding relates to the introduction of a system of WMA, as well as the cessation of RBI participation in primary issuances of government securities before the passage of the FRBM Act at the Centre.

Finally, a proactive approach has been adopted on several issues. For example, a bi-annual conference of state finance secretaries is being convened for over ten years, in which Central government nominees also participate. The conference sponsors several studies and working groups, for which the RBI provides the technical support. Constant feedback from all stakeholders is sought on several issues that happen to be under the consideration of the RBI. Often, even the draft circulars are placed in the public domain for feedback. The RBI's communication policy has now been extended to cover several leading national languages—as will be evident from the RBI website.

NOTES

1. The central board of the RBI includes, as directors, Dr Ashok S. Ganguly, Shri Azim Premji, Dr D. Jayavarthanavelu, Shri Kumar Mangalam Birla, Shri Lakshmi Chand, Shri Y.H. Malegam, Professor Man Mohan Sharma, Shri H.P. Ranina, Professor U.R. Rao, Shi Sanjay Labroo, Smt. Shashi Rekha Rajagopalan, Shri Suresh Neotia, Shri Suresh D. Tendulkar and Dr A. Vaidyanathan.

Prior to 2006, the board, as originally constituted, included as Directors Dr A.P.J. Abdul Kalam, Dr Amrita Patel, Shri D.S. Brar, Shri K. Madhava Rao, Professor Mihir Rakshit, Shri N.R. Narayana Murthy, Professor C.N.R. Rao, Shri Ratan Tata, Shri K.P. Singh, Shri Suresh Krishna and Professor V.S. Vyas.

2. Currently the outside experts in the Technical Advisory Committee on Monetary Policy are Professor D.M. Nachane, Dr R.H. Patil, Dr Shankar Acharya, Shri Suman Bery and Shri S.S. Tarapore.

3. Advisory panel members include Shri Aman Mehta, Dr Ashok Ganguly, Shri Ashok Soota, Dr K.C. Chakraborty, Dr R. Chandrasekar, Shri Gagan Rai, Dr Indira Rajaraman, Dr Jaimini Bhagwati, Shri Mahesh Vyas, Shri Nimesh Kampani, Shri Nitin Desai, Dr Omkar Goswami, Shri Pavan Sukhdev, Dr Rajas Parchure, Dr Rajiv Kumar, Dr Rajiv B. Lall, Dr M.T. Raju, Dr T.T. Ram Mohan, Shri M.B.N. Rao, Shri Ravi Mohan, Smt. Shikha Sharma, Shri Shubhashis Gangopadhyay, Shri U.K. Sinha, Shri Uday Kotak, Shri C.M. Vasudev and Shri M.S. Verma.

   Peer reviewers include Mr Andrew Large, Mr Andrew Sheng, Mr Carl Hiralal, Mr Eric Rosengren, Mr Gregory Johnston, Mr Ian Mackintosh, Mr Michael Hafeman, Mr Neil Patterson, Mr Ranjit Ajit Singh, Mr Shane Tregillis, Mr V. Sundararajan, Dr Sushil Wadhwani, Mr Vito Tanzi and Professor William Buiter.

4. Those who have addressed the conference in the last four years include Dr A.P.J. Abdul Kalam, Shri Anand Mahindra, Shri Azim Premji, Ms Chetna Gala Sinha, Dabbawala Association office-bearers, Dr Devi Shetty, Shri Mohan Das Pai, Dr Pritam Singh, Dr Sandip Rane, Shri Satish Pradhan and Dr E. Sreedharan.

5. These include Professor Jaju, Professor Jhunjhunwala, Professor Krishnamoorthy, Shri T.V. Mohandas Pai, Dr R.H. Patil, Dr Phatak, Shri Rajesh Doshi, Professor Ram Mohan Rao, Professor Sarda and Professor Sivakumar.

17

The Virtues and Vices of
Talking About Monetary Policy
Some Comments*

It is virtually impossible to add value to the comprehensive and incisive analysis of the subject in the paper by the eminent and respected scholar, Professor Alan Blinder (2008). This chapter will basically supplement or elaborate some ideas in Professor Blinder's paper from a practitioner's point of view. To begin with, there will be select comments on each section of the paper, keeping in mind the Indian perspectives. The second part will highlight select issues which appear to be especially relevant to monetary policy communication in EMEs. The concluding part will pose some issues which deserve debate in the search for what Professor Blinder calls 'optimal' central bank communications policies.

INDIAN PERSPECTIVES

Reasons for Communication

There has been significant progress in India in enhancing communication and removing the mystique surrounding monetary

*Previously presented as remarks at the 7th BIS Annual Conference at Luzern, Switzerland, 26 June 2008.

policy. While in the pre-reform period, before the 1990s, communication was relatively easy in a controlled environment, it has become a greater challenge in a market-oriented environment, particularly in the context of global financial market integration. The stakeholders have become larger and wider, and the monetary policy by itself, in terms of its operating framework and instruments, has assumed increasing complexity. There is a clear recognition of the importance of market expectations in the conduct of monetary policy, partly influenced by academic work and partly by the demonstration effect of evolving practices among central banks. Perhaps there are other reasons behind the demand for such enhanced communications in India; for example, increasingly, greater transparency is being demanded as part of public policy in almost all spheres of governance of the public sector, which includes the central bank. The media—we have six business dailies in English, apart from four business channels on television— exerts pressure, seeking information on many issues. In a way, there is both a supply side and a demand side to the communications of the RBI on monetary policy aspects, in the context of evolving market expectations.

On the need for communications, we have no doubt that it enhances the effectiveness of monetary policy in a liberalised market environment. In fact, the Indian experience shows that by itself, the need to communicate compels far more rigorous thinking and analyses, as it is said that the best of learning comes from a compulsion to teach. The compulsions to communicate catalyse the processes aimed at improving the quality of decision-making and provide helpful feedback.

Democratic accountability, as a reason for better communication, is very valid for India too. However, improvements in communication have been taking place in recent years without any formal recognition of the extent of the RBI's independence. I personally feel that improved communication with regard to the thinking and the actions of the RBI has enhanced the *de facto* central bank independence, while *de jure* there has been no noticeable movement to accord greater independence.

Accountability to Parliament, the supreme body of elected

representatives, is very important in the context of the functioning of a central bank in a democracy. In India, the RBI is accountable to the Parliament through the Ministry of Finance, and thus its communication to the Parliament is through the ministry. Whenever the views of the central bank and the ministry converge, there should be no complexities. The RBI is also summoned to give evidence before parliamentary committees, most often along with the officials of the Ministry of Finance. There are some occasions when the committee hearings are restricted to the RBI, generally when the Governor is called in. However, we are sworn to secrecy from making public our submissions to the parliamentary committees, whereas the committee may make use of the material supplied by us when it considers appropriate. In a sense, the RBI's views, as submitted to the parliamentary committees, are not available in their entirety in the public domain.

It is quite possible that there are communications or signals, if not directions, from the Ministry of Finance, often on issues relating to monetary policy or banking, a sector owned predominantly by the government. If these are consistent with those of the central bank, they reinforce the central bank policies; however, if these are divergent, they pose a dilemma for central bank communication and, to that extent, a central bank may be constrained from freely articulating its policies.

These are some noteworthy features of communication in the context of democratic accountability to the Parliament in India.

Limits to Communication

Based on my personal experience, it is possible to mention some limitations on making communication more effective in India. Most often, in any given context, the preferences of market participants may be different from, but not necessarily opposed to, public policy preferences. While transparency and communication in such circumstances helped in a re-ordering of preferences, an element of surprise in the decisions and timing of the communication was more effective when public policy preferences and market preferences were in virtually opposite directions. In the latter case, communicating the reasoning for the actions, either concurrently or ex post, was found to be desirable.

Communication is Not Pre-Commitment

Pre-commitment is generally useful on many occasions as part of monetary policy communication. I have two observations based on our experience in this regard. First, in highly uncertain conditions, a conscious view needs to be taken on the virtues of pre-commitment. Second, even when there is a pre-commitment and some reversal was needed at some stage due to unforeseen circumstances, a detailed and timely explanation for deviating from the assurance helps clarify the situation. Further, degrees of pre-commitment may vary from a 'vague but indicative' to 'a definitive time-table' and our choice has varied depending on the circumstances.

What to Communicate

On what to communicate, Professor Blinder refers to four different aspects of monetary policy, namely overall objectives and strategy, motives behind a particular decision, the economic outlook and future monetary policy decisions. Most difficulties in putting these into practice arise with regard to the future monetary policy decisions. Our effort in this regard has been to explain the stance of the monetary policy that would govern the future, which is currently done at quarterly intervals. The emphasis of this communication is on presenting information and analyses that allow market participants to draw their own inferences; however, the RBI desists from giving any explicit forward guidance.

The RBI is not only responsible for monetary policy, but also for banking regulation and for management of the external sector and government debt. Further, the content of communications relates not only to policy changes, but also to the path of structural reforms, including legal reforms. In our periodical communications, we have adopted a format whereby we present the monetary policy and developmental and regulatory policies in two distinct sections in our annual and mid-term reviews, while the first and third quarter communications are confined to monetary policy. Cross-references are no doubt inevitable. These are in addition to various other forms of communication—regular or ad hoc, and formal or informal.

Central bank communication is generally perceived as synonymous with pronouncements on monetary policy. In fact, a central bank's dilemma is more pronounced with regard to the communication of supervisory issues. On supervisory matters, the central bank communicates to the common person, and does not necessarily confine itself to a specialised audience like financial markets or financial institutions. These market players with knowledge and skills can absorb such communication in the right spirit, despite having specific business interests. What the general public desires to know may at times be at a variance with what market players would like disclosed. The dilemmas of a supervisor, especially in a country like India, are even more complex on account of the level of financial education.

The strategies and content of communication aimed at meeting the challenges to financial stability will be different from those to do with maintaining price stability. In India, several measures, monetary as well as administrative, were undertaken to meet the threats to financial stability, while complementary or parallel recourse was taken to communications. Some examples are: a speech in Goa in August 1997 to 'talk down the rupee'; reassuring statements on market developments in the context of the Asian crisis, combined with a package of measures, in tranches in 1997 and 1998; pre-emptive measures in mid-1998 in the context of the crisis in Russia; reassuring statements issued in the context of border conflicts in 1999; a combination of liquidity injections and reassuring statements along with other measures in the context of 9/11 and, in 2005, to explain the impact of the redemption of the India Millennium Deposits, to the extent of US$ 7 billion, on the foreign exchange markets. There could also be occasions when the central bank may not react to certain instances, for example when some sanctions were imposed on India. However, these decisions are taken thoughtfully and consciously after duly taking into account the need and market sensitivity. In brief, we take recourse to OMO, open mouth operations and open only eyes and ears operations in regard to threats to financial stability.

How to Communicate

The public face of the RBI with regard to formal communications is the Governor, but the deputy governor, who also deals with the subject, interacts more actively, more frequently and in greater depth with the media. These are in addition to the legal reporting requirements and several other documents that are placed in the public domain at periodical intervals. In the absence of a formally constituted Monetary Policy Committee, this arrangement works well in terms of communicating with coherence, clarity and credibility.

On the impact of the RBI's communication on financial markets, the most notable contribution has been the generation of a better understanding, debates and sensitivities among market participants and analysts concerning the issues involved in money, finance and macro-stability. This process has been critical for India, partly because the legacy of a planned economy required un-learning as well as re-learning, and partly because the financial-sector reform process as well as the context has been somewhat more unique in India than in many other EMEs.

Predictability

On the predictability of the monetary policy decision in India, I am unaware of any research work on the subject. Let me therefore take recourse to anecdotal evidence. Since 2004, the RBI has been withdrawing monetary accommodation, strengthening prudential requirements and emphasising risks to price as well as financial stability. Most market participants seemed to have conditioned, at least until recently, their expectations of monetary policy response on what they considered the standard practice in advanced economies. As a result, for some time in the past, the RBI had acquired an unwarranted reputation of always surprising the markets, prompting me to quip at one stage that 'the financial markets always surprise me with their expectations from the RBI'.

As regards the forms of central bank communications, our experience is that formal, structured and periodic statements are normally valued significantly but that there is a markedly heightened interest in speeches and comments in times of unexpected global or domestic developments.

India is not an inflation-targeting country. Democratic pressures have proved a disciplining force so far, and its record over five decades is reasonable relative to most developing countries. Further, the two groups of commodities that carry a large weight in the consumption basket, namely food and fuel, are subject to supply shocks, making it difficult to identify a 'core' that could be meaningfully targeted. Yet there are suggestions, mainly from the academia, for inflation targeting; however, there is little or no support for it in political economy.

There is a reference in Blinder's paper to paying some attention to communicating with the general public. In India, communication strategies are designed keeping in mind the target audience. The RBI communicates with various types of audiences—researchers, analysts, academicians, mediapersons, entities regulated by the central bank, other central bankers, rating agencies, international or multilateral bodies and players in the financial markets. The RBI also endeavours to communicate with other special audiences, such as urban and rural women and men, senior citizens, defence personnel and even school children. Let me illustrate with a communication initiative that the RBI undertook two years ago. The Ombudsman Scheme for banks was revised recently, and hence the objective was to inform as wide a section of our population as possible. A press release might not have fully served the purpose. So, a decision was taken to issue an advertisement in the print media—for which the content was indeed common, but the languages differed. It was interesting to note that the fifteen leading Hindi newspapers with a larger circulation of 8.1 million and a far larger readership of 87.0 million helped us reach an audience that was almost five times larger than the one we could have reached had we advertised in the seventeen leading English newspapers, which have a combined circulation of 6.3 million and a readership of 17.9 million. In fact, in India, fifty-four leading non-English newspapers have a circulation of 21.4 million and a readership of 197.2 million. Given this experience, we made the RBI website available in eleven national languages spoken by a large section of the population, apart from English and Hindi, which are the official languages of the Union Government. Further, in 2007 the RBI launched a Financial Literacy Project to educate the common person, who is generally not financially literate. The project aims to impart information and knowledge about banking, finance and central banking to the common person in her/his own language. The material published under this project has therefore also been made available in the eleven major Indian languages, apart from English and Hindi, through a multilingual website.

These illustrations endorse what Professor Blinder has said in his paper: 'In the end, central banks derive their democratic legitimacy and hence their cherished independence from the consent of the general public' (p. 26).

SELECT ISSUES RELEVANT TO EMES

Let me attempt a few generalisations on the subject, keeping in mind the EME perspectives.

First, it is not very clear whether the empirical research on the subject referred to in Professor Blinder's paper has adequately covered EMEs. For example, the BRIC countries (Brazil, Russia, India and China), South Africa, Indonesia, Saudi Arabia, etc., are emerging as significant players in the global economy. Are their experiences different from those researched so far?

Second, the government happens to be a significant player in many EMEs, especially in the financial sector. In these circumstances, should communication with financial markets, which should admittedly be two-way for optimal results, exclude communication by/with the government? Naturally communication by/with the government, by its very nature, will have a differential and, at times, overlapping impact. But how does it affect the independence of the central bank and its policy effectiveness? This dimension poses a challenge for communication policy.

Third, the education function of central bank communication that Professor Blinder referred to may be more important in EMEs. In fact, such a function, when it carries credibility, may enlarge the role of a central bank in the EMEs. In this regard, let me quote from an undelivered speech of a distinguished central banker on the subject.

> Communication is not just about transparency. It is also about education, guidance and steering things in the right direction. In this, the central bank can be an honest broker between the government and the public and even the parliament.[1]

In fact, a central bank can influence changes in public policy that are relevant to monetary and financial policies. For example, at the cost of modesty, let me quote Mr Tarapore, a respected central banker.

> ...when the definitive history of India's policy on gold is written up, the speech by Dr Y.V. Reddy, Deputy Governor, Reserve Bank of India, at the World Gold Council Conference on 28 November 1996 will stand out as a watershed as it is perhaps the only speech by a senior Indian official which squarely takes on issues on gold policy and it will be appropriately recorded as a forerunner of major policy change.[2]

Fourth, relative to many other institutions in the public sector, central banks in many EMEs happen to have professional skills, experiences and objective and independent thinking, which can be drawn upon by the government especially during the process of reform, in particular reforms in the financial sector. Structural changes involving institutional and legal changes in EMEs may need active inputs from the respective central banks. How do the theory, practice and expectation of a transparent and independent central bank reconcile with these practical compulsions?

Fifth, the issue of financial stability is of great significance and enormous complexity for central bankers in EMEs. These economies vary considerably with regard to their fiscal, current account, openness to the external sector and dependence on oil earnings or oil imports. Yet, analysts in financial markets often treat them as a group, presumably because the EMEs are perceived as high-risk and high-reward destinations for financial capital. That characteristic makes them more vulnerable to volatility in capital flows, sometimes for reasons other than economic fundamentals in the country concerned. As the title implies, the EMEs are emerging from one state to another, namely from lesser market orientation to greater market orientation, and are thus in a state of transition. Consequently, the central banks in the EMEs, in their pursuit of financial stability, face additional challenges: first, to manage the transition in their own economies, which has socio-economic as well as political dimensions and second, to keep a watch on the sentiments affecting foreign capital flows— which could change for reasons other than domestic ones.

There are other reasons why challenges before communication policy are considerably more complex for central banks in the EMEs. Generally, the style and content of communication in EMEs has to evolve over time, consistent with the progress in financial sophistication. Further, in a globalised world, the communications of a central bank in advanced economies have a great impact on financial markets in EMEs. Communications, including the scope for pre-commitment in policy, may have to factor in these complexities.

SOME ISSUES FOR DEBATE

Before concluding, I should admit that Professor Blinder's paper has provoked some thoughts that warrant further debate. I will mention them briefly.

First, communication is a two-way process, and it is all about sharing information. Market functionaries and agents have an equal role in enhancing their disclosure of data and information. However, studies seem to focus on one-sided communication from policymakers. How far could non-transparent and asymmetric markets adversely affect the policy effectiveness of central banks?

The recent sub-prime turmoil is a clear case in point. This may be worth examining.

Second, while discussing the independence of central banks, how do we capture the *de facto* elements as distinct from the *de jure* ones? While it is true that the distinction is specific to the overall governance in the public sector in each country, there may be an explanation for divergences between the two that might either reinforce or undermine the credibility of communication. Further, there may be different degrees of independence being exercised in practice, and it might be interesting to try and understand how these could be captured in future studies.

Third, the exercise of independence has generally been discussed in the context of price stability. The issue becomes more complex in the face of threats to financial stability since crisis management, as distinct from prevention, requires coordination or at least consultation with the government, both in terms of actions and communication. This is particularly relevant if quasi-fiscal costs are involved. The more complex issue of managing the conflicts between the goals of price and financial stability, which on some rare occasions warrant consultation or coordination with the government, is another matter.

Fourth, how much of the recent empirical evidence is adequate to give credit to the effectiveness of the monetary policy of central banks relative to, say, the globalisation of trade in goods and services? At this stage, I must share one concern about the credibility bonus earned by an effective communication policy that I had expressed in 2006:

> Is it possible that such 'hands on' and 'very successful' communication by many central banks with regard to maintaining financial stability have resulted in under-pricing of risks by the private sector, or in a distinct lowering of aversion to financial risks? Is it possible that this credibility bonus is partly responsible for the upward pressure on the housing and equity prices becoming a global phenomenon?[3]

Fifth, is it possible to envisage intermediate arrangements between an individualistic and a mandated Monetary Policy

Committee? We have an example of such an intermediate arrangement in India. We have an Advisory Committee on Monetary Policy, consisting of members drawn from non-executive independent members of the RBI board and outside experts to aid the decision-making process. This arrangement enables participation without diluting the coherence, credibility and flexibility—especially with regard to communication.

Professor Blinder (2005) referred to four prototypical central bank decision-making systems: individual central bank governor (for example, the Reserve Bank of New Zealand); autocratically-collegial Monetary Policy Committee (MPC) (for example, the Federal Reserve System); genuinely-collegial MPC (for example, the European System of Central Banks) and individualistic MPC (for example, the Bank of England). Perhaps India would be a fifth prototype, placed somewhere in the middle, in terms of its proximity to the classic decision-maker of economic theory. It could be called individual central bank governor—voluntarily collegial (the RBI).

Finally, in the debate on accountability and independence, it may be useful to be clear about whom the central bank is primarily accountable to. If a central bank does not enjoy independence, the question of its direct accountability will not arise. Broadly speaking, however, have central banks of late been tending to focus more on accountability to financial markets, by design or necessity, rather than to the government, or the real sector or the public at large?

NOTES

1. Dr I.G. Patel's address at the SAARC Governor's meeting on Communication in Central Banks, which was scheduled for December 2004 but was cancelled because of the tsunami.

2. Excerpts from Mr Tarapore's address at the Gold Banking Seminar of the World Gold Council, New Delhi, 2 August 1997
3. Keynote address at the Regional Seminar on Central Bank Communications, sponsored by the International Monetary Fund, held at Mumbai on 23 January 2006.

REFERENCES

Blinder, Alan S. 2008. 'Talking About Monetary Policy: The Virtues (and Vices?) of Central Bank Communication'. Center for Economic Policy Studies (CEPS) Working Paper No. 164, Princeton University, May.
————. 2005. 'Monetary Policy by Committee: Why and How?' Promontory Financial Group, Princeton University, 12 December.

VI

Managing Capital Account Liberalisation

18

Foreign Exchange Reserves
New Realities and Options*

In the aftermath of the Asian crises, it was widely perceived (a perception supported by academic research and commentators) that large reserves were needed by EMEs to withstand any crisis, and that to some extent, it was a reflection of a lack of confidence in the international financial architecture. As a result, the recent episode of reserve accumulation has been on a much higher scale and was more prolonged than had been seen during the early 1990s. For instance, as reported by the BIS, during 2000 and 2005 the EMEs accumulated reserves at an annual rate of US$ 250 billion (or 3.5 per cent of their annual combined GDP), which was almost five times higher than the level seen in the early 1990s. The bulk of the reserve accumulation was concentrated in Asia, with countries like China, Korea, India, Malaysia and Taiwan (China) witnessing large increases, while countries in Latin America and central Europe had a fairly modest increase in reserves during this period. Lately, many oil-exporting countries have also seen a large increase in their reserves.

It may be useful to recognise that reserve accumulation in some senses reflects the savings-investment balances, and is symptomatic of both domestic and global factors, including self-insurance, a concept difficult to define.

*Previously presented as address, the 2006 Program of Seminars, Singapore, 16–18 September 2006, on the Theme 'The World in Asia, Asia in the World'.

RESERVES INCREASES: MOSTLY DRIVEN BY CAPITAL ACCOUNT SURPLUS

It is important to identify the sources of reserve accretion in this latest episode. There are some countries like Russia where the reserves are built out of current account surplus. In countries like China, Korea and Taiwan, the surplus in both current and capital accounts led to the accumulation of reserves. On the other hand, there are countries like India where the reserves accretion was driven more by capital account surplus and was not due to a current account surplus, broadly implying that the capital inflow was more than what could be normally absorbed in the domestic economy. Net capital flows have remained much larger than the current account deficit in India, as well as in most of Latin America and central and Eastern Europe. In case the reserve accumulation is due to large capital flows, it would be useful to distinguish between debt and non-debt flows, as also between FDI and generally less stable portfolio flows. In fact, both the stock and the flow in each category would be relevant for reserve management. While the marking-to-market of the assets and liabilities may be difficult, it might not be irrelevant.

Thus, while the traditional indicators of adequacy of reserves are based on trade, debt and monetary indicators, or even the 'Guidotti Rule' or 'Liquidity at Risk' rule suggested by Alan Greenspan, they need to be supplemented with what may be described as multiple indicators to assess the adequacy of the reserves of any country at a given juncture.

DIFFICULTIES IN COMPUTING QUASI-FISCAL COST OF RESERVES

A simple method of calculating the net cost of carrying reserves to the central bank is the difference between the interest rate on domestic securities and the rate of return earned on the foreign exchange reserves adjusted for any exchange rate change. The magnitude of the cost, which is often difficult to estimate, varies with the extent of sterilisation and the yield differentials. These are termed quasi-fiscal costs in the literature, since the costs to the central bank are passed on to the sovereign through a lower transfer of profits. In countries where local interest rates are well above international levels, such carrying costs could be positive, while they would be negative if the reverse were true. A recent study by the BIS has shown that carrying costs are negative in a number of countries at current interest rates. The study states that in China, for instance, the one-year interest rate in June 2006 was less than half the comparable US Treasury bond rate. Hence the central bank is earning a positive carry. However, it can be argued that given the inherent cyclical nature of interest rates, such negative carrying costs could reverse over a period of time. Moreover, one has to keep in mind that these hypothetical cost calculations do not capture capital gains or losses. Dani Rodrik of Harvard University has proposed a measure of the social cost of reserves from the national standpoint, which is equal to the spread between the private sector's cost of short-term borrowing abroad and the yield that the central bank earns on its liquid foreign assets. He estimates this cost to be roughly equivalent to 1 per cent of GDP of the developing countries in 2004. Briefly stated, there are difficulties in calculating the precise quasi-fiscal costs or other costs on this account.

While assessing the fiscal cost of holding reserves, it would be worthwhile to set off the benefits that the country may have in holding reserves. In any country risk analysis by the rating agencies and other institutions, the level of reserves generally has high weights. Moreover, it is essential to keep in view some hidden benefits that could accrue to a country holding reserves, which may, *inter alia*, include: maintaining confidence in monetary and exchange rate policies; enhancing the capacity to intervene in foreign exchange markets; limiting external vulnerability so as to absorb shocks during times of crisis; providing confidence to the markets that external obligations can always be met and reducing volatility in foreign exchange markets. It is true that beyond a point, when the credit rating reaches the appropriate investment grade, addition to reserves may not lead to further improvements in the credit rating. It is necessary to recognise that, as in the case of costs, there are difficulties in computing the benefits, too.

CHANGING COMPOSITION OF RESERVES

The available data on the composition of official reserves indicate that progress towards a diversification of reserves has been cautious, which is not surprising, given the very definition of reserves in terms of 'external assets that are readily available ...', as offered by the IMF. An important objective of holding the reserves is to be prepared for contingencies, but the range of instruments available to satisfy this need is limited. Nevertheless, the management of reserves has been changing, and there has been a quest for higher returns within these traditional objectives. To quote Philip D. Wooldridge of the BIS, from his latest article on 'The Changing Composition of Official Reserves' in the September 2006 issue of the BIS Quarterly Review:

> Continuing a trend that began in the 1970s, when reserves were first reallocated from US Treasury bills to bank deposits, reserve managers have been gradually shifting into higher-yielding, higher-risk instruments. They seem most comfortable managing market risk but are beginning to take on more credit and liquidity risk too. The currency composition of their portfolios, while volatile, has not changed as much as the instrument composition.

It is essential to recognise that reserve managers are already shifting into higher-yielding instruments with a higher risk-return equation, presumably as a result of the progressively rising level of reserves. Consequently, the financial returns on the free reserves at the margin could be far higher than the average return. In my view, the marginal return appears to be a more relevant concept in the context of alternative forms of investment of reserves.

QUASI-RESERVES

With the positive shock emanating from large capital flows resulting in significant reserves accumulation in many EMEs, a new development in reserve management is to hold a part of the reserves that could be used by the public sector in a country in a manner different from the strictly defined pattern in which external assets are held by the monetary authorities. Such foreign exchange reserves could be termed quasi-reserves. In terms of its holding, such quasi-reserves are easily retrievable when the situation demands. In Singapore, the Monetary Authority of Singapore (MAS) and the Government of Singapore Investment Corporation (GIC) basically manage the foreign exchange reserves. The GIC is the government's principal investment agent, handling the bulk of the nation's investments, while the MAS holds reserves to maintain the stability of the Singapore dollar. Similarly, Temasek Holdings invests in Singapore as well as manages a diversified global portfolio, with the aim of creating and maximising sustainable value for the shareholders and providing resources to finance pensions and other benefits.

Along the lines of Singapore's GIC, South Korea has recently established the Korean Investment Corporation (KIC). Another interesting example is that of China, where foreign exchange reserves have been utilised to strengthen the banking system without selling foreign securities. China has transferred funds from its international reserves, held with the Peoples' Bank of China (PBC), to a new company, the Central Huijin Investment Company (CHIC), set up in 2003 and jointly managed by the government, PBC, and the State Administration of Foreign ·Exchange. In the PBC's balance sheet, the said amount of reserves was replaced by claims on the CHIC. The CHIC used the assets to purchase shares in banks that were to be recapitalised.

STABILISATION FUNDS

Investment funds are sometimes created by the public sector out of the 'windfall revenue' accruing to a country due to a rise in the export price of, say, oil or other commodities. Such reserves arise due to positive external shocks, which can cause a surge in government revenues and, at times, could be challenging too, as some governments may have to deal with an appreciating exchange rate, undermining export competitiveness with symptoms of Dutch disease'. Many countries such as Chile, Kuwait, Norway, Russia and the United Arab Emirates (UAE) have institutionalised the investment of the surplus arising from the positive shocks of commodity and oil prices by creating sophisticated investment agencies or commodity/oil stabilisation funds to manage reserves, since there is a broader range of investment opportunities for their savings today than there were in the 1970s or 1980s. The management of such a corpus may, in some cases, be entrusted to the central bank, but with an appropriate mandate.

Usually these stabilisation funds are established with one or more of the following objectives: insulate the budget and the economy from excess volatility in revenues; help monetary authorities to sterilise unwanted liquidity; build up savings for future generations or use the money for economic and social development. With regard to oil funds, the transparency and disclosures standards appear to be lower than those for the official reserves, but with some accountability.

An interesting question in this regard is the extent to which windfall revenues can be equated with large capital flows. While there could be a deceleration in the windfall revenues, the reserve accumulation due to large capital flows should reckon with the possibility of potential reversals and outflows with respect to the capital account.

INNOVATIVE IDEAS

It is useful to explore some of the innovative ideas for using reserves that have been put forward in the recent period.

First, in March 2006, Professor Lawrence Summers, while delivering the L.K. Jha Memorial lecture in Mumbai, argued that the level of reserves in many countries far exceeded the traditional measures of reserve levels required to guard against a foreign exchange crisis. While expressing concern about the risk composition of the assets in which these reserves are invested,

Professor Summers suggested that it was time for the IMF and the World Bank to think about how they could contribute to the deployment of the reserves held by some of the major emerging markets. Professor Summers suggested that these two multilateral institutions create an international facility, under which the countries could invest their excess reserves without taking on the domestic political responsibility for the process of investment decision and the ultimate outcome. In turn, the modest fee charged by these two institutions could support the concessional and grant aspects of global development.

The proposal provides an option to a country holding reserves to place a part of these with the IMF/World Bank entities to operate, *de facto*, as external asset managers. The option could be exercised, presuming that it would be permissible, but not obligatory, to place a part of the reserves if the envisaged entity could provide the assurance that it had the expertise to function as such an external asset manager, and provide a higher risk-weighted return than the domestic reserve managers. Further, since the external asset managers for reserve management in the market are usually guided by the parameters fixed by the official reserve management authorities, which may vary from country to country, the proposed entity may also have to have several windows to cater to the varied mixes of safety, liquidity and return preferred by the various client countries. Thus, the critical issue would be the professional expertise of the proposed entity in terms of assuring an acceptable risk-reward equation.

Second, there was a proposal put forward in 2005 by Eswar Prasad and Raghuram Rajan of the IMF for a controlled approach to capital account liberalisation for economies experiencing large capital inflows. The proposal essentially involved securitising a portion of the capital inflows through closed-ended mutual funds that issue shares in the domestic currency, use the proceeds to purchase foreign exchange from the central bank and then invest the foreign exchange so acquired, abroad. It is argued that such an arrangement would eliminate the fiscal costs of sterilising these inflows, provide domestic investors with opportunities for international portfolio diversification and stimulate the development of domestic financial markets; more importantly, it would allow central banks to control both the timing and the quantity of capital outflows. It is advocated that this proposal be a part of a broader toolkit of measures to liberalise the capital account cautiously when external circumstances are favourable.

The merit of this proposal lies in combining three elements—capital account management, financial-sector development and the use of foreign exchange reserves. This proposal for setting up more than closed-ended private-sector foreign asset funds, to be licensed by the central bank, appears relevant under certain circumstances, mainly when there is a likelihood of a significant investor interest for such funds. This, however, would not be realisable if there is a negative carry that such funds could entail. Further, it is not certain whether a private intermediary, licensed by a central bank specifically for this purpose, would entirely obviate the moral hazard, even in the absence of any explicit or implicit guarantee with regard to performance.

In India, domestic mutual funds are permitted to invest in foreign securities, apart from the American Depository Receipt (ADR)/Global Depository Receipts (GDR) of Indian companies, up to an aggregate limit of US$ 2 billion. In addition, a limited number of qualified mutual funds are also permitted to invest cumulatively up to US$ 1 billion in overseas exchange traded funds (ETF). More generally, the pace and sequencing of several measures of liberalisation of the capital account take into account the degree of comfort as one of the relevant factors.

Third, an idea that received some attention in March 2002 during the gathering on 'Finance for Development' in Monterrey, Mexico, is that instead of holding the reserves in US dollars, a new form of global money, akin to the IMF's Special Drawing Rights, namely 'global greenbacks', could be issued, which countries could hold in their reserves. The corpus would be created by countries setting aside a part of their reserves every year as an insurance against contingencies. The amount of money held by these countries in 'global greenbacks' could be given to developing countries to finance their development programmes as well as global public goods like environmental projects, health initiatives, humanitarian assistance and so on. For countries that receive less than the amount they need to put into reserves, the new 'global money' would go into reserves, freeing the dollars that these countries would otherwise set aside. Countries that receive more than they must put into reserves could exchange the new money for conventional currencies. Eventually, all the new money will find its way into reserves, which in effect represents a commitment by the countries to help each other in times of trouble.

It has been argued that the 'global greenbacks' proposal envisages the flow of funds to poor countries according to their needs, while contributing to global economic growth, stability and equity. Opponents of this move have argued that some countries will become 'greenback addicts', and when the handouts end, the economic withdrawal symptoms will be severe.

Fourth, in the aftermath of the Asian financial crisis, two related developments took place. In 2000, the Association of Southeast Asian Nations along with China, Japan and the Republic of Korea (ASEAN + 3 countries) mutually agreed to form a network of bilateral swap agreements to provide mutual protection from financial emergencies, popularly known as the Chiang Mai Initiative (CMI). The success of such an initiative is reflected in the recent proposal of the Asian finance ministers to double the size of the Asian central bank swaps under the CMI.

The Asian Bond Fund Initiative was also launched in 2003, and reflected the efforts to develop a regional bond market for catering to the medium- and long-term financing needs of Asian economies. The Asian Bond Fund provided an arrangement for pooling a portion of the foreign exchange reserves of a few East Asian and Pacific countries, and the Fund's portfolio is invested in the liquid US dollar-denominated bonds issued by the major Asian economies. The second Asian Bond Fund, launched in June 2005, aims to promote local currency bond markets by establishing a Pan-Asian Bond Index Fund (PAIF) and eight single-market funds.

DEGREE OF COMFORT

The concept of the adequacy of reserves is popular, but it is also possible, from a practitioner's perspective, to view reserves in terms of the degree of comfort they provide at various levels. Such a perspective is more dynamic and contextual. Certainly, at a very low level of reserves, which we in India had in the early 1990s, the degree of comfort was very low, and with the rising level of reserves, the comfort also increases. The levels of comfort and discomfort could be linked to the problems of plenty and that of paucity, along a continuum representing the different levels of comfort at various levels of reserves. For a country, it could happen that initially the degree of comfort with the level of reserves might be too low for some time, but with the rising level of reserves, the country might reach a 'comfort zone'; and as the reserves level keeps rising and reaches a still higher level, at some point a portion of the reserves would cease to be strictly foreign exchange reserves and could be characterised as a corpus of funds available for deployment in a higher risk-return portfolio.

Several factors, apart from the exchange rate regime, influence the comfort level with regard to reserves. For example, they would include vulnerability to real-sector shocks, the strength of the fiscal and financial sectors, current account balance, the changing composition of capital flows, a medium-term view of the growth prospects encompassing business cycles, etc. In a sense, the official reserves have to reflect the balancing and comforting factors relative to external assets and liabilities in the context of a rational balance sheet approach.

OPTIONS LINKED TO COMFORT

Let me now link the availability of options with the degree of comfort.

First, it may be useful, for practical purposes, to view the adequacy of reserves in terms of the degree of comfort they offer at a given time.

Second, while considering the level of reserves and the comfort derived from it, it will be necessary to take into account the investment and stabilisation funds, if applicable. Further, transferability from official reserves to such funds and vice versa, and the extent of liquidity required, also need to be considered in assessing the comfort level.

Third, the relative emphasis on safety, liquidity and return keeps changing with the degree of comfort at a given level of reserves.

Fourth, it must be noted that from a national balance sheet point of view, the official reserves have to reflect the potential market infirmities in the private sector. So, if high returns are derived from the high risks assumed due to the larger risk appetite of the external asset managers, then deploying official reserves as well in the high-risk assets would exacerbate the risks. Official reserves may be needed as a cushion when markets become suddenly risk-averse, and hence safety and liquidity should normally have higher orders of priority in the management of reserves.

Fifth, it is possible for a central bank to have tranches—each tranche reflecting a different combination of safety, liquidity and return. Each tranche can be managed by the central bank or an external asset manager, or both in parallel, to benchmark their relative performance.

Finally, and above all, the criticality of the accountability in the use of reserves must be recognised. It is useful to note that reserve management policies normally involve—the joint responsibility of the government and the central bank—irrespective of whose balance sheet they appear in.

CONCLUDING OBSERVATIONS

I would like to recall what I had said in this regard in 2003, at the Annual Fund-Bank meetings in Dubai:

The reserve accumulation could also be seen in the context of the availability of abundant international liquidity following the easing of the monetary policy in industrial countries. The resultant excess liquidity flowed into the emerging markets. In the event of hardening of interest rates in industrialised countries, this liquidity may as quickly dry up; in that situation, emerging markets should have sufficient cushion to withstand such reverse flows of capital.

Now, with the global rise in interest rates, there is always a lurking fear in EMEs that the level of capital flows may not be maintained. Thus, the comfort level of reserves should not be viewed with respect to the current situation alone, but should also reckon the assessment of emerging risks. Moreover, at this moment the global economy has not been tested on the eventuality of a not-so-orderly correction of current global imbalances. Given that eventuality, as experts caution, disruption in financial markets in the form of large cross-currency volatility and a sharp rise in interest rates are not unlikely in the global economy.

To sum up, several factors impinge on the comfort level of reserves, and the relative weights assigned to safety, liquidity and return. When, how and through whom the search for higher returns should be pursued, depending upon the level of comfort, is a matter of convenience and context, and appropriate options should always be kept open.

19

Management of the Capital Account in India
Some Perspectives*

BACKGROUND

During the lecture on Parameters of Monetary Policy in India at the annual conference in Chennai, in January 2002, I made a brief reference to this issue when I said: 'While the twin objectives of monetary policy of maintaining price stability and ensuring availability of adequate credit to productive sectors of economy have remained, capital flows and liberalisation of financial markets have increased the potential risks of institutions—'thus bringing the issue of financial stability to the fore'.

We had introduced two innovative measures, namely the LAF and the MSS, to manage the challenges of monetary policy in the context of large and volatile capital flows, and to assure macro-stability, in particular, financial stability.

While releasing the India Development Report of the Indira Gandhi Institute of Development Research and speaking on 'Indian Economy—Current Status and Select Issues' (January 2005), I had mentioned 'the possible issues that need to be considered if one were to achieve a better management of non-debt components of capital flows that will address emerging concerns'.

*Previously published as inaugural address, delivered at the Annual Conference of the Indian Econometric Society, Hyderabad, 3 January 2008.

At the current juncture, there are several compelling circumstances, both global and domestic, which demand a revisiting of the issues that we discussed earlier, and an elaboration of the emerging concerns in the current context.

THE GLOBAL CONTEXT

Let me first briefly refer to the global context. There have been unprecedented developments in global financial markets. There have been pressures in money and credit markets which are sought to be addressed through coordinated action on the part of several leading central banks to inject liquidity into the overnight as well as term money markets. The impact and outcomes of these recent actions of monetary authorities still appear unclear, both for the immediate future of financial markets and the long term, vis-à-vis the real economy, in terms of growth rate as well as price stability. In the meantime, equity markets in most economies are buoyant, but have been far more volatile over longer periods than in the recent past. There is widespread concern among several central banks in EMEs about the added pressures on monetary management, due to the prevailing extraordinarily strong and volatile cross-border capital flows. These concerns cut across continents, irrespective of the size of economies, the degree of openness, the monetary arrangements and exchange-rate arrangements. While the actions arising from these concerns are varied, they normally involve a combination of monetary policy measures, both direct and indirect, and often involve the management of capital account in several ways without excluding, in some cases, administrative actions. Some countries, recognising the pressures levied by large capital inflows, have taken recourse to countervailing policies in the current account, mainly through greater recourse to stabilisation funds.

Our Finance Minister, while referring to 'Managing Capital Flows' in the Mid-Year Review 2007–8 on 7 December 2007, stated:

While there are international experiences in this regard with some successful and painful adjustment process, the specific Indian context requires innovative policy responses. Going forward, this would be a major challenge (p. 57).

MAINSTREAM ACADEMIC THINKING

While there has been extensive academic work done on the capital account, for the sake of convenience I will refer to a recent comprehensive study on the subject that reflects a fresh thinking among academics. Professor Barry Eichengreen, who admits to seeing 'both sides of this coin' and is a well-respected authority on the subject, wrote a paper titled 'The Cautious Case for Capital Flows' for Rating Agency Malaysia's conference on 'Free Capital Mobility: What's in store for Asia', held in Singapore on 1 August 2007. In this paper, he refers to four schools of thought on free capital flows, and it is instructive to consider them in some detail.

The first school is in favour of an open capital account and is based on the textbook case for a more efficient allocation of capital. Professor Eichengreen is doubtful of this interpretation, and argues that recent experience does not suggest that capital is flowing from developed countries, where it is relatively abundant, to developing ones, where it is scarce. He adds:

A further problem is that liberalizing equity market flows is not the same as liberalizing all capital flows. Experience shows that investment in equities has more favorable effects than investment in debt but that governments are more inclined to liberalize debt flows. (p. 4)

The second school argues that even if the expectations of the first are not fulfilled, there are corollary benefits, since foreign capital comes packaged with technological and organisational know-how. These benefits may be true of equity and FDIs, but are not true of debt finance. Professor Eichengreen adds: 'More generally, evidence of the corollary benefits of capital account liberalisation is open to alternative interpretations'. He says, 'Moreover, there are reasons to worry that capital account liberalisation adopted with an eye toward forcing reform can have costs as well as benefits'.

The third school emphasises the association of capital account liberalisation with crises, and Professor Eichengreen mentions that this view 'unites such otherwise diverse minds as Joseph Stiglitz and Jagdish Bhagwati'. Based on recent developments, he notes two interpretations of this aspect: (a) that the world is being made safer for capital flows and (b) the volatility has been temporarily suppressed, warranting a caution to emerging markets. He considers that the recent rise in volatility, associated with the sub-prime mortgage problem in the US, is open to both interpretations, and concludes as follows: 'The bottom line is the importance of properly sequencing capital account liberalisation with other policies'. In this context, he refers to the 'need to open trade before opening to capital flows', and the need for 'sound and stable monetary and fiscal policies and the more flexible exchange rate regime appropriate to an environment of open capital markets'.

The fourth school of thought refers to the difficulty that Asian countries are having 'in managing capital inflows and the problems this has created for their competitiveness'. There have been extensive strategies adopted so far, including the adoption of measures to limit inflows, their impact and objectives, etc. The most significant comment in this regard relates to the need for fiscal actions, and he says:

> Again, the message is that capital account openness is beneficial when it is appropriately teamed with other policies. And the implication is that countries that are unable to use fiscal policy in this way, perhaps for political reasons, should go slow on capital account liberalization.

Summing up, Professor Eichengreen refers to the two challenges encountered while going forward that authorities in Asia face with regard to the current problem associated with capital flows.

The first relates to the upward pressure on currencies as private capital continues flowing into the region. He comments:

> The main tool for countering appreciation of the currency will be fiscal policy.... If currencies are too strong for comfort, then Asian governments need to raise taxes and cut public spending. This is politically challenging, but it is a necessary corollary of the decision to free capital flows.

The second relates to limiting the risks of instability. On this, he comments:

> If Asian stock and bond markets fall sharply, the negative shock could spread quickly from leveraged investors to the property sector, from there to the banks that have lent to them, and ultimately to the real economy.

To sum up, the first and second schools of thought, which were dominant till recently, have now been supplemented, or perhaps supplanted, by the third and fourth schools. Further, in the second school, there has been a recent recognition of difference between equity and debt flows in the context of downside risks. The third school focuses on the importance of proper sequencing of liberalisation of the capital account with other policies. The fourth school elaborates on issues relating to the management of capital account, and takes a more nuanced approach to it. In brief, the third and fourth schools, which are of more recent origin and are gaining in respectability, are closely aligned with the approach that India has been following.

THE CURRENT INDIAN CONTEXT

The Ministry of Finance placed a review of the trends in receipts and expenditures at the end of the second quarter of the financial year 2007–8 on 7 December 2007. In this document, there is an exhaustive analysis of several contemporary issues relating to the macroeconomic environment. The status and issues relating to the management of the capital account do find a prominent place in the discussion, which refers to the challenges for monetary management and the complexities in managing capital flows in the following passages:

> The predominant issue that continues to confront the monetary authority during the current year has been the steady increase of forex flows and the policy response thereto. (Para 3.1.12, p. 37)
>
> The management of capital flows is a complex process encompassing a spectrum of policy choices, which inter alia, include: the appropriate level of reserves; monetary policy objectives related to liquidity management and interest rates and maintenance of healthy financial market conditions with financial stability. (Para 3.1, p. 56)

The Eleventh Five-Year Plan (2007–12), as approved by the National Development Council on 19 December 2007, makes several observations in this regard. Some of these are reproduced here.

> The problem posed by having to manage large inflows has been discussed in Chapter-10. It arises because of the well known 'trilemma' that it is not possible to achieve three objectives simultaneously, i.e. free capital mobility, an independent monetary policy and a stable exchange rate. Attention should be given to measures to restrain these capital flows and enhanced the absorptive capacity in the economy to avoid running into the classical 'Dutch Disease' situation where non-tradeables become over-priced and erode the competitiveness of the economy in the tradeable sector. (Para 2.30)
>
> The cautious approach to opening the capital account followed thus far as a conscious act of policy has given the government some leeway in limiting inflows of certain categories. (Para 2.33)
>
> These problems illustrate the merit of the cautious approach adopted by the government in the matter of liberating capital inflows. The advantages of accessing pool of capital to finance

development are recognised in the commitment to move gradually to fuller capital account convertibility. But the move is to be made gradually at a pace which enables the authorities to deal with unexpected volatility. In controlling capital flows it is important to recognise the relative attractiveness of different types of flows. In this regard direct foreign investment is the most preferred form of flow. Investments in Indian firms through the stock market and by venture capital funds in unlisted companies are also potentially beneficial. External commercial borrowing and other short term flows are areas where one can introduce an element of control to moderate sudden surges. However, even with capital calibration it is not easy to manage a surge in capital inflows, if it occurs. In such situations, it is necessary to explore ways of limiting the fiscal cost of sterilising large growth of reserves: either by making these flows less attractive or by means that do not require costly sterilisation. (Para 13.75)

It is noteworthy that there has been recognition of the more immediate challenges brought out by the recently observed financial turbulence in global markets, necessitating a focus on domestic factors in the process of growth and stability in our country. The Prime Minister, in his opening remarks at the 54th meeting of the National Development Council on 19 December 2007, *inter alia* said:

There are some clouds on global financial markets following the sub-prime lending crisis. There are worries that the growth of the US and other leading economies may slow down and some may even go into a recession. This may impact both our exports as well as capital flows. Our economy is now increasingly integrated into the global economy with the external sector now accounting for almost 40% of GDP and hence, we cannot be fully immune to international developments. This is not to say that one must be pessimistic and must be less ambitious in our growth targets. It only implies that we need to redouble our efforts to maintain the domestic drivers of growth and ensure that policy facilitates even faster growth.

To sum up, the public policy in India recognises that—

(a) appropriate management of the capital account is critical for both growth and stability; (b) the cautious approach to capital account has given us leeway; (c) there are preferences with regard to different types of capital flows; (d) some fiscal costs are consciously incurred as necessary on account of sterilisation and (e) monetary and exchange rate management are very complex in the context of the well-known trilemma, and in the current complex global environment, India cannot be immune to global development but should maintain domestic drivers to growth.

POLICY PERSPECTIVES

Admittedly there are several dilemmas, trade-offs and judgements in the process of managing the capital account. The intensified pressures due to large and volatile capital flows in an atmosphere of global uncertainties make the task significantly complex and critical. I propose to summarise the possible approaches in this regard, mainly in terms of analysis.

First, a view needs to be taken, however difficult it may be, as to whether the capital flows are of an enduring nature or are temporary. Prudence demands that in terms of initial reaction all large capital inflows be treated as temporary, and if these flows result in excess volatility in the forex markets, some intervention becomes necessary. The judgement about excess volatility will depend not merely on the quantity of the flow, but also to some extent on the quality in terms of the components of the capital flow. While the flows on account of equity and FDI into green field issues may be considered to be of a more permanent nature, flows on account of buy-outs through channels that are only technically FDI may not constitute a stable element. Overall, the portfolio investments could be expected to be less stable than FDI. Market participants' views on what constitutes excess volatility are also critical in this regard.

Second, large and lumpy quantities, even when expected, tend to disturb the markets, and hence there is a need to even out the impact of such lumpy flows through policy interventions and statements, which can appropriately manage expectations in the market.

Third, while interventions have the objective of containing volatility in the forex market, intervention over a long period, especially when the exchange rate is moving in one direction, might be less effective. However, a critical question is: what would be the impact on expectations about future movements in forex markets if no intervention takes place? The challenges of intervention and the management of expectations will be particularly daunting when financial contagion occurs, since such events are characterised by suddenness, high speed and large magnitudes of unexpected flows, in either direction. The quintessence of a relevant monetary policy is the speed of adjustment of policy measures to rapidly changing situations.

Fourth, a related issue is whether there should be sterilised intervention, and if so, the timing and quantum of such interventions. There is usually a cost attached to sterilisation operations. At the same time, it is also necessary to assess the indirect cost of not sterilising if there are signs of a 'Dutch disease' caused by flows in the capital account. Often it is not a question of whether to sterilise or not, but how much to sterilise. That is an important judgement that needs to be made in conjunction with domestic monetary and liquidity conditions.

The fifth issue relates to the choice of, and an appropriate mix of instruments for, sterilisation. Each instrument, namely the MSS, LAF and CRR, has different features and interactions. The utilisation of each will also depend on the permanency of the components of the flows and how they should be sterilised in the aggregate. Further, each instrument can be used in different ways. The LAF is able to take care of very short period flows. The MSS handles the longer-term flows slightly better than the LAF, and the CRR is more appropriate to address fairly longer-term flows. However, the effectiveness of the MSS will depend more on the initiatives of market participants than on the decisions of the RBI. Operationally, the issue is often not 'which' instrument but 'how much' of each instrument needs to be utilised, with due regard to capital flows, market conditions and monetary as well as credit developments.

Sixth, the market interventions for containing volatility in exchange rate and the consequent sterilisation operations may need to be complemented with measures for effective capital account management, as needed. Just as stabilisation funds take care of current account shocks, capital account management and market interventions are justifiable to take care of capital account shocks.

Seventh, the continued focus on financial market development would mitigate the challenge of capital flows in the medium term. However, it is important to recognise that the maturation of financial markets takes time. Hence, capital flows have to be managed through other tools in the short term, while continuing to work on the development of financial markets. Our preference has been for time-tested and proven 'gradual' approach. In brief, the issue is not either financial market development or management of the capital account, but how much of each approach should be adopted in a given situation and over time.

Eighth, an increase in the absorptive capacity of the economy could be another mitigating factor. However, it is not easy to develop the absorptive capacity of an economy in the short run, and in any case it is very difficult to calibrate the absorptive capacity of an economy to match the volatile capital flows. Further, the level of current account deficit that is generally considered sustainable by global financial markets with respect to EMEs is currently lower than the large amounts of capital inflows. Hence, enlargement of the absorptive capacity is an appropriate approach, but only up to the limit of sustainable levels, and is achievable over the medium term under normal circumstances.

Finally, it is sometimes suggested that encouraging outflows would be a good solution to managing surging inflows. Liberalising outflows may not be of great help in the short run, however, because a greater liberalised regime generally attracts more inflows. Hence, while recourse to some encouragement to outflows—such as the liberalisation of overseas investment by our corporates in the real sector—is helpful, it has to be combined with other measures to manage the flows, depending on their intensity.

A PRAGMATIC APPROACH

It should be evident from the description of policy perspectives in managing the external sector that the latter is essentially pragmatic, iterative and evolving. I propose to briefly narrate some of the reasons for what may appear a more pragmatic but less clearly defined policy of external-sector management.

First, international financial markets do not treat EMEs like India as full-fledged market economies, but only as economies in the process of marketisation. Hence, financial markets respond differently to the same macroeconomic or political development depending on whether it is an EME or an advanced economy. Hence, EMEs have to follow a more pragmatic and contextual policy.

Second, the self-correcting mechanisms in markets, particularly financial markets, are expected to operate smoothly in the absence of capital controls. However, such mechanisms happen to operate more efficiently in advanced economies and far less efficiently in EMEs. While there is an advantage in developing the financial sector with appropriate self-correcting mechanisms, it is not possible to achieve this in the short term, and it is particularly difficult to achieve during highly uncertain global economic conditions. Hence, the extent or lack of self-correcting mechanisms in an economy should be treated as a given in the short term, and a suitable policy of intervention has to be pursued accordingly.

Third, the real-sector flexibilities may be far less in EMEs. For example, opening or closing a business in India requires a considerable amount of time. Hence, the real-sector responses to exchange rate movements are not likely to be as flexible as in the advanced economies. One has therefore to make a judgement on the extent of the existence of such flexibility in the real sector. Policy makers undoubtedly have to encourage the real sector to change and become more flexible to cope with the exchange rate dynamics. At the same time, the pressure to change cannot be to such an extent that the volatile exchange rate movements seriously disrupt the business environment.

Fourth, there is a problem in differentiating between flexibility and volatility in exchange rates, in view of the evolving situation in EMEs. The distinction has to be based on the preparedness of the markets and market participants. It is necessary to encourage expectations of greater flexibility and give notice to market participants about increasing flexibility so that they are prepared, equipped, and enabled to adjust to the greater flexibility. Over a period, what was volatile yesterday becomes flexible tomorrow. This is the process by which we, in India, have been moving gradually towards greater flexibility in exchange rate.

Finally, generalisations about the effectiveness or otherwise of capital control may not be entirely appropriate. The effectiveness of capital account management should be viewed from several angles. Let me mention a few. First, the impact on exchange rate expectations. Second, the counterfactual, namely what could have happened without capital controls at a particular juncture. Third, the short-term impact versus long-term effectiveness. Fourth, the overall regime of current account management in the country concerned, to thwart capital account transactions in the guise of current account. The regimes governing repatriation and surrender are also relevant here. Fifth, the administrative framework and the overall effectiveness of administration in the country, in a given legal and institutional framework. Finally, by all accounts, in terms of both growth and stability, China and India, who do manage the capital account rather actively, have performed exceedingly well in recent years.

The Committee on Global Financial System and the BIS have constituted a working group to report on the issue of capital flows to EMEs, in view of their implications for the overall financial stability. It is commendable that Dr Rakesh Mohan, deputy governor, RBI, has been chosen to head the working group. We hope to gain from the deliberations of the group in evolving our policies to meet emerging challenges.

CONCLUSION

In conclusion, I would like to submit that management of the capital account has become an important element of public policy in India.

The emerging challenges to the management, both in the short term and over the medium term, have been recognised by policymakers at all levels.

While the immediate focus is on managing excess capital inflows and some volatility with regard to the excess, I believe that it will be prudent to not exclude the possibility of some change in course due to any abrupt changes in sentiments or global liquidity conditions, despite the strong underlying fundamentals of the Indian economy. Strategic management of the capital account would warrant preparedness for all situations, and the challenges in managing the capital account during unexpected events would normally be quite different.

The RBI considers it prudent to continue to analyse and monitor different scenarios and possible contingencies, so that the capital account and monetary management continue to facilitate high growth, while maintaining price and financial stability.

REFERENCE

Eichengreen, Barry. 2007. 'The Cautious Case for Capital Flows'. Paper presented at the conference on Free Capital Mobility: What's in store for Asia, Rating Agency Malaysia, Singapore, 1 August.

20

Government-owned Investment Vehicles and Capital Flows
Indian Perspective*

We know that government-owned investment vehicles (GIVs), also referred to as SWFs, have existed for a long time; however, they have acquired significance very recently due to their proliferation, growth in size, and, above all, active participation in capital infusion in the aftermath of the recently observed financial turbulence. The IMF has to be complimented on its pioneering work and excellent documentation on the subject. The role of SWFs in global capital flows is also being debated in several fora, namely the OECD, the G7 Ministers, the European Commission (EC), the Peterson Institute for International Economics, the Central Banking Publications, the G-30, the Institute of International Finance and the World Economic Forum.

TOWARDS GREATER TRANSPARENCY

It is useful to recognise in the above context that, of late, there have been initiatives to increase the transparency of all kinds of pools of capital, as evidenced by the reports of the UK Hedge Fund

*Previously presented as remarks, at a session on 'The Role of Government-owned Investment Vehicles in Global Capital Flows' at the International Capital Markets and Emerging Markets Roundtable held at Washington D.C., 14 April 2008.

Working Group (January 2008), led by Sir Andrew Large, and the Private Equity Working Group on Transparency and Disclosure (November 2007), led by Sir David Walker.

Briefly stated, while there has been intense debate on the subject of comfort with SWFs in global capital flows, the present discussion could be considered both a part of the wider and significant debate on transparency and the regulation of certain broad categories of investors and as one that addresses specific factors relevant to one category, namely SWFs. It is useful to recognise in this regard that there is an overlap among the categories in terms of sources of finance, since SWFs invest on their own account as well as through hedge funds and private equity funds. In other words, one of the broader issues is that of the regulatory safeguards in place with regard to a certain kind of investors who might not necessarily assure regulatory comfort to the host country. A related (in a way the other side of the coin) aspect is the transparency and governance arrangements with regard to the operation of SWFs in the home country. It is heartening to note that the IMF has begun covering, in addition to SWFs, issues relating to hedge funds and private equity funds in its Global Financial Stability Report.

PUBLIC POLICY INITIATIVES ON SWFS

The OECD approach with regard to SWFs is that international cooperation can build mutual trust and keep markets open. The OECD Investment Committee and its non-OECD partners have agreed that over the coming period, they will follow a two-track approach to these issues. The first track would involve dialogue among governments, SWFs and the private sector to improve the understanding of both home and host country approaches to foreign investment. The second track would involve the exchange of experiences in relation to national security protection, and developing shared views on investment policies which observe the principles of proportionality, transparency, predictability and accountability and which also avoid unnecessary restrictions on international investment, including by SWFs.

On 4 April 2008, the OECD released a report intended to develop guidance for recipient country policies toward investments from SWFs. It also proposed to work on how governments could maintain their commitment to open international investment policies— including for SWFs—while also protecting essential security interests. The resulting framework was expected to foster mutually beneficial situations, where SWFs could enjoy fair treatment in the markets of recipient countries and these countries could in turn confidently resist protectionist pressures.

The EC has been proposing a common EU approach to respond to concerns over SWFs, and enhance the transparency, predictability and accountability of SWFs' investments while maintaining an open investment environment. It has laid out the principles that should shape this approach. These are: (i) commitment to an open investment environment, both in the EU and elsewhere, including in third countries that operate SWFs; (ii) support for multilateral work in international organisations such as the IMF and OECD; (iii) the use of existing instruments at EU and member state levels; (iv) respect for EC treaty obligations and international commitments, for example in the WTO framework; and (v) proportionality and transparency.

The recent joint release by the US, Abu Dhabi and Singapore sets out policy principles for SWFs as well as countries receiving SWF investment. The responsibilities enjoined upon SWFs relate mainly to greater transparency in areas such as purpose, investment objectives, institutional arrangements and financial information, strong governance structures, internal controls and operational and risk management systems, as well as the need to respect host-country rules by complying with all the applicable regulatory and disclosure requirements of the countries in which they invest. The prescriptions for SWF host countries stress transparent inward investment rules, which are 'publicly available, clearly articulated, predictable and supported by strong and consistent rule of law' and favour non-discriminatory treatment for SWFs vis-à-vis other foreign investors.

Of particular interest from a host country perspective is the media release of the treasurer of the Commonwealth of Australia in February 2008, which lays down a set of principles to enhance the transparency of Australia's foreign investment screening regime. These principles set out the main factors that are considered during the screening of foreign investment, including considering the investment proposal on a case-by-case basis and assessing their consistency with the national interest. While assessing the national interest in any given case, a balanced view against principles is proposed. The principles set out the additional factors that need to be considered in relation to investment proposals by foreign governments and their agencies, over and above those that apply to normal private sector proposals. While the Australian government welcomes foreign investment, the purposes behind Australia's foreign investment screening is to ensure consistency with their national interest. The treasurer can reject proposals that are deemed contrary to the national interest, or impose conditions on them that require them to address national interest concerns. These concerns may relate to Australia's national security or economic development. The examination includes implications for other government policies, competition and the operations of Australia's businesses.

Recent reports suggest that Germany is contemplating a legislation that will enable it to block 'unwanted' investments by SWFs. The proposed law is expected to enable a scrutiny of all investments in cases where the investor's stake in the investee entity is likely to exceed 25 per cent, even up to three months after the investment has been made. This concern seems to stem from the suspicion that some of the SWFs are driven by 'political and other motivations', and not by purely economic and commercial considerations.

INDIA AS A HOST COUNTRY

In India, the regulatory regime governing capital inflows does not recognise SWFs as a distinct category. Hence, their investments are subject to the normal regulations governing capital flows under the categories of FDI and Foreign Institutional Investments (FIIs).

With regard to some sectors such as banking and financial market infrastructure companies, there are limits on individual holdings, and the investment proposals are subjected to due diligence processing with regard to fit and proper requirements. For this purpose, no discrimination is made between a domestic investor and a foreign investor or between SWFs and others as long as the policy criteria are met. Let me further elaborate on this position.

The existing FDI policy permits investments under the 'automatic route' and the 'approval route' in most, though not all, activities. Under the automatic route, investors are allowed to invest in the identified sectors up to the threshold specified for those sectors without the need for prior approval from regulators or the FIPB. As far as the other sectors are concerned, the investors will need the prior approval of the FIPB before undertaking any investment. The FIPB functions under the aegis of the Ministry of Finance and comprises of representatives of various government departments, who are expected to ensure that the proposed investment addresses the administrative and other concerns before allowing investments in the concerned activity. Similarly, under the FII route, the FIIs registered with the securities market regulator (the Securities and Exchange Board of India—SEBI) can invest in the secondary market without prior approval, subject to certain limits on individual FIIs and an overall aggregate limit for all FIIs as a category, as well as the sectoral thresholds and other conditions applicable to FDI. SWFs can also invest directly as an FII or indirectly as a 'sub-account' of a registered FII, which includes hedge funds and investment funds. Accordingly, any SWF can invest under the FDI route (automatic or approval routes, as the case may be) or the FII route, either directly or indirectly. Thus, on the inflows, there is generally no discrimination either on the basis of the country of origin of the foreign investor, or on the basis of the category of foreign investors.

The policy, however, does provide for a framework with regard to the ownership and management of the entity investing in some sectors, particularly the financial sector, which is applicable equally to resident and non-resident investors.

With respect to banks and the acquisition/transfer of shares, acknowledgement from the RBI is required for all cases of acquisition of shares that will take the aggregate holding (direct and indirect, beneficial or otherwise) of an individual or group to the equivalent of 5 per cent or more of the paid-up capital of the bank. The relevant factors for a 'fit and proper' assessment of the investor include the source of funds for the acquisition, and, where the investor is a body corporate, its track record and reputation with regard to operating in a manner consistent with the standards of good corporate governance, financial strength and integrity. The process also envisages a higher level of due diligence when the shareholding of the investor exceeds 10 per cent in the investee bank's paid-up capital, which includes 'fit and proper' status of the investor entity.

An amendment to the Banking Regulation Act has been proposed, which envisages the prior approval of the RBI in cases concerning the acquisition of more than 5 per cent of the paid-up share capital of a bank by any investor 'directly or indirectly, by himself or acting in concert with any person'. The approval will be accorded after ensuring that the investor would be 'fit and proper' from the perspectives of public interest, the interest of banking policy, emerging trends in banking and international best practices and the interest of the banking and financial system in India.

In the case of investments in financial market infrastructure companies, such as stock exchanges, the guidelines stipulate a desirable dispersal of ownership. Investments by individual entities, including investments by persons acting in concert, are subject to a threshold of 5 per cent of the equity in these companies.

With regard to Securitisation and Reconstruction Companies (SRC), the RBI conducts due diligence on the sponsors/investors before giving a certificate of registration to the SRC. Any subsequent investment by an individual entity in excess of 10 per cent of the paid-up equity capital of the SRC also acquires the status of a 'sponsor' and the prior permission of the RBI, which, as the regulator, is required to satisfy itself of, among other things, the 'fit and proper' credentials of the investor.

Foreign investment in an Indian company in the financial services sector through acquisitions requires the prior permission of the RBI, which allows such investments only after ensuring that the regulatory concerns, if any, are appropriately addressed and that the bona fides of the overseas investor are satisfactory. Wherever necessary, the clearance or comments of the home country regulators of the investing entity are also sought while examining the requests.

In case of investments by foreign investors in activities other than those of the financial services sector, where there are security or other administrative concerns, for instance in defence and strategic industries and print media and broadcasting sectors, investments are allowed only under the 'approval route'.

In order to assess the eligibility of an entity to be registered as FII or as Foreign Venture Capital Investor, the SEBI takes into account all factors relevant to the grant of a certificate, in particular the applicant's track record, professional competence, financial soundness, experience, general reputation of fairness and integrity and whether the applicant is regulated by an appropriate foreign regulatory authority.

In brief, India is yet to consider a policy that addresses investments by SWFs, except as a part of due diligence with regard to all investors.

INDIA AS A HOME COUNTRY

In India, the foreign exchange reserves are on the balance sheet of the RBI and are managed as per the provisions of the RBI Act, consistent with global best practices. The RBI adheres to the appropriate prudential norms and transparency and data dissemination standards with regard to reserves management.

Given the significant increase in the level of foreign exchange reserves, there is an increasing expectation with regard to returns.

The returns on foreign exchange reserves under the present framework are constrained by the mandate to the RBI, which understandably lays a greater emphasis on safety and liquidity.

It may, however, be possible to argue that a part of the reserves, which may be considered in excess of the usual requirements, be managed with the primary objective of earning higher returns. Given the limitations placed on the central bank by its mandate, it can be held that it would be appropriate to bestow this responsibility on a different sovereign entity. If and when the country considers setting up a SWF for the purpose, one of the methodologies could be to fund the SWF by purchasing the foreign exchange from the central bank, to the extent required. These foreign currency funds could then be used by the sovereign entity to seek higher returns by investing in assets, which a central bank's mandate may not permit. As the SWF will be a public enterprise, it will be required to conform to the applicable governance, transparency and disclosure standards.

While it is possible to make a case for an Indian SWF, there are also weighty arguments for caution in this regard. First, it would be very difficult to reckon in the Indian context—as is the case with many other countries, the 'reserve adequacy' in a dynamic setting and on that basis diverts a part of the 'excess' reserves for a higher return from riskier assets. The current reserves management policy recognises this, based on experience during periods of both net inflows and outflows. Therefore, the overall approach to the management of India's foreign exchange reserves takes into account the changing composition of the balance of payments, and endeavours to reflect the 'liquidity risks' associated with different types of flows and other requirements.

Second, while most other countries that have set up SWFs have amassed large reserves, either through persistent current account surpluses or due to revenue gains from commodity exports, in particular those of oil and gas, the Indian economy has twin deficits—a current account deficit as—well as a fiscal deficit. India's export basket is diversified and does not have any dominant 'exportable' natural resource output which might promise significant revenue gains at the current juncture.

Third, India has experienced consistent but manageable current account deficits, barring very few years of a modest surplus. India also has a negative international investment position (IIP) with liabilities far exceeding the assets. The large reserves have been built, over time, mostly on account of capital flows like FDIs, portfolio flows through FIIs, external commercial borrowing and short-term credit. Further, the increasing reserves also reflect, in part, the lower absorption capacity of the economy, which may pick up with the economy moving on to a higher growth trajectory.

In brief, the public policy is yet to take a conscious view on the desirability of establishing a SWF.

SPV FOR USE OF RESERVES

In the context of growing developmental needs, particularly of the infrastructure sector, a step in the direction of using a small part of the reserves for development has recently been taken after considerable deliberation. An announcement was made by the Finance Minister in the Budget Speech 2007–8 on 28 February 2007 to 'use a small part of the foreign exchange reserves without the risk of monetary expansion' for the purpose of financing infrastructure development projects. Accordingly, a scheme has been finalised which envisages the RBI investing, in tranches, up to an aggregate amount of US$ 5 billion in fully government-guaranteed foreign currency denominated bonds issued by an overseas SPV of the India Infrastructure Finance Corporation Ltd. (IIFCL), a wholly owned company of the Government of India. The funds thus raised are to be utilised by the company for on-lending to the Indian companies implementing infrastructure projects in India, and/or to co-finance the external commercial borrowings of such projects for capital expenditure outside India without creating any monetary impact. The lending by the SPV under this arrangement would be treated as external commercial borrowings and would be subject to prescribed reporting and disclosure requirements. The bonds will carry a floating rate of interest. The investment by the RBI in the foreign currency denominated bonds issued by the SPV will not be reckoned as part of the foreign exchange reserves, but will be a foreign currency asset on the RBI balance sheet.

It is noteworthy that this arrangement is distinct, in the sense that India is both a home and a host for the IIFCL's subsidiary, as it is basically an SPV for channelling foreign exchange funds to meet the requirements of the Indian private sector for infrastructure projects in India, by drawing upon the foreign exchange reserves of the country available with the central bank.

SUMMING UP

To sum up, India has not yet considered regulatory initiatives that specifically address SWFs. The existing provisions with regard to 'fit and proper' or take-over codes are, however, applicable to all investors, including SWFs. Currently, the pros and cons for the establishment of an Indian SWF, as generally understood now, are still under debate. India is monitoring recent developments with regard to enhancing transparency and disclosure with respect to hedge funds, private equity and SWFs. In particular, India is watching with great interest the development of global codes, standards and practices with regard to SWFs, both in view of the presence of SWFs in the Indian financial markets and the ongoing debate on establishing an Indian SWF.

VII

Global Financial Imbalances
and Crisis

21

Implications of Global Financial Imbalances for EMEs*

Although fast-growing economies are generally grouped together as EMEs, some of their major macroeconomic indicators present a wide spectrum. While some EMEs are running large current account surpluses (such as China, the Russian Federation, South Korea, Venezuela, Malaysia, Taiwan and Brazil), some others are running current account deficits (such as Turkey, Hungary, South Africa, Mexico, India and the Czech Republic), and their current account balances range from a deficit of US\$ 20 billion to a surplus of US\$ 69 billion. While savings rates for select EMEs range from 9 per cent to 43 per cent of the GDP, in most EMEs the rates have increased and overtaken those in industrial countries, with particularly high savings rates as in China, Malaysia and Russia. Likewise, while some EMEs have fiscal surplus (Russia), several others have fiscal deficit (Turkey, India, the Philippines, Argentina and several others). Also, while some EMEs such as India are largely domestic-demand driven, some others, particularly in East Asia (for instance, Malaysia and the Philippines), are largely dependent on exports to sustain their

*Previously presented as remarks at the round table discussion at the International Symposium organised by the Banque de France, Paris, 4 November 2005.

growth, and their exports of goods and services range from 15 per cent to over 120 per cent of the GDP. It is useful to note that while some EMEs are net oil exporters, some others are net oil importers.

Thus, given the diverse nature, macroeconomic conditions and policy regimes of the EMEs, it may be difficult to consider all of them as contributing to global financial imbalances, and treat them in the same manner; nor would all EMEs be identically affected by the adjustment of global financial imbalances. It may thus be somewhat difficult to speak about the implications of global financial imbalances for EMEs as a group. I will therefore focus primarily on India; however, the analytic framework could perhaps be of some help in appreciating the implications for different EMEs.

It is worth mentioning that there are some factors that could adversely impact the EMEs as a group, albeit with varying intensity. Global developments, particularly those in the world financial markets, have the most direct and serious impact on financing conditions in emerging markets. An abrupt and sharp adjustment of currencies may potentially lead to a significant portfolio rebalancing by foreign investors, which could cause sharp changes in the long-term yields. This in turn could result in volatility in the level and cost of capital flows, with direct implications for the EMEs.

Volatility in financial markets could adversely affect the EMEs in many ways, as well as in complex and interrelated fashions. For convenience of analysis, the impact may be classified broadly as: (*a*) the impact on the financing conditions under which EMEs operate (*b*) impairment of the balance sheets of the banking sector and (*c*) hampering the growth prospects in the real sector. Even within the same EMEs, the impact could vary across different entities such as the government, the corporate sector, the households and the financial sector, depending upon the country-specific and institution-specific operating environment, the stage of development and the degree of integration with and exposure to international financial markets. In view of the diversity of EMEs and the complexity of the impact of any unpredictable unwinding of global imbalances, it is proposed to analyse the possible implications with reference to India.

RECENT MACROECONOMIC DEVELOPMENTS IN INDIA

There are several noteworthy features of India's recent macroeconomic performance. First, the investment climate has improved and industrial and service sector activity has picked up. Second, buoyant exports have emerged as the driver of the demand for a broad spectrum of industries. Third, there has been a modest attempt at and a commitment to achieving fiscal consolidation. Fourth, the trend inflation has declined over the years and inflation expectations stabilised. Fifth, India has been successful in managing liquidity against the backdrop of continuing capital flows. Sixth, India has emerged as a preferred destination for foreign investors, and has received about a quarter of the global portfolio flows to EMEs in 2004. Seventh, India's foreign exchange reserves are in excess of the total outstanding external debt of the country. Eighth, the performance of the corporate sector has improved, and some corporates are now listed on the international stock exchanges. Ninth, India's financial markets have deepened, widened and become vibrant over the years with a robust institutional framework and market infrastructure in place. Tenth, the profitability and soundness indicators of the banking sector have improved. Finally, India has been adopting international benchmarks for financial standards and best practices with suitable adaptations for Indian conditions.

The Indian economy today is characterised by an environment of confidence, positive business expectations, a renewal of rule-based fiscal consolidation, stable and orderly financial markets and institutions, and progressive integration with the global economy. Real GDP growth for 2005-6 (April-March) was conservatively projected at around 7.0 per cent and was then revised upwards to a range of 7.0 to 7.5 per cent. Despite the sustained strength of export performance, the merchandise trade deficit was expected to be somewhat higher in 2005-6 than in the previous year, mainly on account of the substantially higher oil prices and non-oil import demand for investment. For the year as a whole, while invisibles financed a large part of the enlarged trade deficit, the current account deficit was expected to widen during 2005-6, but remain within acceptable limits that could be financed by normal capital flows. The headline inflation was expected to lie in the range of 5.0–5.5 per cent. Consolidation of Central government finances was the goal of the fiscal policy at the Centre—the targets—were the GFD of 3.0 per cent of GDP and the elimination of revenue deficit by 2008–9. The fiscal position of state governments also continues to undergo slight correction in terms of key deficit indicators.

Against this background, it may be useful to analyse the implications of global financial imbalances for India in terms of its likely impact on four separate balance sheets—of the government, the RBI, the corporate sector and the banking sector.

IMPACT ON THE GOVERNMENT

The Government of India does not raise resources from international capital markets to finance the fiscal deficit, although bilateral and multilateral sources do provide a moderate amount of foreign currency funds. The government could, therefore, be affected indirectly through the spillover impact of external developments on domestic interest rates. What is of relevance, *inter alia*, is the nominal international interest rates and domestic interest rates, adjusted for inflation differential. To the extent that there is a rise in domestic interest rates, there could be an increase in the cost of government borrowings. Since most of the outstanding debt is at fixed rates and not on floating rates, the rise in the borrowing cost will be incremental. This situation also provides greater headroom for a flexible monetary policy to adjust policy rates, as and when warranted, without any excessive impact on the fiscal deficit.

IMPACT ON THE RESERVE BANK'S BALANCE SHEET

The fiscal position of the government could also be indirectly impacted through the nature of the management of foreign exchange reserves held by the RBI. Volatility in the foreign exchange market exposes foreign exchange reserves to both operational and market risks. Depreciation in the value of any reserve currency vis-à-vis the domestic currency would result in an equivalent decline in the value of the reserves held, although the impact may be mitigated to some extent through the appreciation of other currencies in which foreign exchange reserves are held. Also, an increase in the global interest rates would entail capital losses on the corresponding assets, including fixed income securities. Valuation and capital losses could impact the income of the RBI and thus its surplus transferable to the government, which in turn would have fiscal implications. It is pertinent to mention that the RBI, as a matter of prudent practice, follows conservative accounting norms, whereby the valuation gains/losses on foreign exchange reserves and gold are not taken to the profit and loss account, but are instead booked under a separate reserve head.

IMPACT ON THE INDIAN CORPORATES

As a result of the deterioration in global financial market conditions, spreads on corporate debt might widen suddenly due to a shift in investor confidence in global financial markets. Increase in the global interest rates may also have an impact on other benchmarks such as Libor. A sharp rise in yields may entail an increase in the cost of the variable-rate debt contracted by the corporates. This could be offset to some extent if there is a depreciation of the relevant currency and a consequent decline in the value of the existing debt contracted by corporates in that currency.

Indian corporates, as also some public-sector enterprises, raise resources from international capital markets. While a part of their external commercial borrowings is at variable interest rate, a part is at fixed interest rates. In order to avoid any serious impact of the changes in the exchange rate on the balance sheet of the corporate sector, the RBI has been advising banks to regularly monitor the unhedged position of the corporates, and has also been exhorting corporates to hedge their foreign exchange exposures. Thus, India's corporates could be affected by the deterioration in financing conditions only to the extent that they are not hedged, either by foreign-currency cash flows in the normal course of business or through recourse to appropriate hedging products. Corporates would, however, be affected to the extent that interest rates firm up in the domestic market, depending on their exposure to debt relative to other liabilities.

IMPACT ON THE BANKING SECTOR

Banks in India are dependent mainly on domestic deposits, predominantly at fixed rates, for their resource requirements. They would therefore be impacted significantly only if the adverse developments in the international capital markets are particularly severe. In general, banks also do not hold stock of securities in foreign currency. Banks in India thus have a relatively small exposure to the foreign exchange market. Their foreign currency borrowings are subject to the prudential limit of 25 per cent of their Tier-I capital, and they are also required to maintain capital against the net open position. Foreign currency borrowings by banks are permitted beyond this ceiling, which is linked to the net worth, exclusively for the purpose of export finance.

Like many other EMEs, the credit extended by banks in India has increased sharply in recent times. Credit growth, which was earlier seen largely in housing and retail loans, has now become quite broad-based, with agriculture and industry also joining in to drive up the credit demand. The credit growth in some sectors, especially those related to assets experiencing price volatilities, is being monitored closely.

Banks are allowed to lend to resident exporters in foreign currency at internationally competitive rates of interest from their foreign currency lines of credit, as well as out of funds available in exchange earners' foreign currency accounts, resident foreign currency accounts and foreign currency non-resident bank

(FCNRB) accounts. These loans are intended to finance domestic and imported inputs for export production. Foreign currency loans to exporters are generally hedged against credit risk, since they are extended for bona fide underlying activity, viz., export production. They are also usually covered for exchange risk since they are denominated in foreign currency. Banks are also allowed to extend loans in foreign currency to NRIs against their FCNRB deposits. Funds in foreign currency deposits can also be utilised for lending to domestic corporates for working capital requirements in India, import financing, purchase of indigenous machinery, repayment of rupee term loans and external commercial borrowings.

Banks have also been extending credit for investment in the asset market. Like many other EMEs, asset prices in India have also risen sharply in the last couple of years. Should there be a reversal of capital flows, asset prices may decline sharply, exposing the banks' balance sheets to credit risk. There is a risk that a rise in interest rates in general could impact housing prices and expose the balance sheet of households to interest rate risk, leading to some loan losses for banks. The overall banking sector's exposure to housing loans is relatively small and may not have serious systemic implications. Likewise, the equity market has also seen a sustained uptrend. A reversal of capital flows could impact the equity market, and some of the advances extended for investments in the equity market might turn non-performing. Again, Indian banks do not have a large exposure in the asset market, although it has increased in the recent past. A decline in asset prices could cause loan losses and capital losses (if the decline is significant), even though the impact on banks' balance sheets might be muted, given their small exposure to the asset market.

The most significant impact on banks' balance sheets, however, could be felt through their investment portfolios. Banks in India hold substantial investments in government and other fixed income securities. Such investments amounted to US$ 173 billion, constituting 35.1 per cent of their total assets as on 16 September 2005. To the extent that a rise in international interest rates impacts the domestic interest rates, it would entail marked-to-market losses on the investment portfolios.

The banking sector, however, has acquired some added strength to absorb such probable shocks, largely aided by regulatory actions. Apart from having built up a significant capital base, reflected in the CRAR for the sector of 12 per cent, specific steps have been taken to meet the interest rate risk. First, a separate provision for capital against market risk has been introduced. Second, a gradual building up of Investment Fluctuation Reserve up to 5 per cent of the marked-to-market portfolio (out of tax-free profits) by March 2006 was mandated and several banks achieved the target. Third, an enabling risk management environment has been provided to banks to hedge their risks through vanilla derivative instruments. Fourth, the conservative accounting norms followed did not allow banks to book unrealised gains. Fifth, as a one time measure, banks were allowed to transfer securities to HTM after booking the mark-to-market losses against these. Thus, in general, banks in India have the resilience to withstand some rise in interest rates.

IMPACT ON THE REAL SECTOR

A readjustment of the currencies would also have implications for the real sector. A significant readjustment of the currencies and rise in interest rates could slow down the global growth. This would entail a reduction in export opportunities and in the investment demand for EMEs in general, many of which depend on export demand to sustain their growth. Rise in interest rates, by slowing down spending, may have a negative impact on the global economic growth. Thus, readjustment of the currencies may affect several EMEs in a significant way.

The impact of any slowdown on India may be assessed with reference to two factors. First, India's economy is largely domestic-demand driven. While India's exports constituted 11.5 per cent of GDP, its share in the world trade is only 0.8 per cent. Second, India's exports basket is fairly diversified.

Some concerns arise with regard to the implications for employment in case of a slowdown in the exports sector, especially with regard to the significant specialisation in business process outsourcing (BPO)/IT Enable Services. A rapid job growth that absorbs the huge supply of agricultural labour into its industrial workforce is necessary for socio-economic stability in India. Any negative impact on employment, resulting in a substantial decrease in real earnings and widening income inequality, is likely to reduce the overall welfare and increase the cost of the structural adjustments required, especially in the absence of meaningful social safety nets.

MONETARY AND PRUDENTIAL MEASURES AS RESPONSES

The outlook for output growth in India has improved in recent months, particularly with the momentum gained in the manufacturing sector. However, the persistence of global imbalances and high oil prices with a significant permanent component do pose some risks. Furthermore, credit growth in recent times has been extremely strong, possibly impacting credit quality, while money supply is overshooting the anticipated trajectory and strong investment demand, coupled with high oil prices, is turning the current account surplus into a deficit (which, however, is modest and manageable through normal capital flows). These developments pose new challenges to maintaining price and financial stability while ensuring momentum in growth. Consequently, in the Mid-Term Review of Annual Policy Statement for the year 2005–6, released on 25 October 2005, several measures have been announced to contain and manage the downside risks.

First, the reverse-repo rate (overnight liquidity absorption by the RBI) has been increased by 25 basis points to 5.25 per cent, keeping the spread between reverse repo and repo at 100 basis points. The Bank Rate, being the signalling rate for the medium term, is retained at 6.00 per cent.

Second, rationalisation of the limits on banks' exposure to the capital market has been announced, restricting it to 40 per cent of a bank's net worth while simplifying the exemptions and coverage.

Third, the general provisioning requirement for standard advances has been enhanced from the present level of 0.25 per cent to 0.40 per cent, except with regard to banks' exposures to laggards in credit growth, namely agriculture and small and medium industries.

Fourth, a decision had been taken to treat the entire balance under Investment Fluctuation Reserve as Tier I capital, thus providing some head room to banks to raise the Tier II capital in the future.

Fifth, revised guidelines are being issued on the corporate restructuring mechanisms to be followed by banks in the light of experience gained.

Sixth, keeping in mind the recent trends in credit markets, the RBI is initiating a SRP with select banks that have a significant exposure to some sectors, namely real estate, highly leveraged NBFCs, venture capital funds and capital markets. The purpose of such a review is to ensure that effective risk mitigants and sound internal controls are in place to manage such exposures.

SOME REFLECTIONS

From the above discussion it is clear that the impact on India would depend on the pace and extent of currency and current account readjustments, and changes in global interest rates. While India by itself hardly contributes to global financial imbalances, any large and rapid adjustments in major currencies and related interest rates or the current accounts of trading partners could indirectly impact the Indian economy.

From the case of India, it is also clear that readjustment of the currencies and a rise in interest rates would impact different EMEs differently. Despite the rise in short-term interest rates, long-term interest rates, instead of rising, have moderated, leading to a further flattening of the global yield curve and a narrowing down of credit spreads. EMEs have taken advantage of favourable financial conditions. During the first half of 2005, EMEs focused on operations aimed at meeting domestic and external obligations and lengthening maturities. However, higher global interest rates could contribute to a widening of emerging market bond spreads, particularly those with a high debt to GDP ratio. In view of the expected deceleration in financial conditions, some emerging markets have cushioned themselves by advancing their external financing, taking advantage of the current benign financial market conditions. EMEs have, however, continued to improve their debt structures in an effort to reduce their vulnerability to external shocks. They have carried out active liability management operations aimed at meeting their financial requirements, while minimising the cost of debt and its risks. Some countries have taken steps to develop their local markets, and have reduced the amount of foreign currency-linked domestic debt while gradually improving the maturity profile. Some of the EMEs have also reduced the share of domestic debt indexed to the exchange rate.

Compared to past crises, EMEs in general are now resilient and in a better position to absorb financial shocks. They have developed resilience to shocks by improving their macroeconomic conditions and regulatory frameworks. EMEs have been achieving a healthy growth with more or less stable inflation, and have reduced their dependence on external demand. There has also been an improvement in fiscal positions, supported by the development of domestic securities markets. The external debt burden has declined and the composition of financial flows has changed, with lower reliance on borrowings from international banks. Several EMEs have addressed the weaknesses that led to the earlier crisis by strengthening prudential regulation and supervision, bringing them more in line with international best practices. Banks' balance sheets have improved and capital ratios have risen. Corporate governance practices have also improved. To the extent that EMEs have introduced flexibility in their exchange rates, their vulnerability to external shocks has declined. All these factors have reduced the vulnerability of EMEs. The large reserves held by EMEs should also enable them to cope with the volatility arising out of a sudden shift in market sentiment.

While the macroeconomic fundamentals of several EMEs are strong, placing them in a relatively better position to withstand deterioration in international financing conditions, the economic performance of some EMEs has been found to be less robust. The conditions in these economies may be accentuated by the adjustment of global financial imbalances and high and volatile oil prices. A possible volatility in the global financial markets, emanating from a rise in interest rates, could magnify and propagate the problems associated with the less than satisfactory performance in some EMEs, making them vulnerable to a sudden reassessment of country risk. Such threats are real, as the default rates of sub-investment grade borrowers could increase. Credit derivatives, which have proliferated in recent years and whose pricing has depended on relatively untested models and default correlation assumptions, may be particularly vulnerable to corrections.

The main challenge before EMEs is to continue to take advantage of the current favourable external financing conditions, and at the same time pursue the domestic macroeconomic and structural reforms necessary for long-term stability. In fact, some EMEs have well-advanced external financing, which in some cases even included pre-financing for 2006. EMEs have made significant gains in terms of healthy growth, stable inflation, large trade surplus, greater exchange rate flexibility and lower debt burden. While EMEs are preparing themselves to face sudden shocks, efforts need to be made by all concerned towards an orderly adjustment of global financial imbalances. While coordinated policy action would minimise the cost of rebalancing, a stress testing by all the concerned regulators in the EMEs to assess the extent of resilience could perhaps be helpful.

The EMEs, despite their diversity, seem to generate expectations of high growth, and are generally characterised by less-than-fully developed markets, especially financial markets. Consequently, there are significant cross-border capital flows with market perception of high risk and high reward in EMEs. It is useful to note that implicit in the word 'emerging' in the very title given to EMEs as a group is the notion that they are undergoing a rapid change or transition. We must recognise that the transition embraces demographics, political institutions, social dimensions and related attitudes. These all-encompassing changes have an in-built potential for uncertainties, and possibly some volatility, but this gets exacerbated by the international capital flows, particularly when the changes in such flows happen to be unrelated to domestic fundamentals. In such a situation, managing the transition turns out to be a critical challenge for policymaking, and the management requires a more difficult and dynamic trade-off between commitment and flexibility in policy.

Overall, while added risks—both upside and downside—are inevitable with increasing global financial and economic integration, the EMEs may consider strengthening their resilience not only through sound macroeconomic management, but also through the adoption of appropriate prudential measures. Over a period, coordinated efforts, both at regional as well as global levels, could also help EMEs to cushion themselves better against the risks of financial globalisation.

ANNEX

Select Economic Indicators—Select EMEs

(US $ billion)

Country	GDP (growth rate)[1]	Inflation rate[1]	Trade Balance[2]	Current Account[2]	Foreign Reserves[3]	External Debt[4]	Overall Budget Balance to GDP[5]	Export of goods and services to GDP[@]
1	2	3	4	5	6	7	8	9
Argentina	10.1	9.7	11.2	2.8	24.4	166.2	−3.3	24.0
Brazil	3.9	6.0	40.1	12.5	54.6	235.4	−1.5[@]	22.5
Chile	6.5	3.0	8.7	0.6	15.8	43.2	−0.3	38.0
China	9.5	1.3	93.1	68.7	711.0	193.6	−1.7[@]	40.2
Colombia	5.3	4.9	1.8	−0.8	14.9	33.0	–	19.1
Czech Republic	5.1	1.7	1.3	−4.1	30.2	34.6	–	–
Egypt	4.7	4.7	−9.5	4.4	18.5	31.4	–	25.5
Hungary	4.1	3.6	−3.4	−9.2	18.0	45.8	–	–
India	7.0	4.1	−34.7	−6.4	133.6	113.5	−4.5[@]	15.4
Indonesia	5.5	8.3	27.8	7.8	31.0	134.4	−1.2	31.3
Israel	4.8	1.6	−7.7	1.3	27.8	–	–	–
Malaysia	4.1	3.7	23.6	16.7	78.0	49.1	–	121.3
Mexico	3.1	4.0	−9.6	−8.4	66.4	140.0	−0.3[@]	30.1
Peru	4.9	1.2	4.0	0.4	12.8	–	−1.8	19.6
Philippines	4.8	7.2	−0.7	2.9	15.3	62.7	−4.0	52.0
Poland	2.8	1.6	−3.3	0.3	39.4	95.2	–	22.6
Russia	6.1	12.4	110.6	69.2	146.0	175.3	4.4[@]	25.6
South Africa	4.5	3.9	−2.3	−8.6	17.2	27.8	−1.0	28.2
South Korea	3.3	2.0	26.0	21.3	206.6	–	–	–
Taiwan	3.0	3.6	1.7	13.3	254.1	–	–	–
Thailand	4.4	5.6	−7.3	−2.2	47.3	51.8	−2.8	–
Turkey	4.2	7.9	−38.9	−20.0	42.9	145.7	−19.6	27.0
Venezuela	11.1	14.8	24.7	17.7	23.1	34.9	–	35.7

1. Percentage change one year ago.
2. The latest twelve months.
3. Excluding gold, except Singapore; IMF definition.
4. Relating to 2003.
5. Relating to 2001.
@ Relating to 2004. = Not Available.

Note: Indicators are based on the latest available data, and therefore relate to different periods for different countries.

Source:
1. *The Economist*, 1–7 October 2005.
2. *Global Development Finance*, 2005.
3. *World Development Indicators*, 2004, World Bank.

22

Global Imbalances
An Indian Perspective*

The international perspective on global imbalances is considered by raising three issues: (*a*) the essential features of the global imbalances as they stand today; (*b*) the possible causes of these imbalances and (*c*) the emerging consensus on policy responses. This is followed by a discussion on India's perspective on the global imbalances, covering: (*a*) India's role in the global imbalances; (*b*) the approach to global consensus on causes and policy responses; (*c*) the possible impact of global imbalances on India and (*d*) the emergence of oil as a new factor in the policy debate on global imbalances. The concluding part explores a possible agenda for analysis to enable a better understanding of global imbalances.

GLOBAL PERSPECTIVE ON GLOBAL IMBALANCES

Essential Features of the Global Imbalances

It is useful to understand that in different countries, the existence of a current account surplus or deficit is inevitable among economies

---

*Previously presented as an address at The Financing for Development (FFD) Office, Department of Economic and Social Affairs (DESA), United Nations, New York, US, 11 May 2006.

at any given time. In particular, one of the arguments in favour of global integration is that capital may flow from developed economies to the capital-starved developing economies, implying that there would be current account deficits in the latter. The problem is not the existence of current account deficits or surpluses per se, but the persistence of large current account deficit and large current account surplus, particularly in large and systemically important economies, which give rise to fears of unsustainability and disruptive unwinding.

Possible Causes of Global Imbalances

The current global imbalance is reflected in large mismatches in the current account positions of some countries, and its mirror image in the form of domestic saving-investment mismatches. For instance, the US current account deficit was 6.4 per cent of GDP in 2005 and stood at US$ 805 billion, while the current account surplus of Japan and emerging Asia accounted for about 60 per cent of the current account deficit of the US. Now, with rising oil prices, the oil-exporting countries also exhibit large current account surpluses.

Some argue that since the late 1990s, the growth processes in many EMEs, especially those from Asia, have come to rely heavily on external demand. In such a scenario, it has been felt that many of these countries tried to maintain their external price competitiveness by keeping their currencies undervalued. This process led in turn to large trade and current account surpluses for the Asian EMEs and large trade and current deficits elsewhere in the world, most noticeably in the US.

It is also clear that the sharp deterioration in the saving-investment balance in the US in recent years, along with the sustained rise in consumption demand, could only be met by rising imports; hence the rising, large current account deficits in the US. The adverse shift in the saving-investment balance in the US has been reflected both in the high budget deficit since 2002 and the deterioration in net personal saving since 1998.

The Emerging Consensus on Policy Responses

The global imbalance as it stands today may get corrected on its own, and there could perhaps be chances of a less favourable outcome of disorderly correction. One possible scenario could be that an orderly private sector led adjustment in imbalances would materialise even without policy action. It is argued that, however slim the chances of a disorderly adjustment, keeping in mind its huge costs, public policy cannot but strive for relatively orderly adjustment. In any case, it is felt that there is a need for a better understanding of policy issues with a view to taking appropriate policy actions as also minimising the cost of adjustments were it to take place in a not very orderly fashion.

We have realised, like many others here, that the sustained and increasing imbalances in current account positions across the globe could entail serious risks for the functioning of the international monetary system. Rebalancing is best seen as a process with many moving parts, involving all the major actors in the global economy. The successful execution of rebalancing will require a careful application of traditional macro-policies—monetary, fiscal and currency policies—as well as the implementation of a comprehensive micro-agenda of structural reforms.

A significant part of the debate seems to be about the relative weights to be accorded by each country to the various elements of the package and the various aspects of coordination among the countries that are appropriate. With regard to the current global initiatives to correct global imbalances, the Communiqué issued by the International Monetary and Financial Committee, released on 22 April 2006, highlights that action for an orderly medium-term resolution of global imbalances is a shared responsibility, and will be of greater benefit to members and the international community than actions taken individually by countries. The key elements of the strategy towards an orderly resolution of the global imbalance as suggested in the Communiqué are: (*a*) raising national saving in the US with measures to reduce the budget deficit and spur private saving; (*b*) implementing structural reforms to sustain growth potential and boost domestic demand in the euro area and in several other countries; (c) further structural reforms, including fiscal consolidation, in Japan; (d) allowing greater exchange rate flexibility in a number of surplus countries in emerging Asia and (e) promoting efficient absorption of higher oil revenues in oil-exporting countries with strong macroeconomic policies.

In the light of the above, the adjustments that are generally advocated in individual economies and regions may be summarised as follows:

i. A major challenge for US authorities could be to seek policies that strike a balance between measures to boost personal saving and those to cut consumption. However, US policies would need to delicately balance a gradual withdrawal of fiscal stimulus without hurting the recovery. It should be noted that demand compression could result in another recession, which would not be in the interest of the global economy. A gradual realignment of the real exchange rate of the US dollar coupled with measures targeted towards fiscal consolidation is generally advocated. Having said that, proper calibration would hold the key to the success of such a policy mix, and this is an important public policy issue.

ii. The Euro area, which continues to depend largely on external demand, could pursue some structural reforms, especially product and labour market policies, to boost the domestic demand and broad-base the recovery. While there are signs of recovery in investment, many recognise that further progress would be helpful in fostering a better integration of labour, healthcare, product, pension and financial market reforms. It is recognised that structural reforms are by their nature complex, and their impact could at best be only over the medium term.

iii. We can already see that the Japanese economy is on its way to recovery; the current account surplus has begun to narrow against the background of strengthening domestic demand, which is critical. Thus, the Japanese economy is expected to continue to take some concrete measures to strengthen its financial system, restructure the corporate sector and reduce large fiscal imbalances.

iv. As for the emerging economies, especially in Asia, some experts suggest that the growth strategy could be reoriented towards domestic demand to offset possible declines in exports to the US. There are already some signs of strengthening in the domestic demand in this region. It is considered important to improve the investment climate to support higher private investment in the emerging economies. Some argue that the exchange rate policy may require the attention of policymakers in the region. However, some others are of the view that exchange-rate adjustments may not serve the interests of output and employment in these countries, while the effectiveness of such exchange-rate adjustments by themselves in unwinding the imbalances is not conclusive.

v. The oil-exporting countries have recorded large trade surpluses, the investment of which in the domestic market and abroad would help to rebalance the global demand. It is suggested that these countries could boost expenditures to some extent in areas where social returns are high, like education, health, infrastructure and social security. It is felt that structural policies to strengthen the legal and economic infrastructure in these countries may help to promote investment. However, it is also argued that in many oil-exporting countries the scope for domestic absorption is limited in the short run.

INDIA'S PERSPECTIVE ON GLOBAL IMBALANCES

India's Role in Global Imbalances

Since independence, India has moved from the moderate growth path of the first three decades (1950 to 1980) to a higher growth trajectory since the 1980s. Over the last two and a half decades, India has emerged as one of the fastest growing economies of the world, averaging about 6 per cent growth rate per annum, and the ranking of the country in terms of size of the economy, especially in purchasing power parity (PPP) terms, has improved. In the last three years, we have averaged a growth rate of 8 per cent.

Apart from registering an impressive growth rate over the last two and a half decades, India's growth process has been stable. Studies indicate that the yearly variation in growth in India has been one of the lowest. During this period, we have faced only one crisis in 1991. This crisis was followed by a credible macroeconomic structural and stabilisation programme, encompassing trade, industry, foreign investment, exchange rate, public finance and the financial sector. The Indian economy in later years could successfully avoid any adverse contagion impact of shocks from the East Asian crisis, the Russian crisis during 1997–8, the sanction-like situation in the post-Pokhran scenario and the border conflict during May–June 1999.

In this context, it is appropriate to view the evidence showing that the policies followed by India have not in any way contributed to the widening of current global imbalances:

i. Between 2001–2 and 2003–4, India registered modest current account surpluses, but this was more a reflection of a phase of business cycle, and with the turn-around in the business cycle, India has registered a modest current account deficit in the last two years. In fact, going by the current indication and the projections of the Tenth Five Year Plan, India is likely to maintain a modest and sustainable current account deficit in the near future.

ii. It is observed that generally, current account surplus accounted for a considerable proportion of reserve accumulation in most Asian EMEs and Japan during 2000–5. For India, the current account surplus has been a minor source of reserve accretion. In our case, capital flows, as opposed to current account surpluses, played an increasingly important role in the accumulation of reserves.

iii. Our approach, aimed at a market-determined exchange rate with no predetermined target, along with market interventions to essentially manage volatility, has served us well. At the empirical level, the flexibility of the Indian exchange-rate policy is captured by the marked two-way movement of the Indian rupee against the major currencies, including the US dollar. Recent international research on viable exchange rate strategies in emerging markets has lent considerable support to the exchange-rate policy followed by India.

iv. The main driver of growth in India has been the domestic demand. An impressive growth in exports and imports does strengthen the economy, but the ratio of exports to GDP in India is lower than most EMEs.

v. The overall improvement in GDP growth during the reform period has also been facilitated by an improvement in the rate of aggregate domestic saving. For instance, in the high growth phase of 2002–3 to 2004–5, the saving rate rose by 5.5 percentage points from 23.5 per cent in 2001–2 to 29.1 per cent in 2004–5. The gross domestic investment rate, for the first time, remained above 30 per cent in 2004–5, mainly on account of private investment growing at 19.7 per cent. With the FRBM Act in place, the fiscal situation in India has shown an improvement in recent years. The fiscal consolidation process envisages a phased reduction in the key deficit indicators. Monetary policy, while being supportive of investment demand, places emphasis on price and financial stability, and has succeeded in containing inflation expectations. These factors give confidence to the possibility of sustaining the present growth momentum—a GDP growth of close to 8 per cent per annum.

India has thus been following policies which have not only served it well, but have also contributed to global stability. As mentioned by then Finance Minister Mr P. Chidambaram, we do not expect any change in the basic framework of our policies, both in terms of growth based on efficient use of capital and stability assured by sound macroeconomic policies.

Approach to Global Consensus on Causes and Policy Responses

We believe that global developments, particularly those in the world financial markets, have the most direct and serious impact on financing conditions in the emerging markets. Any abrupt and disorderly adjustment to global imbalances may have serious adverse implications. Recognising these developments, the Prime Minister of India, Dr Manmohan Singh, in his welcome address to the Board of Governors of the Asian Development Bank (ADB) at the Thirty-Ninth Annual General Meeting in Hyderabad, highlighted the importance of correcting these imbalances.

> While to some extent mismatches in current account positions are to be expected—and even desirable—in the global economy, large disparities raise concerns about unsustainability and hard landings. The process of correcting imbalances can be disruptive if it is sudden and unexpected. The present level of global imbalance cannot be sustained forever. It calls for action both from countries having current account surpluses and those having current account deficits. A coordinated effort is necessary to correct the imbalances to prevent a sudden down turn. International financial institutions need to play a proactive role in this regard.

During the same annual meeting of the ADB, Finance Minister P. Chidambaram, while dwelling at length on the issue of global imbalances, highlighted the need to address global imbalance in such a manner that the benefits of global integration continue in an uninterrupted fashion. He pointed out that Asia has an important role to play in conjunction with other countries in the process of unwinding global imbalance. I quote from his address: 'I must reiterate that to sustain the recovery process and to correct the global imbalances in an orderly manner, there is an imperative need for a cooperative approach.'

We had raised the issue of global imbalances in the RBI's *Annual Report* of 2002–3, realising at the time that this problem has the potential to occupy the attention of global economies in the future. The report observed:

> Although growing imbalances may seem to be an integral feature of globalization, there are nonetheless limits to the accumulation of net claims against an economy that are implied by persistent current account deficits. The cost of servicing such claims adds

to the current account deficit and, under certain circumstances, can be destabilizing.

In retrospect, the apprehensions expressed proved warranted.

At this juncture, it will be appropriate to list some important considerations that should govern initiatives with regard to the resolution of global imbalances, recognising that such policy initiatives may be broadly in consonance with the emerging consensus described earlier.

First, it is necessary for multilateral institutions like the IMF to be seen as symmetrical in their analysis of national economies and their relative positions in the global economy. This would add credibility to the policy advice that could be considered by each country.

Second, at the same time each country's action will be governed by an enlightened national interest. It is necessary for multilateral institutions to analyse, explore and be convinced of how the policy actions would serve the long-term national interest.

Third, it is desirable to convince policymakers in each country that the actions considered appropriate are in the long-term interest of the country itself. In this regard, the contextual challenges for each economy should be given due weight. For example, in countries like India, employment and poverty reduction need to be given the highest priority.

Fourth, it is essential to recognise that coordination is necessary, given the complex situation where neither causes nor solutions are clear-cut. As a first step, there could, however, be a broad agreement on the directions and first principles that are most appropriate. An emphasis on harmony in policies and a search for cooperative solutions appears appropriate.

Possible Impact of Global Imbalances on India

As highlighted by the Finance Minister of India during the ADB annual meeting, apart from the impact on the real and external sectors, it is felt that developments in the currency and capital market are intrinsically intertwined with global imbalance, and therefore, in the eventuality of a disorderly correction, disruption in these markets in the form of large cross-currency volatility and a sharp rise in interest rates are likely in the global economy. What could be the possible impact of a less than orderly adjustment of global imbalances on the Indian economy?

India does not depend on the international capital market for financing fiscal deficit, because of which the adverse consequences of global developments would be muted to some extent. However, there could be a spillover effect of global developments on domestic interest rates, and thus on fisc as well. The fiscal position of the government could also be indirectly impacted through the nature of the management of foreign exchange reserves held by the RBI.

Similarly, any abrupt adjustment in global imbalances may affect corporates, banks and households in India, even though the impact may be less than in some other emerging economies.

With respect to the impact on corporates, if there is a widening of spreads due to a shift in investor confidence in international markets, those corporates who have borrowed at variable rates may possibly suffer more than those who have taken loans on a fixed rate basis. Corporates that have hedged against currency and interest rate risks may escape the adverse effects. It may be noted that the RBI has been urging banks to encourage corporates to hedge their foreign currency exposures. Further, exposure of the corporate sector as a whole to external debt has been limited by the indicative ceilings on external commercial borrowings imposed by the government and the RBI. The level of the total external debt of India is currently less than the foreign exchange reserves.

Although banks in India have their deposit bases predominantly in rupees and their investment in foreign currency assets is not large, they have been financing investment in assets, home loans and the retail market, as well as equities. As in many EMEs, asset prices have risen sharply in India, too. Should there be a reversal of capital flows, asset prices may decline; however, the banks' exposure to risky assets has been severely restricted by the RBI's regulatory actions. Likewise, the equity market has also seen a sustained uptrend, but efforts have been made by the RBI to cap the banks' exposures. Further, banks in India have invested significantly in government debt and other fixed income securities. If a rise in international rates gets reflected in the domestic interest rates, banks will have to mark down the value of their investment portfolio. To the extent that a rise in international interest rates impacts the domestic interest rates, it would entail marked-to-market losses on the investment portfolios. However, the banking sector has acquired some added strength to absorb such probable shocks, largely aided by regulatory actions.

As regards the impact on households, there is a risk that a rise in interest rates in general could impact the housing market and expose the balance sheet of households to interest rate risk, increasing the risk of loan losses for banks. Since the overall banking sector's exposure to housing loans is relatively small, adverse developments may not have any systemic implications for the banking sector.

The Emergence of Oil as a New Factor

The emergence of large current account surpluses among oil-exporting countries is an important recent development. The current account surplus of oil-exporting countries increased from 6.2 per cent of their GDP in 2001 to 19.1 per cent in 2005. Less than a third of the combined current account surplus of oil-exporting countries has been reflected in their foreign exchange reserves, which rose by US$ 90 billion in 2005. The IMF (*World Economic Outlook*, April 2006) has highlighted that to the extent that higher net savings by oil exporters have driven down the global interest rates, and these lower rates have boosted the demand in economies with market-based financial systems, such as the US, the oil price shock may also have had an additional negative effect on the US external position.

The fact remains that rising oil prices would result in further widening global current account imbalances as, according to consensus forecast, the current account balance of the US was projected to deteriorate further in 2006. Other industrialised economies were projected to run a combined surplus, led mainly by Japan and Germany. The aggregate current account surplus of the major oil-exporting countries is expected to increase further in the near term.

In this regard, it may be noted that India's oil import bill had amounted to 2.9 per cent of GDP in 2001–2; however, the bill climbed to 5.5 per cent of GDP in 2005–6, although in volume terms the increase was marginal.

AGENDA FOR ANALYSIS

In view of the complex nature of global imbalances and the way forward to minimise the risks of disorderly adjustments, it may be useful to explore a possible agenda for further analysis.

First, national balance sheets could be given special attention to get a fuller picture of the financial claims that countries make against other countries. Looking at the national balance sheets would also help us acquire a sense about the potential for adjustment, and of the possible impact of relative price changes on the value of assets and liabilities. The composition and size of the liabilities and assets of national balance sheets are crucial, as we could get a global picture by viewing them together. However, we should look deeper into the balance sheets in terms of disaggregating them into public and private-sector components, and the incomes generated in the process. A relevant observation here is the perceived higher returns to external assets held by the US relative to US assets held by the rest of the world. A disaggregation enables an analysis of the role of the private and public sector in perpetuation, as well as the resolution of imbalances. There could be a dominance of bilateral claims of the private sector of one country to the public or the private sector of another country. Could such dominant bilateral claims become a noticeable force which allows, at times, non-economic factors to play a role in the whole process of engagement?

Second, following the experience of the East Asian crisis of 1997–8, where private-sector vulnerabilities rather than public-sector imbalances played a key role in precipitating the crisis, the third-generation models have explicitly brought to the fore the role of balance sheet mismatches in causing financial crises. A country's balance sheet, as evident from traditional macroeconomic aggregate, could be quite sound, and yet an analysis of the composition and size of the liabilities and assets of the balance sheets of domestic entities may be useful in assessing vulnerability to the manner of unwinding imbalances. It would therefore be useful to analyse the impact of global imbalances on various balance sheets within the country, such as the government sector, the financial sector—including banks and financial institutions—the non-financial private sector, including corporates and households.

Third, as mentioned earlier, the surplus of oil-exporting countries has emerged as a new factor in the debate on the global imbalance. There are some indications that the oil surpluses are being deployed in more diversified avenues than official reserves. Oil exporters appear to have taken advantage of emerging investment opportunities in stock markets and real estate. Such inflows could have helped to keep long-term interest rates as also the emerging market bond spreads low, even as policy rates rise. An interesting issue would be the nature of their responses to the unwinding of global imbalances.

Fourth, in a way global imbalance is a reflection of incomplete globalisation. If there were complete globalisation, the surplus in the saving of one country could be utilised by a country with a deficit in saving, as happens among different states in India or the US. It could be argued that as the global economy integrates further, the resolution of global imbalances might be smoother.

Fifth, what is the evolving role of viewing exchange rate regimes in influencing the domestic economy? Some argue that the emerging evidence indicates that domestic price movements remain somewhat immune to considerable exchange rate movements. If so, the possibility of bringing about a global rebalancing through exchange-rate adjustment by itself may not be very encouraging. No doubt the exchange rate would have an important role to play in global rebalancing, but the issue is its relationship with other components of the whole package, like saving-investment, fiscal deficit, raising investment, structural reforms and domestic output, as well as employment. The linkages among the various components described here could be very country-specific.

Sixth, there is wide diversity among the Asian economies in terms of saving and investment rates, fiscal deficit, drivers of growth (domestic versus external demand) and the degree of flexibility in their exchange rates. Thus, it may be difficult to treat all of them as contributing to global financial imbalances in the same manner; neither would all the Asian economies be identically affected by the adjustment of global financial imbalances. Correspondingly, the policy response of each country to the issue would be tailored to the circumstances. More importantly, with the growing integration among Asian economies, how would the process of rebalancing affect them, depending on the manner in which dominant economies in Asia manage the process?

Seventh, given the potential for investment demand in the region, we must find ways of making better use of savings and finding investment avenues within the region. In this regard, an important issue would be the generation of demand within the region, so that the aggregate current account surpluses are absorbed in the region itself. This process of demand generation would help in the orderly correction of the global imbalances.

Eighth, one wonders whether there is a dissonance between the perception of financial markets and that of policymakers with regard to global imbalances. Policymakers appear to be signalling some concern, but the response of the financial markets is often out of alignment with the signals. Interestingly, anecdotal evidence shows that analysts in financial intermediaries are sensitive to the downside risk of imbalances, but that the conduct of the participants does not reflect the awareness. No doubt this sense of dissonance is not new; for example, stock markets went up after Alan Greenspan's statement regarding irrational exuberance. If such dissonance is true, and persistent, what would be the effectiveness of public policy initiatives?

Ninth, is there an advantage in assessing non-quantifiable factors to explain the persistence of what has been stated as a stable disequilibrium to describe the current status of the global economy? For example, the signature value of the US in terms of the confidence of financial markets as a lasting safe haven could be a factor, although the issue is whether it will be valid interminably. The perception of continuing productivity gains in the US due to its proven flexibilities could be another. The lack of alternatives to deploy global savings, which have been expanding, may also be relevant. These are undoubtedly not quantifiable, but do not cease to be relevant for analysis and assessment.

Finally, is it possible that there are several intermediate scenarios between orderly adjustments and disruptive or disorderly adjustments? A series of marginal adjustments, often in spurts, could take place, which may appear random yet move towards a gradual lessening of imbalances through an interactive and iterative process encompassing markets, national policies and global cooperation. The agenda for analysis proposed here may facilitate the exploration of such intermediate scenarios of unwinding global imbalances.

CONCLUSION

To conclude, the performance of the Indian economy since 1980, and in particular since the reforms in the 1990s, is in many ways an impressive success story, both in terms of growth and stability. The Indian economy has responded well to the rising global competition with gradually increasing integration within the world economy. The current high growth phase of the Indian economy has also coincided with rising domestic saving rates. While India by itself hardly contributes to the current global financial imbalances, any large and rapid adjustments in major currencies and related interest rates or current accounts of trading partners could indirectly, but significantly, impact the Indian economy. We therefore have a large stake in the process of unwinding of global imbalances, and are willing to play our part in ensuring successful outcomes from current initiatives.

23

Globalisation, Money and Finance
Uncertainties and Dilemmas*

In the recent period, a reassessment of the costs and benefits of globalisation seems to be taking place. Already, the share of the emerging countries in world exports has surged to 43 per cent from 20 per cent in 1970. Domestic structural reforms in emerging economies are unlocking the pent-up domestic demand, and in turn enabling a greater realisation of the huge potential for growth. So, what is causing the rethink in both the developed and the emerging economies? Several factors seem to be at work.

First, the traditional postulate that capital flows from the capital-surplus or developed countries to the capital-scarce or developing countries seems to have been disproved in recent years. Today, we are confronted with the puzzle of capital flowing uphill, that is, from the developing to the developed countries. The world's largest economy, the US, currently runs a current account deficit, financed to a substantial extent by capital exports from EMEs.

Further, the level of financial development per se does not seem to determine the direction of capital flows. It is argued that the phenomenon mainly reflects the limited absorption capacity of developing countries in the context of relatively lower financial development. However, this explanation can be turned around. The US, which has perhaps the most well-developed financial

*Previously presented as valedictory address at the FICCI-IBA Conference held in Mumbai, 28 September 2006.

system, is currently importing capital. As the developing countries catch up in terms of sophistication and depth in their financial systems, would the pattern of capital flows change, and if so, how? In the interregnum, the export of capital from the developing to the developed countries has no doubt revitalised global growth. But will this, or can this, go on?

Second, in a globalising world, the policymakers seem to be confronted with new realities, which are sometimes hard to fully comprehend. In a way, the context in which monetary policy is set leads to a confrontation with the impossible trinity—independent monetary policy, open capital account and managed exchange rate. The theory holds that at best, only two out of the three would be feasible. In practice, however, there is a shift in preference away from the corner solution with respect to financial imbalances. Currently, intermediate solutions, which were earlier regarded as—'fuzzy', are now becoming increasingly relevant. Moreover, in recognition of the differences between trade and financial integration—first pointed out by Jagdish Bhagwati—there is less certainty today about the corner solutions than there was in the past.

Third, at a practical level, the recent experience seems to indicate that globalisation may have had accentuated potential conflicts that can impact the fabric of our societies. Outsourcing to low-wage countries to derive the benefits of lower costs has generated a restiveness in the labour markets of advanced countries, particularly in the skilled segment of tradable services that are more exposed to foreign competition. The geographical fragmentation of the production base is being increasingly used by big firms as a bargaining tool with workers. Increased emigration from developing and emerging countries has depressed wages in the advanced economies and heightened social tensions. In recent years, the contractionary effects of the cooling of housing markets may also be building up further pressure against globalisation.

Fourth, there are widespread concerns about the gaps in international trade rules and regulations, the impasse in multilateral trade negotiations and, consequently, the rising number of regional and bilateral trade arrangements, which could rule out the use of the very policy measures that were instrumental in the development of today's mature economies and late industrialisers.

Fifth, the rapid pace of globalisation in monetary and financial relationships has not been accompanied by an improvement in the international financial architecture. The provision of liquidity to enable countries to weather payment difficulties has arguably been inadequate. Managing financial crisis remains largely a national responsibility. As the UNCTAD's *Trade and Development Report*, 2006 has noted: 'The bulk of adjustment in case of external imbalances is often concentrated on a group of developing and transition economies, despite the fact that the source of such imbalances may occur in the developed world' (Overview, pp. 38–9). This seems to have provoked an accumulation of foreign exchange reserves in the emerging countries.

In the wake of these developments, there is a growing expression of heightened sensitivity to the costs associated with globalisation. In the ultimate analysis, public policy has an important role in managing the costs and benefits of globalisation. When the going is good, public policy is viewed with disfavour. In the face of adverse conditions, however, public policy intervention is often the only sought-after solution. Accordingly, it is public policy which has the best chance of preserving the benefits of globalisation and ensuring that these are widely shared so as to maintain support for free trade and stem protectionism, thereby providing globalisation with the popular legitimacy which, at present, seems to be sometimes lacking. 'Making Globalisation Work' is the challenge before policymakers, so that the benefits of globalisation are sufficiently shared and demonstrably exceed the attendant costs. To quote Chairman Bernanke:

> Further progress in global economic integration should not be taken for granted ... as in the past, the social and political opposition to openness can be strong ... much of it arises because changes in the patterns of production are likely to threaten the livelihoods of some workers and the profits of some firms.... The natural reaction of those so affected is to resist change, for example, by seeking the passage of protectionist measures (Bernanke, 2006).

GLOBALISATION AND MONETARY POLICY

While considerations relating to maximising output and employment weigh as much upon monetary authorities as maintaining price stability, particularly in developing countries, domestic inflation has increasingly become less sensitive to the domestic output gap, and potentially more sensitive to the world output gap. It is therefore necessary for each country to take a holistic approach vis-à-vis the trinity of free flows of capital, freely floating exchange rates and independent monetary policy. At a practical policy level, the trinity can be regarded as implausible and difficult, yet manageable through intermediate solutions that adapt to the country-specific situations. For monetary authorities, the new realities perhaps provide unknown challenges in an uncertain future, heightening the dilemmas in policymaking.

Central banks are often concerned with the stability/variability of inflation, rather than the level of prices. However, inflation processes have become highly unclear, with soaring commodity prices coexisting with low consumer prices in an environment of high asset prices. Amidst these uncertainties, central banks are faced with the need to recognise the importance of inflation perceptions and inflation expectations as distinct from inflation numbers. The distinction between inflationary expectations and inflation perceptions in the context of inflation policy is also worth bearing in mind. More often than not, it is the expected change rather than the actual change in real interest rate, following a change in the policy rate, that drives the actions of the economic agents. Thus, the ability to condition inflation expectations, rather than the decisions on the policy rates, is of fundamental importance to monetary policymaking now. In this context, credible communication and creative engagement with the market and economic agents has emerged as the critical channel of monetary transmission, as against the traditional channels.

The presence of administered interest rates, even in segments of a financial system, could hold back appropriate adjustments in real rates as a sequel to changes in the policy rates. What is surprising, however, is that the financial market rates could also display such impervious behaviour, and thereby act as the source of nominal rigidities in the economy. The recent 'conundrum' in the financial markets *a la* Greenspan is a case in point. As a result, long-term real rates in financial markets have changed, but not in the desired direction, posing challenges to the effectiveness of monetary policy even in a market-based system. Therefore, it is not only the change in real rates but also the direction of change following changes in the policy rates that are important for the effectiveness of monetary policy.

In a relatively more stable economic environment, the need, extent and duration of policy interventions becomes less and less. Central banks are now taking baby steps—sometimes more frequently and at other times after a long gap, and in both directions—to respond to what appear to be ripples rather than huge waves in the sea of economic activity. For instance, what is considered a 'neutral rate' of interest in the present period appears to be much lower when compared to several years before. The significant issue here is whether the neutral rate with respect to the EMEs, which has been coming down in tandem with the global rates, will tend to be distinctly higher than in developed economies. If so, how much higher would be appropriate?

Even a moderate inflation rate poses a dilemma in an increasingly open-economy framework. If the domestic inflation rate of an economy, however low it may be, is higher than the average inflation rate of its trading partners, it puts pressure on the exchange rate. In this context, the question of the simultaneous balancing of the internal and external sectors becomes a major issue. The conduct of monetary policy inevitably involves a careful judgement on the relative weights assigned to the domestic and the global factors, and a constant reassessment of these in response to evolving circumstances.

In a dynamic setting, where financial markets are continually evolving and payment systems and technology are changing rapidly, one may not find a clear-cut evidence of stability in monetary rules and intermediate targeting. In such circumstances, monetary authorities are being constrained to look at all relevant indicators, following a menu or a 'check list' approach. Discerning news from noise is a persistent dilemma in conducting monetary policy.

Since external capital flows to emerging economies cannot be easily predicted and can also reverse even in the presence of sound fundamentals, monetary authorities have to often make choices with regard to exchange rate and monetary management. The appropriate management of monetary policy may require monetary authorities to consider offsetting the impact of foreign exchange market operations, partly or wholly, so as to retain the intent of monetary policy. The monetary authority has to decide on the extent of offset as also the means of offset—market-based or non-market based or a combination of the two.

Financial stability considerations may require the use of an interest rate tool in conjunction with other prudential measures. At times there could even be a trade-off between raising the short-term interest rate and tightening prudential norms if the risks are perceived to originate from certain segments of the market. The highly leveraged lending operations against the backdrop of asset-price bubbles might require adjustments in the lending margins and risk-based capital requirements. An issue in this regard is the extent to which these should be considered akin to the erstwhile selective credit controls.

GLOBALISATION AND THE FINANCIAL SECTOR

The international financial markets are currently dominated by private equity funds like hedge funds, which largely operate outside the 'Know Your Customer'/'Know Your Investor' norms. Hedge funds have long used arrangements that allow them to execute trades with several dealers, but there is now an increasing tendency on their part to consolidate the clearing and settlement of their trades at a single firm, the 'prime broker'. Prime brokerage poses some unique challenges for the management of counter-party credit and operational risk.

It is commonly observed at the global level that hedge funds are 'opaque'—that is, information about their portfolios is typically limited and infrequently provided. The information a fund provides may also vary considerably, depending on whether the recipient of the information is an investor, a counter-party, a regulatory authority or a general market participant. From a policy perspective, transparency to investors is largely an issue of investor protection, which in turn depends on the nature of investors. The need for counter-parties to have adequate information is a risk-management issue. Concerns about hedge fund opacity and possible liquidity risk have motivated a range of proposals through which regulatory authorities can create and maintain a database of hedge fund positions.

There are some uncertainties associated with the settling of trades in newer types of over-the-counter (OTC) derivatives, particularly credit derivatives. As part of the recent financial innovations, the credit-derivative and structured-credit markets have grown rapidly during the past few years, allowing for the dispersion of credit risk by financial players. Perhaps it is necessary to evolve mechanisms to ascertain the size and structure of risk components, the scale and direction of risk transfers and therefore the distribution of risk within the economy.

In recent years, the issue of institutional mechanisms for the prevention and resolution of financial crises at the multilateral level has assumed importance. There are four aspects to the question of whether the international financial architecture is now in a position to give comfort if a country were to have a problem. First, undoubtedly the resilience of the world today, particularly that of private capital markets, has improved enormously since 1997. Macroeconomic policies and approaches of international financial institutions, as well as the resilience of markets have improved. Second, even though in terms of magnitude the official/bilateral flows of funds are miniscule, the very intent of such flows, guided by broader societal consideration, gives them strength in the face of private flows. Third, as we are aware, risks are never eliminated, but are only mitigated. The existing international financial architecture is inadequate when it comes to preventing or mitigating the domestic and external effects of financial crisis, particularly in large economies like China and India. Fourth, the impact of instability in times of crisis appears to be largely borne by the home or domestic public sector, rather than the global private sector. Avoiding crisis is ultimately a national responsibility. In such a milieu, policymakers are often confronted with competing positions and need to make choices in the face of daunting dilemmas.

CONCLUDING REMARKS

In a recent survey of the world economy, *The Economist* (16 September 2006) predicted that the emerging economies are set to give the world economy its biggest boost since the industrial revolution. A greater integration into the global system of production and trade, supported by buoyant capital flows, is driving a widening wedge between the emerging and the developed countries in terms of growth rates. Already accounting for more than half of the world GDP in PPP terms, they will raise their share to two-thirds of the global output in twenty years' time. It took fifty years for Britain and America to double real income in the nineteenth century when they were industrialising; China is achieving the same feat in nine years! Over the next decade, almost a billion new consumers will enter the global marketplace, providing an enduring stimulus to economic activity across the world.

In all humility, it needs to be recognised that despite soaring economic growth, real per capita incomes, and therefore standards of living in the developing countries, remain well below those in the developed countries. As the BRIC report of Goldman and Sachs (2003) had thoughtfully projected, the average per capita income in America would still be three or four times higher than that in China even in 2040. The IMF has estimated that if India's relative per capita income rises by under 2 per cent, it will take more than 100 years to close half the distance from the developed countries' per capita income levels. If India's per capita income grows by 3 per cent in real terms, it will still take sixty-nine years to close half the gap. More importantly, faster growth alone will not automatically eradicate poverty; it depends on how inclusive that growth is, and how the benefits of globalisation are shared.

The future will, in all likelihood, call for some radical thinking, perhaps even new vistas of development in operational and institutional frameworks of monetary policy. So far, it is claimed that the emerging economies have made the work of monetary authorities a lot easier by subduing inflation—both commodity prices and wages—and have in fact gifted credibility to monetary policy. Yet, the question that is often asked is whether the emerging economies have facilitated the holding of interest rates at very low levels by central banks in the developed countries. In the face of the consequent build-up of liquidity, elevated asset prices and soaring consumer indebtedness, is there a dark side to the future? The intellectual edifice on which monetary policy is founded is rooted in the management of aggregate demand. However, a supply shock arising from globalisation can produce vastly different growth-inflation outcomes, which monetary policy by itself is not fully equipped to manage. Indeed, a question that has been asked in this context is whether price stability is enough as a goal of monetary policy, and how sacrosanct it is at times when, for example, central banks have to contend with financial imbalances, even if it means overshooting inflation targets.

At the end, it will be remiss of me to not address the relationship between the real and the financial sectors in India in the context of globalisation. Economists have for long recognised the strong complementarities between the real and the financial sectors. Financial development contributes to growth in either a supply-leading or a demand-following sequence; that is, either the financial sector development creates the conditions for growth or the growth generates demand for financial services. It is important to recognise that the financial sector in India is no longer a constraint on growth, and that its strength and resilience are acknowledged, although improvements need to take place. On the other hand, without the real sector development in terms of the physical infrastructure and improvement in supply elasticities, the financial sector can even misallocate resources, potentially generate bubbles and possibly amplify risks. Hence, public policy may have a crucial role to play in ensuring a balanced reform in both the real and the financial sectors. The criticality for policymakers is not only to ensure that there are no financial-sector constraints on real sector activity, but also to assure that the financial-sector reforms have complementarity with the pace and process of reform in the real sector in India, along with, no doubt, fiscal empowerment— as consistently emphasised by the RBI.

REFERENCES

Bernanke, Ben S. 2006. 'Global Economic Integration: What's New and What's Not?', Speech at the Federal Reserve Bank of Kansas City's Thirtieth Annual Economic Symposium, Jackson Hole, Wyoming, 25 August.

UNCTAD. *Trade and Development Report*. 2006. Geneva. August.

Epilogue
The Global Financial Crisis and India

The financial crisis, which assumed global proportions in 2008, is, at the time of writing, far from over. In fact, many facets of the crisis are still unfolding, while many of the policy responses are yet to bear fruit and the road to recovery is uncertain. The landscape for the future, beyond the crisis, is sought to be designed by the collective wisdom of the heads of governments of several countries on the basis of lessons learned from the crisis. At this stage, therefore, there is merit in asking the right questions on the global crisis and its implications for India, and exploring the possible answers.

WHAT CAUSED THE CRISIS?

The explanations offered for why the crisis occurred can be broadly divided into those relating to macro-economic management and those concerning the financial sector, in particular the behaviour of financial markets, although in reality both must have reinforced each other to bring about the distress conditions.

Macro-Economic Explanations

Explanations in terms of macroeconomic management may be summarised as follows:

First, some countries, notably the US, built large current account deficits. Some others, notably in Asia, built significant current account surpluses and lent to or invested in the US. Since these recurring imbalances persisted and increased over the years, correction was warranted by the markets.

Second, in many countries, macroeconomic policies in the recent past resulted in gross inequalities in income and wealth. For example, median wage was constant in real terms despite the growth in output in the US. Consequently, there has been a deficiency in aggregate demand, which did not manifest as long as the illusion of economic activity was maintained by the excessive development of the financial sector. These excesses in the financial sector created an illusion of sustainable activity in the real sector for quite some time, but it could not last. The sub-prime crisis in the US was only one of the symptoms of the lack of aggregate demand, coupled with excessive financialisation of the economy and excessive leverage (that is, utilising a far larger proportion of borrowed or others' money relative to one's own in undertaking risky business).

Third, in view of the underdeveloped nature of financial markets in some developing economies, such as in China and other Asian economies, the domestic savings in those economies could not be fully channelled into the required domestic investments, and hence there was a surplus of savings in these countries.

Fourth, the monetary policy, especially in the US, was excessively accommodative (that is, allowing the supply of money to be plentiful and interest rates low relative to appropriate levels) for several years, resulting in excess liquidity. This excess liquidity caused investors to search for yield and either under-price risks or take excessive risks. Such excess liquidity found its way into speculative activities, causing asset bubbles. (Large increases in the prices of assets like real estate or equity were based mainly on the belief that such prices will keep increasing in future.)

Fifth, some central bankers were focused exclusively on price stability, and many of them were mandated to focus on this through inflation targeting regimes. In addition, there was no formal mandate to any particular institution to maintain financial stability, hence the relatively low emphasis of such stability in public policy. (Financial stability implies the existence of uninterrupted financial transactions as well as an acceptable level of confidence in the financial system, and an absence of excess volatility that unduly and adversely affects the normal real economic activity.)

Sixth, many central banks were persuaded to be very transparent and provide forward guidance to financial markets on their policy stance, especially on the future course of monetary policy. Such forward guidance provided excessive comfort to financial markets and enabled them to under-price risks.

Seventh, even when some of the central banks perceived the under-pricing of risks, financial market agents asserted that the central banks could not sit in judgement on prices set by a competitive market, and assured policymakers that markets would correct themselves automatically. The central banks were informed by financial market agents time and again that the dangers of policy mistakes were more than the prospect of markets not correcting themselves smoothly. The central banks were obviously persuaded by these arguments, and as a result did not act or intervene.

Eighth, some of the central banks perceived that there were excessive risks in the system, but concluded that due to the emergence of new intermediaries like hedge funds and new derivatives instruments, such risks were dispersed widely, especially among those who could afford to bear them, with no impact on the financial system as a whole, even though the risks did not disappear. Overall, the central banks seem to have ignored the economic imbalances and asset bubbles that were building up, and thus failed to act in a counter-cyclical fashion to moderate, though not eliminate, the boom bust cycle.

Ninth, multilateral institutions like the IMF, which were charged with the responsibility of surveillance, gave warnings about macroeconomic imbalances. They, however, did not bring out the extent of the vulnerabilities of the global economy in general, and the systemically important economies in particular. The multilateral institutions were constrained partly because they were dominated by select countries that were unwilling to subject their economies to objective surveillance, and which had in fact encouraged the institutions towards an excessively market-oriented ideology.

Finally, there is only one significant reserve currency (that is, a currency in which global reserves can be held), that is, US dollar. The global economic system was thus subject to the undue influence of the policies of one country. This dependence of the global economy on one currency by itself had the potential for instability, and in any case could have facilitated excessive risk-taking by the public policy in the US. This could also partly explain the smooth financing of the twin deficits (in the current account of the balance of payments in the external sector and the fiscal account of the government) of the US by the rest of the world for several years, resulting in a huge build-up of global imbalances.

A critical examination of all the above explanations would indicate that they might be interrelated, and that each of them may at best provide only partial explanations of the macroeconomic factors that could have contributed to the crisis. The imbalances did enable the excesses in the financial sector, which were an important reason for the crisis. It can be argued that there was no deficiency in the aggregate demand but actually a deficiency in aggregate savings, both in the household and government sector in the US, a very relevant country in this context. With regard to the role of central banks, they had allowed excess liquidity and ignored asset bubbles in the system since the central banks were not equipped to conclude *ex ante* that there was a bubble, and asset prices were not part of the central banks' focus on monetary policy. They had also apparently underestimated the concentration of risks within the financial sector. Multilateral bodies like the IMF pointed out the need to focus on macroeconomic imbalances and the bubbles in the housing sector, but missed diagnosing the extent of vulnerabilities. It has been noted that the US did not subject itself to the Financial Sector Assessment Program (FSAP) of the IMF, although it is a moot point whether it was material, considering the experience of FSAP with Argentina and Iceland. The UNCTAD, in its Trade and Development Reports, has been warning about the vulnerabilities of the financial sector, but these were largely ignored by most of the policymakers. Finally, the continued dependence on the US Dollar as a reserve currency could have imparted some vulnerability to global financial stability.

In sum, while there is no single explanation in the realm of macroeconomic management that could have exclusively contributed to the crisis, there is a common thread that runs through most of the explanations, viz., a serious underestimation of the potential for market failures, as it relates to the macro economy in general and the financial sector in particular. Further, the growth and development of the financial sector seems to have acquired a momentum of their own in public policy, without due regard to its links with the growth of the non-financial or real sector.

Regulation of the Financial Sector

A second set of explanations relates to the regulatory environment in which financial markets were functioning. It is well recognised now that the problem of sub-prime lending for housing in the US was only a proximate cause or simply a trigger, and that the problem was far deeper and widespread. The sub-prime lending was also a case of irresponsible lending and ignorant borrowing, rather than a programme of financial inclusion. Moreover, such lending was facilitated by a regulatory environment that was driven by vested interests which benefited from excessive lending in the deregulated financial environment. While there may be differences of opinion on the nature of the sub-prime problem in the US, there is a consensus now that the problem in the financial sector is more fundamental and globally relevant, and essentially related to the functioning of the sector. The explanations most commonly advanced in this regard are summarised here.

i. The regulators in the financial sector did not have the adequate skills to cope with the rapid growth in the variety and complexity of market innovations in financial products.

ii. The principle-based regulation adopted by some of the regulators left too much of discretion to the regulated entities to manage their own risks.

iii. The regulators concentrated on mitigating the entry-level risks in the individual-regulated institutions through micro-prudential regulation, rather than the risks to the system through macro-prudential monitoring and regulation. The regulators did not recognise the need for counter-cyclicality in regulation, thus amplifying the boom and bust cycle (that is, the need to tighten regulation when the economy was experiencing an excessive exuberance and relaxing it during a period of unjustified pessimism).

iv. The liquidity risks in the operations of financial entities were ignored, and this was also not built into the Basel 2 prudential norms. While the prudential norms focused on the quality of assets, they did not take into account the pattern of funding of such assets; for example, there are consequences of funding long-term assets with short-term funds.

v. The off-balance sheet items and investment vehicles and their potential impact on capital adequacy were not fully captured by the regulators.

vi. The regulators focused on regulating commercial banks, ignoring the developments in what has been described as the shadow banking system. Non-bank entities such as investment banks, hedge funds, private equity firms, etc., remained unregulated, and hence turned out to be sources of risk. In other words, the ambit of regulations was not as comprehensive as it should have been.

vii. The regulators relied heavily on ratings assigned by credit rating agencies, particularly in implementing Basel 2. They failed to adequately regulate the Credit Rating Agencies even though they were relying heavily on the ratings. The ratings proved to be unreliable, and possibly motivated by the prevailing framework of incentives and conflicts of interests.

viii. The regulatory structures were inadequate since multiple regulators facilitated regulatory arbitrage by the market participants, and thus exacerbated the risks.

ix. The global framework for cross-border institutions' regulation and supervision was weak, although the financial markets and institutions were globalised.

x. In a bid to attract the financial services industry to their jurisdictions, regulators in international financial centres such as London and New York adopted a policy of relatively soft regulation, or what has been described as 'light touch regulation'. The eagerness to develop some centres as global financial centres resulted in a race to the minimal regulation.

It is generally accepted that the environment in which market participants operated also contributed to the crisis.

i. The accounting standards were pro-cyclical, especially due to the policy of mark-to-market rules of valuation of assets and liabilities. The mark-to-market rules require that the assets and liabilities be valued from time to time as per the prevailing market values, which tend to give a high valuation when the economy is in a boom and depress values when the economy is in a bust.

ii. The incentive framework, especially in investment banks' hedge funds and private equity funds, etc., encouraged excessive risk taking. The remuneration policies for senior management in particular were set in such a way that gave no incentive to encourage prudent behaviour, since they got hefty bonuses based on short-term performance irrespective of the long-term risks assumed in the process.

iii. The banks developed a business model wherein they originated loans but distributed the credit risks inherent in such loans to others. This led to a manifold increase in the leverage. The securitisation was a convenient tool to avoid additional regulatory capital. These practices were carried to excesses, resulting in a huge increase in the overall leverages in the financial sector.

iv. Greed became an accepted and generally respectable norm of behaviour in the financial sector, resulting in a build-up of excessive risks.

v. Complexity in financial instruments helped profit-seeking by ensuring savings on regulatory capital requirements, and defeated the purpose of transparency prescribed by the regulator.

vi. The global financial system was dominated by a few large financial conglomerates, and these were fully aware that they were too big to fail. Such awareness by itself provided incentives to become big enough and then take up riskier ventures. The crisis originated in large, globally significant financial institutions.

vii. The tax havens and bank secrecy laws provided opportunities for maximising profits through tax avoidance and the avoidance of applicable regulations.

A critical examination of the above explanations indicates that some of them may be more relevant than others, while a few other explanations are not central to the crisis. In analysing the causes of the financial crisis, it is necessary to learn lessons from the countries that were host to serious financial crisis—such as the US and the UK—and those that faced less serious crisis— such as Canada and India.

Most of the explanations apply to the two most significant international financial centres, the US and the UK. Their regulatory philosophy was in recent years characterised by progressive deregulation, greater dependence on markets, eagerness to attract the global financial services industry, and erosion of the special status and integrity of traditional commercial banking activity, viz., accepting retail deposits and disbursal of credit to their clients. Many other countries adopted a regulatory philosophy similar to the one described above, though with varying degrees of commitment.

AN OVERVIEW OF CAUSES

In view of the above, the critical question is whether there was a regulatory capture that could have led to wrong assessments or inappropriate actions or deliberate inaction by central banks and regulators. A close examination of various events in recent years, such as legal changes, regulatory actions, policy analysis, and even media focus in most economies, especially the advanced economies, may point to the possibility of a regulatory capture. However, this capture may be of a more comprehensive variety than the typical one described in the literature. The typical one entails the capturing of the regulator by the regulated, essentially based on information asymmetry. The financial markets had developed far more rapidly than the real economy, and in the process fostered considerable linkages with the political economy, made possible by excessive profitability in the financial sector. The financial markets and institutions strongly influenced opinion-making through the media. Many high-profile economic analysts tended to be overly optimistic about the benefits of financial-sector development and the deregulation of the financial sector. All these may have reinforced the traditional regulatory capture. There was a lurking suspicion in some quarters that the performance of central banks and regulators was in fact being significantly judged only by the regulated, viz., the financial markets. In this light, it can be justifiably held that it was significant political economy factors that drove the actions and inactions of both central banks and governments, and that they explain both the excessively accommodative monetary policy and the soft regulation in many economies. (A cynic remarked that under socialism, the government took over the banks, and under capitalism banks took over the governments.)

This line of explanation would consider the failure of both the market and the state as reasons for the crisis. In other words, it may be held that the crisis reflects a failure of governance in both private and public sectors. The failure of governance is also evidenced in the failure of all relevant institutional defences against serious financial instability. Thus, the Board, the management, risk management practices, and internal controls all allowed excesses. The rating agencies, the advisors, the analysts and the auditors failed to alert us to the build-up of risks, possibly due to incentives or counter-party dealings. The financial regulators allowed these excesses to happen. Finally, the market discipline, on which reliance has generally been placed and which may include the media and public opinion, did not prevent these excesses.

There is a view that the failure of governance at all levels is indicative of the failure of the whole economic system, or what some have described as a failure of capitalism. In this view, there is a possibility that the current crisis is not merely a cyclical one that could be easily resolved through the self-regulating character of capitalism. A suitable redesign of international and domestic institutions may aid the process of recovery, but it would still be temporary. In this line of thinking, the current crisis is a product of the hegemony of global finance and is a structural crisis, and hence should lead to what is described as a collapse of capitalism.

There is some merit in viewing the crisis as a significant intellectual failure, in the sense that it was essentially a network crisis caused by a lack of a systemic view of networks. Strong network linkages have developed in the financial sectors, enabled by technological developments and financial deregulation. These network linkages helped to take advantage of economies of scale, obtain capital efficiency, and reduce transaction costs. While these had several beneficial effects through interconnectivity, they also added complexity and risks which were not comprehended by economists or policymakers or finance experts. In sum, it is possible to hold the view that the crisis was caused by several factors which include both moral and intellectual failure in both the private and public sectors.

HOW UNIVERSAL ARE THE CAUSES?

The explanations for the crisis described above are very broad generalisations, and are not universally applicable to all economies for several reasons. While there may be excess or deficient savings in an economy or a region, for the global economy as a whole there cannot be excess, since the global economy is a closed economy. Furthermore, many economies like the Euro area and India did not contribute to global imbalances. Moreover, the banking systems in some countries such as Canada, China and most of Asia appear to be relatively well-capitalised. Some economies did take recourse to counter-cyclical monetary and regulatory policies. Hence, the causes for the crisis could vary from country to country. At the same time, the crisis is global in the sense that all economies are affected through contagion. Some of them, especially many developing countries, are affected despite having sound macro-policies and no serious flaws in the functioning of their financial sector.

It is useful to track the evolution of the crisis in terms of origin and contagion. The crisis surfaced with the bursting of the bubble in sub-prime mortgages in the US as reflected in the credit markets, especially due to the explosion of derivatives markets in the US and the proliferation of the originate to distribute model of banking. In view of the deep integration of domestic financial markets and the existence of large conglomerates operating in several segments of financial markets, the stress was transmitted to the various financial products. With significant global financial integration, some of the instruments that later proved toxic in the derivatives market were distributed across several economies. The cumulative effect was a serious cross-product and cross-border spread of contagion of distress in financial markets and institutions in such globalised economies.

Households and corporates accustomed to high asset values in such globalised economies were adversely affected by the bursting of the asset bubbles, and contributed to sudden and severe contractions in demand and loss of confidence. These developments resulted in drastic reductions in activity in the real sector, a process that is still unfolding at the time of writing (April 2009). Thus, the initial problems in the financial sector were transmitted to the real sector with adverse feedback effects. At the same time, the contagion was felt by many economies that did not have significant financial integration due to contagion through real sectors.

Developing economies were affected through several channels. The transmission channel varied with respect to different developing economies, depending on the nature of their integration with the global economy. The developing economies, which are export-dependent in a significant manner, were more seriously affected by the trade channel through a drastic reduction in earnings from the export of goods and services. There have been spillover effects on invisibles through lower remittances from non-residents and earnings from tourism. The finance channel has been operating both on the current account and the capital account. On the current account, export earnings are also affected by disruptions in trade finance for the export and import of goods, since cross-border banking is essential for trade. On the capital account, the capital is flowing out from the developing to the advanced economies, both because the latter requires additional capital or liquidity and because the investors find safety in mature financial markets, even though some of these are at the epicentre of the crisis. Borrowings in international capital markets have become difficult and expensive. The moderation in capital inflows— and in some cases the net outflows on the capital account—put pressure on the balance of payment and exchange rates. The cumulative effect of the above is on real-sector activity, which in turn may have an adverse impact on the NPAs of banks in the future, and of course on tax revenues. The most seriously affected among developing countries appear to be those with large current account deficits, with limited fiscal manoeuvrability, and a considerably open capital account. Furthermore, economies with a large share of short-term debt in their external liabilities were also vulnerable. In brief, the crisis has affected all economies, and the explanations encompass dynamic interactions between national and international factors. The contagion spread in several ways and, put simplistically; within the financial sector in the advanced economies, then across financial sectors in the advanced economies; followed by feedback from the financial to the real sectors in such economies. Contagion also spread through the financial and real sectors from the advanced to the developing economies, followed by a feedback from the real to the financial sectors within all the economies.

It is possible to argue that the crisis is essentially that of the US, in terms of both origination and impact. There were enough warning signals about the asset bubble, which were ignored by the US either because of over confidence or political economy considerations. The US was undoubtedly leading the global boom in economic activity, and naturally in the bust cycle the impact is felt in the rest of the world. It would logically follow that if the problems in the US were to be fixed, recovery will follow soon. It is noteworthy that the US continues to be the leader in the global debate on the measures needed for recovery and the agenda for reforms. In a way, the US has globalised what is essentially its own crisis, and the fundamental flaws in the systems of that country may in the bargain be dealt with in a myopic manner. The Group of Twenty (G-20) seems to have been co-opted in the design of recovery and reform led by the US. In the process, there is a danger that the policies of some of the G-20 countries may be stretched beyond what is required, based on the fundamentals of the said economies. Traditionally, the Group of Seven (G-7) had been brought in line with the thinking of the US, but now attempts are being made to bring EMEs in alignment with the design of recovery and reform led by the US.

In some ways, the crisis and its management may become an excuse for reversing and loosening policies that had been assiduously put in place by some countries. Unlike the US, which is in a unique position to manage its problems, some of the EMEs may face difficulties in managing the long-term consequences of the approach described above. It can be argued that in some cases, the very same policies that contributed to the crisis are being followed aggressively. For instance, some fiscal measures, particularly those aimed at bailing out the banking system, may be justified, but the limits to the extent of the overall fiscal stimulus in the case of EMEs with a large overhang of public debt must be reckoned with. Similarly, the limits to expansionary monetary policies in the context of vulnerabilities in the external sector of some EMEs cannot be ignored. Recent evidence indicates that the crisis has hit many of those EMEs which had twin deficits.

In brief, there is a view that the crisis originated in the US; there has been a contagion to other countries even though they did not pursue policies similar to those of the US; the design of recovery and reform is also being led by the US; and that the long term consequences of such an approach could be serious for some of the countries unless they remain on constant guard on a continuing basis.

WHY AND HOW DID THE CRISIS HIT INDIA?

It will be useful to explore the relevance of the various causes of the crisis described above for India. On the macroeconomic front, India had, in recent years, experienced a marginal current account deficit. Hence, India did not contribute to the global imbalances. While the income inequalities appear to have increased, in India there has been no evidence of a deficiency in the aggregate demand in the domestic economy. Most of the domestic investment was financed by domestic savings, although the trade and financial linkages between India and the global economy increased significantly. Relative to the trends in many other countries, especially the US, monetary policy in India tended to be counter-cyclical. The RBI defined for itself financial stability as an important consideration, and articulated the same in its various policy statements. Price stability continued to be a priority, but not at the cost of neglecting other considerations consistent with its mandate. The RBI's communication policies made it clear that it does not provide forward guidance to financial markets, and only shares its analysis with market participants. The build-up of risks in the global financial system had been articulated especially since 2005, and there was recognition of the fact that there was no clear knowledge of where the risks reside. The RBI conceded that it could not take a view on whether there were asset bubbles or not, but it did note the possibility of such a build-up of bubbles in the domestic economy. Consequently, to protect the banking system from a possible adverse impact, counter-cyclical regulatory measures were undertaken while the monetary policy was leaning against the wind of excessive growth in credit and money supply. The conduct of policy was conscious of the limitations of the global financial architecture, and hence gave importance to self-insurance through the build-up of forex reserves, especially in the light of strong capital inflows, with a dominance of the more volatile portfolio flows. Some moderation of capital inflows was attempted while outflows were liberalised, especially for corporates and households. While it is difficult to pass judgement on whether the policies and actions of the RBI were appropriate, it is possible to hold that they were, broadly in a direction that did not contribute to the current crisis of the global economy, and, in fact, they attempted to minimise the vulnerabilities in the domestic economy.

The regulatory environment in India was counter-cyclical and took both micro and macro prudential measures. The liquidity issues were specifically addressed through the regulation. Banks were encouraged to concentrate on what may be termed traditional retail banking, relative to wholesale or capital market operations. The banking regulation took cognisance of the benefits as well as the complexity of the financial innovations. The extent of the adequacy of skills in the financial system, both in the markets and institutions, was noted, in order to take extensive recourse to such new instruments. The regulatory framework was extended to systemically important financial institutions, and a policy of identifying and regulating conglomerates was adopted during recent years. The operations of overseas NRI corporate bodies as a distinct category were banned in view of their opacity, and concerns were expressed about not only the quantity, but also the quality of such cross-border flows. In brief, the regulatory framework in India did not exhibit many of the weaknesses that are adduced as reasons for the current global crisis.

Despite the policies described above, which should not have allowed any crisis in India, why and how did the global crisis hit the Indian economy? It is essential to explore the reasons behind the phenomenon. It should be noted that India's integration with the global economy contributed noticeably to India's accelerated growth while the global economy was prospering. Hence, it is logical that India would feel the impact of adverse developments in the global economy. From this perspective, the issue is whether a calibrated policy of gradual integration with the global economy reduced or minimised the transmission of such risks to India, and whether domestic policies contributed adversely to global stability.

India is not prominent in the debate on the contribution to global imbalances for four important reasons. First, domestic savings and investments have been broadly in balance, with only marginal deficits. Second, the domestic demand has been leading growth, thus avoiding a possible collapse in aggregate demand due to global developments. Third, the policy has in recent years strengthened the efficiency and resilience of the financial sector, especially banking institutions. Fourth, the infrastructure and trade practices in financial markets were considerably strengthened as a process of gradual deregulation was undertaken. Hence, global factors are primarily responsible for the impact the crisis had on India, while domestic factors did lend some defence against the distress arising from the global factors. The transmission of the global crisis to India has to be viewed in terms of the pace, extent and the nature of its integration with the global economy, on account of trade and finance. With regard to the trade channel, the slump in export demand is very important, although one should not ignore the relief to the economy gained from corrections in commodity prices, especially oil. With regard to invisibles, India is relatively a large net earner of forex, and hence some impact on the export of services or the level of inward remittances is to be expected. It must be noted that with regard to the export of goods, India has relatively diversified the trade basket, while remittances also flow from both the developed and the developing economies. Diversified trade and diverse sources of workers' remittances are not very helpful in moderating the impact when the collapse in demand happens to be universal. The externally-induced slump in export demand affects not only the export sector, but also related domestic activity, and thus has the effect of dampening the overall economic activity.

With regard to the finance channel, it is useful to consider both markets and institutions. Equity markets were affected due to the withdrawal of liquidity by FIIs. The domestic bond markets were affected marginally, since the government securities market and the corporate bond markets were not significantly opened up. They were, however, affected indirectly, since the drying up of bond and credit markets globally made corporates substitute overseas funds with domestic funds. Cumulatively, these impacted the forex markets, warranting the use of forex reserves and the management of liquidity in money markets. It is also important to recognise that there could have been disruption in the availability of trade finance, in view of the virtual temporary collapse of banking in other economies. The domestic credit markets were affected due to the reluctance of banks to lend and the reluctance of borrowers to borrow, because of the considerable uncertainties in the level of economic activity. As regards financial institutions, their direct exposure to global financial markets has been somewhat limited. While the banking system continued to be resilient, there has been an indirect impact on some of the Non-Banking Financial Companies and Mutual Funds, which had significant exposures to highly appreciated domestic assets. The second-order effects of moderation in the real sector, especially export, real estate, and consumer demand on the level of NPAs in the banking system, should not be ignored.

Can the slowdown in real economic activity be attributed solely to the global crisis? It is difficult to ignore the possible domestic factors that could have in any case caused some slowdown in real activity. For example, it is difficult to establish that the growth in physical infrastructure or its quality in recent years has matched the growth in aggregate output, and that hence, autonomous moderation in growth momentum could have taken place quite apart from global influences. It was difficult to sustain the continuing and very high growth in the profitability of corporates, especially large corporates with cross-border presence or linkages, by the growth in the real economy. With respect to some large corporates, the non-operating income was large due to changes in the valuation of forex liabilities and treasury operations, and these were in any case expected to moderate over a period. It is therefore possible to argue that the global forces that dampened the domestic economic activity were to some extent coterminous with a possible downturn in the domestic economic cycle.

WHAT HAVE BEEN THE POLICY RESPONSES TO THE CRISIS?

The initial reaction to the crisis came from select central banks of advanced economies, particularly the US, the Euro, the UK, Switzerland and Japan. The response was in terms of providing liquidity (assured liquidity for an extended period and an expanded menu of collaterals for central bank funding, etc.) through coordinated action. It soon became evident that there might be several issues of insolvency in the process of restoring normalcy in the functioning of financial markets. Globally significant financial intermediaries lost confidence in each other. Hence, bail out of some of such financial intermediaries became necessary to restore confidence in each other and in the financial system. Refusal to bail out one of the large entities added to the panic. The fiscal implications of large-scale and unprecedented operations of central banks in these advanced economies to revive markets warranted close coordination between fiscal authorities and central banks. There has also been unprecedented growth in the balance sheets of central banks, along with an increase in the riskiness of their assets involving potential fiscal costs. Hence, finance ministries dominated the process of decision-making, although central banks continued to be the front line of defence and often the public face of recovery plans. In fact, the magnitude and nature of the responses of monetary authorities have increasingly blurred the distinction between monetary and fiscal stimulus.

The evolution of the financial crisis into an economic crisis was soon followed by a threat of social unrest. At the same time, the inadequacy of the prevailing arrangements in the global financial architecture came to the fore, while some emerging and developing countries approached the IMF and the World Bank for resources. The global dimensions of the crisis have so far triggered two meetings of the G-20 leading economies that account for over 70 per cent of the global population, income, trade, wealth and financial sector. The membership of G-20 comprises finance ministers and chiefs of central banks of the twenty countries, including the EU. The G-20 met at the level of Heads of Government in November 2008. Several actions as per the Washington Action Plan at the national level, encompassing fiscal, monetary, regulatory and governance issues, were broadly agreed upon. Some actions with regard to multilateral bodies were also recommended. Most countries took simultaneous action on several fronts broadly consistent with the consensus, but with varying emphasis on different components. Protectionism in both trade and finance persisted, especially in advanced economies. As mentioned above, the Heads of Government of G-20 (since expanded to include two more countries) met again in London on 2 April 2009 to review the actions taken and chart out further actions at the national level.

The actions taken thus far are in five broad areas. First, central banks in most countries are reducing policy interest rates and injecting ample liquidity. Second, the central banks are willing to intervene in all financial markets and in almost all products, liquid or not, toxic or otherwise, and domestic or foreign currency. Thus, the central banks and governments have been injecting capital to financial intermediaries, lending to such intermediaries, nationalising banks, providing blanket insurance to depositors, and on the whole closely interacting with financial intermediaries to avoid large-scale insolvency and loss of confidence, and restoring normality, especially in credit markets. Fourth, fiscal stimulus has also been provided, albeit in different degrees, through expenditures in terms of support to financial sector and subsidies, reduction in revenues through tax rebates, etc., and guarantees on a large scale. Close interactions between governments and market participants and discretionary fiscal dispensations are being resorted to. Fifth, other related measures to restore confidence are being undertaken, and these are quite varied—ranging from protectionism to changing prudential or accounting standards, or launching innovative ad-hoc institutional structures with an underlying public-private partnership. Sixth, the lendable resources of the IMF have been increased significantly to enable it to provide assistance to the needy developing countries affected by the crisis.

The IMF has responded with a new set of conditionality and credit facilities as appropriate to resolve the ongoing crisis. Finally, it is essential to recognise that while the policy responses of each country were varied, most of the responses have been along the lines described above.

Several issues have been debated with regard to the various policy responses, and these may be summarised as follows:

i. The initiatives taken by national authorities, especially in advanced and systemically important economies such as the US, to revive the domestic economy may have consequences for other countries. These externalities could be positive or negative. Furthermore, while concerted and coordinated action may be needed, the extent of the fiscal or monetary stimulus and the measures differ across countries, based on the public policy preferences of the time at the national level, as warranted by country-specific circumstances. Thus, issues of adequacy and the appropriateness of actions of individual economies in a global context remain while considering the appropriate global response. A large number of countries feel left out in the process of multilateral initiatives on managing the crisis for want of representation in the G-20 initiatives. The fundamental issue of adequacy of policy space, particularly for developing economies, in a globalising world dominated by a few advanced economies and with one economy's currency being the global reserve currency, are very complex and are naturally yet to be addressed. More generally, policy autonomy is needed for national authorities in view of the externalities of the financial sector, and such autonomy has to be reconciled with the global obligations warranted by the rapid globalisation of the financial sector.

ii. The London Summit G-20 communiqué includes a commitment to refrain from raising new barriers to investment or trade in goods and services. In practice, however, this restricts the freedom of the developing countries more than that of the advanced economies. Developing countries have considerable scope to increase their applied tariffs under the WTO regime, since they are lower than the committed tariffs in many cases. The communiqué also commits support for the WTO Doha Round without recognising the fact that some of the proposals on the table are based on the further liberalisation of financial services. The lessons from the crisis with regard to the risks in further liberalising financial services have thus not been taken into account.

iii. Subsidisation of commercial and financial activity in advanced economies in this context places developing economies at a disadvantage, since they cannot subsidise their industry in view of the limited resources available. Thus, the recapitalised entities in advanced economies could undermine the level playing field in global competition. Several Free Trade Agreements have binding provisions among contracting parties on matters relating to cross-border investments, and hence the issue of a level playing field assumes special significance. Indeed, in view of the lessons learnt from the crisis, the provisions relating to financial services in Free Trade Agreements may have to be reviewed.

iv. There are medium-term implications of the short-term actions taken to ensure recovery. In particular, the fiscal stimulus involving a huge debt or contingent liability for the government could have an inflationary potential. In brief, the fiscal sustainability of current actions should be constantly assessed, in terms of their implications for both the national economy and global balances. For example, if significant fiscal stimulus is undertaken by countries which have large fiscal and current account deficits, there could be a cumulative impact. Such an impact may aggravate the existing macroeconomic imbalances over the medium term. Pump priming in general is appropriate if the crisis were only of a cyclical nature; however, if it turns out to be a structural crisis, pump priming may aggravate the misallocation of resources. In any case, pump priming by itself may have the effect of postponing, if not undermining, the required structural changes.

v. The mix of fiscal and monetary measures would depend on several factors, and there could be a temptation to place a disproportionate burden on the central banks. The possible threat to price stability on account of current activity has to be reckoned, and expectations of future actions carefully modulated. Under some circumstances, monetary measures may themselves have an inflationary potential for the future, and could, beyond a point, induce a liquidity trap. A liquidity trap generally implies that the expansion of base money by monetary authorities ceases to have the desired multiplier effect, thus rendering the easy monetary policy significantly ineffective for a prolonged period.

vi. The bail-out strategies may create moral hazards, although during extreme distress moral hazard should not be a compelling consideration. Furthermore, the conditions attached to bail outs are critical, both for achieving the intended purpose and for mobilising public opinion in favour of such bail outs. It is also essential to ensure that the bail out serves the main purpose of restoring normality in the financial sector, and does not merely serve the interests of the management, shareholders and bond holders of the institution concerned. There may be issues about the wisdom of utilising some elements of the financial sector to restore normality, if such elements are perceived as the so-called 'greedy' elements or 'toxic wastes' that caused the problem in the first instance.

vii. In a crisis scenario, public policy generally acquires a larger policy space and greater discretion to manage the crisis and restore normality. Not only should such discretion be given up once the recovery commences, but participants in the financial sector should also cooperate in establishing new rules of the game. This would indeed be the 'exit' problem, and the issue is whether attention is being paid to an 'exit' strategy while undertaking the actions aimed at restoring normality in a crisis situation. In other words, the danger of a build-up of vested interests in carrying out the measures taken for crisis management should not be ruled out.

WHAT HAS BEEN THE POLICY RESPONSE IN INDIA?

The monetary measures included a reduction in policy rates, reduction in the bank reserves to be deposited with the central bank, and the liberalisation of refinance facilities. Some measures uniquely appropriate to Indian conditions were also undertaken, such as the rupee-US dollar currency swap window for banks, refinance to apex institutions catering to small industries, export and housing, and refinance to banks' lending to mutual funds and non-banking financial companies. In addition, a special arrangement was also made for the non-banking financial companies under stress, whereby liquidity support is provided by the RBI, but the solvency risk is borne by the government. In responding to the stress in financial markets, the RBI had the ability to provide foreign currency from reserves and manage liquidity in money markets through the multiple instruments originally designed to manage volatility in capital inflows. The policy with regard to access to external commercial borrowings, which had emerged as an active instrument for management of capital flows, was relaxed in a counter-cyclical move after the flows started reversing. In fact, the position was more than reversed to one that had existed before the tightening process had started. A small window was opened for NBFCs to avail of foreign currency borrowing from multilateral financial institutions and government-owned development financial institutions. Corporates were allowed the flexibility to buy back the Foreign Currency Convertible Bonds (FCCBs) earlier issued by them.

The response of the Indian authorities has been along predictable lines. The central government invoked the emergency provisions of the FRBM Act to seek relaxation from fiscal targets, and launched fiscal stimulus packages from December 2008. These fiscal stimulus packages included additional public spending, government guaranteed funds for infrastructure spending, cuts in indirect taxes, expanded guarantee cover for credit to micro and small enterprises, and additional support to exporters. These packages came on top of an already announced expanded safety net for the rural poor, a farm loan waiver package, and salary increases for government staff, all of which were expected to have stimulated demand.

With respect to prudential measures, India had acquired considerable policy scope, since counter-cyclical measures had already been put in place during the period of excessive growth in credit. Recognising that the sudden and significant turn of events could impair assets down the line, counter-cyclical measures such as higher risk weights and provisioning requirements for certain sectors witnessing very high credit growth, which had been put in place in 2006, were restored to their original levels. In order to preserve the economic and productive value of the assets affected by the sudden and sharp deterioration in external conditions, banks were asked to take action for the quick detection of weaknesses and a careful assessment of viability, and put in place, in a time-bound manner, restructuring packages for viable accounts. As a precaution, it was emphasised that the basic objective of restructuring is to preserve the economic value of units, not the ever-greening of problem accounts. Other measures include relaxation in accounting standards, in relation to the foreign currency obligations of corporates.

WHAT IS THE AGENDA FOR REFORMS?

In view of the intensity and spread of the crisis, there is a wide spread and deep interest in undertaking reforms, especially in the financial sector, that would minimise the prospects of such crises in the future, and equip the global community as well as national authorities to manage future threats to financial stability. The academic work on the subject is already extensive, and takes into account the historical background as also the unique features of the current crisis. Multilateral institutions such as the UN, UNCTAD, World Bank, IMF, regional development banks, ILO, OECD, etc., have reported extensively on the implications of the crisis, the immediate response needed, and the reforms that appear appropriate. Ad hoc groups have been constituted by several authorities to render advice on specific issues. In the US, the UK and the Euro area, national authorities, including parliamentary bodies, are making extensive enquiries and proposing comprehensive reforms. Of these, two initiatives are of particular importance. G-20 initiatives represent a consensus at the level of select governments on the various reforms that are appropriate. These are of considerable operational significance. The draft report of the Commission of Experts of the President of General Assembly on Reforms of International Monetary and Financial System is more comprehensive, and tries to combine measures that are both desirable and feasible. It has the added benefit of inputs from all member countries of the United Nations, and does not suffer from the problem of defending any particular legacy. The Commission has wide representation from policymakers and academicians from different parts of the world.

The set of reforms proposed by all these bodies can be divided into three broad areas, viz., macro-aspects, financial sectors and global issues. With regard to macro-aspects, serious attention had been paid to reviewing and rebalancing competing considerations in public policy. In the financial sector, there is an impressive agreement on the fundamental directions in which reforms are needed. Essentially, it is a review of a philosophy of deregulation in favour of redesigned regulation. On issues relating to global economy, considerable complexities remain, although the main issues have been flagged for discussion and further consideration.

At the macro level, a fundamental review of the role of the state vis-à-vis the market is underway. It is recognised that in the recent past, market failures have been underestimated. There is no longer a presumption that the markets are always right. The mainstream opinion is in favour of continuing with market orientation with a greater role for governments. Furthermore, the realistic roles of the real and financial sectors are being revisited. There is an increasing recognition that the financial sector, though critical for a modern economy, is only a means to an end, and that while the financial sector enables growth, it may not necessarily lead to or sustain growth. This is more akin to the classical view which states that money or finance is only a veil, and that what matter significantly are the real forces operating in the economy.

The adverse consequences of inequalities in income and wealth are better recognised, and the stabilising role of social security measures better appreciated. The confining of the role of monetary policy to inflation targeting is questioned, although the importance of both price stability and financial stability is recognised. Finally, there are great concerns with regard to governance in both public and private sectors.

As regards the financial sector, there is a reasonable convergence on the fundamental directions in which regulatory reform has to take place. There are, however, differences with regard to the extent to which regulation should be tightened and the extent to which global regulation should take precedence over the national-level regulation. There is better recognition of the importance of the stability of the commercial banking system relative to other financial institutions. It is generally recognised that regulation should be counter-cyclical, comprehensive, system-oriented and conscious of liquidity considerations. There is less explicit recognition of the dangers to counter-cyclical regulation, since counter-cyclical regulation should not mean dropping regulatory standards below the desirable norm. While financial innovations may add to efficiency, it is noted that all innovations may not be good for the system, and hence regulators have to carefully maintain the appropriate balance between the safety and usefulness of innovations in the financial sector. Issues of conflict of interests, transparency and governance in all institutions relevant to the financial sector have gained great prominence. The importance of host regulators compared to home regulators is being recognised. The possibility of modifying accounting standards to reduce pro-cyclicality is being debated. Moreover, a developmental focus is sought to be given to the financial sector, in the sense that financial inclusion and other socially desirable objectives should not be ignored in the search for efficiency and stability in the financial sector. The role played by central banks in the financial sector is being reviewed in order to strengthen their authority to discharge the mandate for maintaining financial stability.

The deficiencies in the current global monetary system and global financial architecture have been noted. An important source of the crisis is thought to be macroeconomic imbalances, which is a consequence of the current arrangements making the US dollar the reserve currency. While there is considerable interest in moving to a more stable and yet flexible, while being universally acceptable, reserve currency, there has been no serious formal consideration of this matter in policy circles. While this may reflect the reality of how complex the problem is, and the difficulties in the transition from current arrangements, there is a concern in some circles that perpetuating the existing arrangements may give rise to a crisis again in the future. There is greater recognition of the importance of cooperation at regional levels and bilateral swap arrangements among central banks. The importance of even handed surveillance of the external sector, and the financial and broader economic policies and practices of national governments is conceded, but no practical steps are forthcoming. There is better appreciation of the need for capital account management, especially during difficult times. The risk of globalisation of the financial sector relative to trade has been noted in many circles. There is a greater sensitivity to the problems arising from tax havens and the prevalence of bank secrecy in some jurisdictions.

As regards international financial institutions, the Financial Stability Forum has been expanded into the Financial Stability Board with a more formal mandate on all matters relating to global financial stability. It is not clear, however, whether this would make it any more effective than the Financial Stability Forum in predicting or managing crisis. The deficiency in governance arrangements in International Financial Institutions has been conceded, and the need for corrective actions accepted. Immediate prospects for a significant change are, however, not apparent, though the beginning of a reform is indicated with regard to the IMF and the World Bank. In the meantime, they have been authorised to operate with additional borrowed funds, and possibly IMF-created global liquidity in the near future. Above all, the fundamental issue of policy space needed for national authorities to maintain stability and strengthen globally binding arrangements is yet to be satisfactorily resolved. In particular, developing economies are left with a perception that they have no policy space to withstand the adverse consequences of globally transmitted problems.

There are some structural and fundamental issues being debated, and there is merit in addressing some of them, even as policies are designed to ensure recovery of the economy and bring about institutional reforms. At one end of the spectrum is the contention by a few that this crisis represents the end of capitalism, while most others feel that this is only a problem of policy mistakes and market failures, both of which can be fixed by the reforms under consideration. While a few argue that this is the end of globalisation, most others feel that open trade and investment policies globally should still be the goal. While this may not be the end of financial globalisation, there is considerable discomfort with the financial globalisation and deregulation. The relevance of policy space for national regulations, and indeed of development finance, is being revisited. On the issue of a regime of global regulation or global coordination of regulatory regimes, lessons need to be drawn from the experience of the Euro area. The multiple fiscal authorities and single monetary authority, viz., the European Central Bank (ECB), has led to severe problems of coordination. In the global environment, there are multiple fiscal and multiple monetary/regulatory authorities that would make significant coordination extremely difficult. Further, the issue of multiple versus a single regulator at the national level remains by and large unresolved.

As explained above, several factors of a policy and structural nature have contributed to this crisis, whose full contours remain to be known. Several policy initiatives have been taken by all the countries to manage the crisis. An international consensus, however weak and broad, is now available for the most part of the immediate course of action. The beginning of 2009 represents a watershed in the process of cooperation at the global level on policy issues relating to the globalisation of finance. A new journey has been initiated. It can only be hoped that the difficult journey will gather strength, and that all sustained efforts will be made not only to ensure recovery, but also to address some of the structural issues that the global crisis has revealed.

WHAT IS THE POSSIBLE IMPACT OF THE GLOBAL CRISIS ON INDIA?

At the time of writing this Epilogue, the consequences of the global crisis are being felt in all economies, and the duration as well as the severity of the impact is still uncertain in the rest of the world. Similarly, the policy measures taken in India are yet to fully impact the economy. Hence, the narrative is confined to some significant factors that would determine the overall impact of the crisis on India.

First, the banking system as a whole remains reasonably strong, and is fairly well-poised to generally withstand a possible impairment of their asset quality due to a slowdown in the real economy, and the bursting of asset bubbles. Empirical evidence indicates that resolving a banking crisis takes longer, say two to three years, and is often very burdensome on the tax payer.

Second, the financial markets have shown considerable resilience, and stress has been confined to frictional liquidity for a temporary period. The RBI has at its command multiple instruments, which it has been deploying as and when necessary. The financial markets draw comfort from the commitment of the RBI to moderate excess volatility. This should facilitate recovery in India.

Third, except for a few large corporates with close linkages with non-banking financial companies and mutual funds, other corporates and most households are not excessively leveraged. The balance sheet of the government has insignificant foreign currency exposures, and most of its debt is at fixed rate. Overall, the balance sheets of households, corporate and financial intermediaries are not excessively vulnerable.

Fourth, the external sector derives comfort from the level of reserves and manageable current account deficit, even after the slump in exports and remittances. The strong domestic demand makes India fairly resilient. Moreover, a large part of volatile portfolio flows may have already exited from India.

Fifth, the slowdown is affecting vulnerable workers, particularly in the construction sector. Among the most adversely affected are export-intensive sectors like gem and jewellery, ready-made garments, textiles and ancillaries. More generally, small and medium industries are adversely affected whenever there is a stress in the financial and real sectors. However, depending on the adequacy of sectoral reliefs and stimulus, there may be some relief. There are some safety networks which may mitigate to some extent the serious effect on the unemployment and underemployment that arose from the slowdown in the real sector.

In responding to the crisis, public policy is therefore able to draw on the strengths in the financial and external sectors, but it is essential to resist the temptation to excessively focus on measures recommended by the global fora and ignore the unique features of the Indian economy. While the financial sector and, to some extent the external sector, are sources of strength, financial markets assess the fiscal situation as weak. Moreover, fiscal stimulus, as already announced by the government, may take fiscal deficit as a per cent of GDP to double digits, while the public debt to GDP ratio in India is among the highest in the world. Bottlenecks in infrastructure continue to prevail, and supply management could be critical to the future path of inflation. While the headline inflation could be low, the relevant indicators for purposes of comparison with the policy stances of other economies should be consumer price indices. In this regard, there is a need to respect the underlying inflationary pressures that persist in India, while determining the magnitude of fiscal and monetary stimulus. The prevalence of administered interest rates add to the rigidities relating to the transmission mechanisms of monetary policy and limits the flexibility available for monetary policy.

In sum, there are some unique strengths and cognisable weaknesses that could determine the impact of the global crisis on India. Indeed, there is some anecdotal evidence to show that the ongoing global crisis has brought to light the resilience of the Indian economy, despite its vulnerabilities. For instance, in its issue dated 17 November 2007, *The Economist* ranked India along with Turkey and Hungary as the riskiest economies among select leading EMEs. The article states, *inter-alia,*

Those with current-account deficits are vulnerable to a sudden outflow of capital if global investors become more risk averse. Economies where inflation and credit growth are already high and budget deficits large, such as India, have less room to ease monetary or fiscal policy if the economy weakens (pp. 75-7).

In its issue dated 28 February 2009, India is rated low in financial vulnerability. India comes fourth, after China, Malaysia and Taiwan, in terms of being low in financial vulnerability (p. 75). While being less vulnerable to serious financial or external-sector problems, India is likely to continue to clock the second highest growth rates in the world.

Select Bibliography

Acharya, Shankar. 'Global Financial Crisis: Asian View', *Business Standard*, 12 February 2009, www.business-standard.com/india/news/shankar-acharya-global-financial-crisis-asian-view/348801 (accessed 17 April 2009).

_____. 'A Cloudy Outlook', *Business Standard*, March 2009, www.business-standard.com/india/news/shankar-acharya-cloudy-outlook/351430 (accessed 11 March 2009).

_____. 'Spring Fever', *Business Standard*, 9 April 2009.

Ahamed, Liaquat. *Lords of Finance: The Bankers Who Broke the World*, New York: Penguin, 2009.

Akerlof, George A. and Robert J. Shiller. *Animal Spirits: How Human Psychology Drives the Economy, and Why It Matters for Global Capitalism*, New Jersey: Princeton University Press, 2009.

Akyüz, Yilmaz. *The Management of Capital Flows and Financial Vulnerability in Asia* TWN Global Economy Series 13, Penang, Malaysia: Third World Network, 2009, http://www.twnside.org.sg/title2/ge/ge17.pdf.

Bank for International Settlements (BIS). *Annual Report*, 2007, www.bis.org/publ/arpdf/ar2007e.htm.

_____. *Annual Report*, 2008, www.bis.org/publ/arpdf/ar2008e.htm.

Bernanke, Ben S. 'The Crisis & the Policy Response', Stamp Lecture at the London School of Economics, London, January 2009,'http://www.bis.org/review/r090115a.pdf.

_____. 'Financial Reform to Address Systemic Risk', speech'at the Council on Foreign Relations, Washington D.C., March 2009, http://www.bis.org/review/r090313a.pdf.

_____. 'On AIG', Testimony before the Committee on Financial Services, US House of Representatives, Washington D.C., March 2009, http://www.bis.org/review/r090325a.pdf.

_____. 'The Financial Crisis and Community Banking', speech at the Independent Community Bankers of America's National Convention & Techworld, Phoenix, March 2009, http://www.bis.org/review/r090324a.pdf.

Bhagawati, Jagdish. 'The capital myths: The Difference between trade in widgets and dollars', *Foreign Affairs*, Vol. 77, May–June 1988.

Bookstaber, Richard. *A Demon of Our Own Design: Markets, Hedge Funds, and the Perils of Financial Innovation*, Hoboken, New Jersey: John Wiley & Sons, 2007.

Brunnermeirer, M. Andrew Crockett, Charles Goodhart, Avinash D. Persaud and Hyan Shin (eds). *The Fundamental Principles of Financial Regulation*, The ICMB-CEPR Geneva Report, Geneva: Centre for Economic Policy Research, 29 January 2009.

Buiter, W. 'Regulating the New Financial System' *Vox*, 9 March 2009, www.voxeu.org/index.php?q = node/3232

Chandrasekhar, C.P. 'India and World Economy', January 2008, http://www.networkideas.org/themes/world/jan2008/we25_World_Economy.htm.

_____. *Financial Liberalisation and the New Dynamics of Growth in India*, TWN Global Economy Series 13, Penang, Malaysia: Third World Network, 2009, http://www.twnside.org.sg/title2/ge/ge13.pdf.

Charlton, Andrew. 'Capital Market Liberalisation and Poverty', in'*Capital Market Liberalization and Development*, The Initiative for Policy Dialogue Series,'Joseph E. Stiglitz and Jose Antonio Ocampo (eds), New York: Oxford University Press, 2008.

Cohan, William D. *House of Cards: A Tale of Hubris and Wretched Excess on Wall Street*, New York: Random House, 2009.

Committee on Financial Sector Assessment. *India's Financial Sector: An Assessment*, Chairman, Rakesh Mohan, Mumbai, Reserve Bank of India, March 2009, www.rbi.org.in.

Corrigan E, Gerald. *The Credit Crisis: The Quest for Stability and Reform*, G-30 The William Taylor Memorial Lectures, 2008, http://www.group30.org/pubs/pub_1452.htm.

Das, Satyajit. *Traders Guns & Money: Knowns and Unknowns in the Dazzling World of Derivatives*, London: Prentice Hall, 2006.

'Dizzy in Boomtown', *The Economist*, 17 November 2007, pp. 75–77.

Dodd, Randall. 'Consequences of Liberalising Derivatives Markets', in'*Capital Market Liberalization and Development*, The Initiative for Policy Dialogue Series,'Joseph E. Stiglitz and Jose Antonio Ocampo (eds), New York: Oxford University Press, 2008.

'Domino Theory', *The Economist*, 28 February 2009, p. 75.

Draghi, Mario. 'Fact-finding on issues affecting the Banking & Financial System', testimony before the Financial Committee of the Chamber of Deputies, Rome, March 2009, http://www.bis.org/review/r090330b.pdf.

_____. 'The Global Recession', speech at the 15th Congress of the AIAF-ASSIOM-ATIC Forex, Milan, February 2009, http://www.bis.org/review/r090226b.pdf.

Eichengreen, Barry and Richard Baldwin. *What G20 Leaders must do to stabilize our economy and fix our financial system*, Centre for Economic Policy Research, 2008. •

Eichengreen, Barry. 'Should there be a coordinated response to the problem of global imbalances? Can there be one?' DESA Working Paper No. 69, September 2008, http://www.un.org/esa/des/papers.

Ellis, Charles D. *The Partnership: The Making of Goldman Sachs*, New York: Penguin, 2008.

Epstein, Gerald, Ilene Grabel and K. S. Jomo, 'Capital Management Techniques in Developing Countries: Managing Capital Flows in Malaysia, India, and China', in *Capital Market Liberalization and Development*, The Initiative for Policy Dialogue Series, Joseph E. Stiglitz and Jose Antonio Ocampo (eds), New York: Oxford University Press, 2008.

European Parliament. *Financial Supervision and Crisis Management in the EU*, Economic and Scientific Policy, European Union Policy Department (IP/A/ECON/IC/2007–069).

Feldstein, Martin S. 'Rethinking the Role of Fiscal Policy', NBER Working Paper No. 14684, 2009.

Financial Services Authority, *A Regulatory Response to the Global Banking Crisis*, Turner Lord Adair, Discussion Paper 09/2, March 2009, http://www.fsa.gov.uk/pubs/discussion/dp09_02.pdf.

Frenkel, Roberto. 'From the Boom in Capital Inflows to Financial Traps', in *Capital Market Liberalization and Development*, The Initiative for Policy Dialogue Series, Joseph E. Stiglitz and Jose Antonio Ocampo (eds), New York: Oxford University Press, 2008.

Frost, Ellen L. 'India's Role in East Asia: Lesson from Cultural and Historical Linkages', RIS Discussion papers, 2009, www.newasiaforum.org.

G-20 Working Group 1. *Report on Enhancing Sound Regulation & Strengthening Transparency*, Chairman, Rakesh Mohan, Mumbai: Reserve Bank of India, April 2009, www.rbi.org.in.

_____. 'Declaration on delivering resources through international

Financial institutions', 2 April 2009, www.g20.org.pub_communiques. aspx.

————. 'Declaration on strengthening the financial system', 2 April 2009, http://g20.org/Documents/Fin_Deps_Fin_Reg_Annex_020409_-_1615_final.pdf.

————. 'Progress report on the actions of the Washington action plan', 2 April 2009, http://g20.org/Documents/Final_Annex_On_Action_Plan.pdf.

————. 'The Global Plan for Recovery and Reform', Leaders' statement, 2 April 2009, http://g20.org/Documents/final-communique.pdf.

G-30, Financial Regulatory Systems Working Group, *The Structure of Financial Supervision: Approaches and Challenges in a Global Marketplace*, 2008, http://www.group30.org/pubs/pub_1428.htm.

Geneva Reports on the World Economy 11, *The Fundamental Principles of Financial Regulation,* January 2009, http://www.voxeu.org/index.php?q=node/2796.

Goldestein, Morris. 'Addressing the Financial Crisis', speech presented at a Peterson Institute, 7 October 2008.

Gopinath, Shyamala. 'Some Reflections on the Recent Global Financial Turmoil: An Indian Perspective', speech delivered at Annual Conference of FEDAI, Kolkata, 10 January 2009.

Griffith-Jones, Stepheny and Avinash Persaud. 'The Pro-Cyclical Impact of Basel II on Emerging Markets and its Political Economy', in *Capital Market Liberalization and Development*, The Initiative for Policy Dialogue Series, Joseph E. Stiglitz and Jose Antonio Ocampo (eds), New York: Oxford University Press, 2008.

Guillén, Mauro F. 'The global economic and financial crisis: A timeline', The Lauder Institute, University of Pennsylvania, March 2009, http://lauder.wharton.upenn.edu/pdf/Chronology (accessed 9 March 2009).

ICRA Journal on Money and Finance. *Economic Assessment and Outlook*, March 2009, www.icraratings.com.

Institute of International Financial. *Final Report of IIF Committee on Market Best Practices: Principles of Conduct and Best Practice Recommendations*, Washington D.C. July 2008.

International Monetary Fund. *'The recent Financial Turmoil'—Initial Assessment, Policy Lessons, and Implications for Fund Surveillance*, Washington D.C. April 2008, www.imf.org/external/np/sec/pr/2008/pr0878/htm.

Jayadev, Arjun and Anush Kapadia, 'When the facts change: How can the financial crisis change minds?' *Economic & Political Weekly*, March 2009, www.epw.in/epw/uploads/articles/13359.pdf,

Khor, Martin. 'Statement at the UN General Assembly Extraordinary Thematic Dialogue on the World Financial and Economic Crisis and its impact on developments', New York: South Centre, 25 March, 2009, www.southcentre.org.

Khor, Martin. 'The Malaysian Experience in Financial-Economic Crisis Management: An Alternative to the IMF-style Approach', in *Capital Market Liberalization and Development*, The Initiative for Policy Dialogue Series, Joseph E. Stiglitz and Jose Antonio Ocampo (eds), New York: Oxford University Press, 2008.

Kindleberger, Charles P. and Robert Aliber, *Manias, Panics, and Crashes: A History of Financial Crisis*, Fifth Edition, Hoboken, New Jersey: John Wiley & Sons, 2005.

Krugman, Paul. 'The Market Mystique', *The New York Times*, 26 March 2009.

Kumar, Rajiv, Mathew Joseph, Dony Alex, Pankaj Vashisht and Debosree Banerjee, 'Indian Economic Outlook 2008–09 and 2009–10', Indian Council for Research on International Economic Relations (ICRIER), Working Paper No.234, March 2009, http://www.icrier.org/publications/working_papers_234.html,

Ludwig, Eugene A. 'Lessons Learned from the 2008 Financial Crisis', G-30, The William Taylor Memorial Lectures, March 2009, http://www.group30.org/pubs/pub_1444.htm.

Mason, Paul. 'Has the bubble finally burst for capitalism', *The Sunday Times: Business*, 12 April 2009.

Mohan, Rakesh. 'Global Financial Crisis & Key Risks- Impact on India & Asia', Remarks at the IMF-FSF High Level meeting on the Recent Financial Turmoil & Policy Responses, Washington, October 2008, www.rbi.org.in.

————. 'Financial Globalisation and Emerging Markets Capital Flows', BIS Working Paper No.44, December 2008, www.bis.org/publ/bppdf/bispap44.htm.

Mohanty, M.S. and P. Turner. 'Foreign exchange reserve accumulation in emerging markets: What are the domestic implications?' *BIS Quarterly Review*, September 2006.

Nachane, Dilip M. 'The fate of India unincorporated', *Economic & Political Weekly*, March 2009, www.epw.in/epw/uploads/articles/13352.pdf.

Ocampo, Jose Antonio and Rob Vos (eds). *Uneven Economic Development*, London: Zed Books, 2008.

Ocampo, Jose Antonio and Jose Gabriel Palma, 'The Role of Preventive Capital Account Regulations', in *Capital Market Liberalization and Development*, The Initiative for Policy Dialogue Series, Joseph E. Stiglitz and Jose Antonio Ocampo (eds), New York: Oxford University Press, 2008.

Ocampo, Jose Antonio and Joseph E. Stiglitz, 'Capital Market Liberalisation and Development', in *Capital Market Liberalization and Development*, The Initiative for Policy Dialogue Series, Joseph E. Stiglitz and Jose Antonio Ocampo (eds), New York: Oxford University Press, 2008.

Organisation for Economic Cooperation & Development (OECD). *OECD Strategic Response to the Financial and Economic Crisis*, December 2008, www.oecd.org/dataoecd/33/57/42061463.pdf.

Persaud, Avinash D. 'Causes, Cures and Myths', *Economic & Political Weekly*, March 2009, www.epw.in/epw/uploads/articles/13345.pdf.

Philippon, Thomas and Ariell Reshef. 'Wages and Human Capital in the US Financial Industry: 1999–2006', NBER Working Paper No. 14644, 2009.

Rakshit, Mihir. 'India Amidst the Global Crisis', *Economic & Political Weekly*, March 2009, www.epw.in/epw/uploads/articles/13350.pdf.

Ram Mohan, T.T. 'The Impact of the Crisis on the Indian Economy', *Economic & Political Weekly*, March 2009, www.epw.in/epw/uploads/articles/13351.pdf.

Reinhart, Carmen and Kenneth Rogoff. 'Banking Crisis: An Equal Opportunity Menace', National Bureau of Economic Research (NBER) Working Paper No 14587, December 2008.

Rojas-Saurez, Liliana. 'Domestic Financial Regulations in Developing Countries: Can They Effectively Limit the Impact of Capital Account Volatility?' in *Capital Market Liberalization and Development*, The Initiative for Policy Dialogue Series, Joseph E. Stiglitz and Jose Antonio Ocampo (eds), New York: Oxford University Press, 2008.

Schmukler, Sergio L. 'The Benefits and Risks of Financial Globalisation', in *Capital Market Liberalization and Development*, The Initiative for Policy Dialogue Series, Joseph E. Stiglitz and Jose Antonio Ocampo (eds), New York: Oxford University Press, 2008.

Schneider, Benu. 'Do Global Standards and Codes Prevent Financial Crises?', in *Capital Market Liberalization and Development*, The Initiative for Policy Dialogue Series, Joseph E. Stiglitz and Jose Antonio Ocampo (eds), New York: Oxford University Press, 2008.

Sheng, Andrew. 'From Asian to Global Financial Crisis', Third Lall Memorial Lecture, New Delhi, February 2009, www.icrier.res.in and www.andrewsheng.com.

Sheng, Andrew. 'The First Network Crisis of the 21st Century: A Regulatory Post-Mortem', *Economic & Political Weekly*, March 2009, www.epw.in/epw/uploads/articles/13347.pdf.

Shiller, J. Robert. *The Sub-prime Solution*, New Jersey: Princeton University Press, 2008.

Soros, George. 'Peripheral care should be the central concern', *The Financial Times*, 22 March 2009, http://www.georgesoros.com/articles-essays/entry/peripheral_care_should_be_the_central_concern.

Stiglitz, Joseph E. *Making Globalization Work*, New York: W.W. Norton & Company, 2006.

Stiglitz, Joseph E. and Jose Antonio Ocampo (eds), *Capital Market Liberalization and Development*, New York: Oxford University Press, 2008.

Stiglitz, Joseph E. 'Capital Market Liberalisation, Globalisation, and the IMF', in *Capital Market Liberalization and Development*, The Initiative for Policy Dialogue Series, Joseph E. Stiglitz and Jose Antonio Ocampo (eds), New York: Oxford University Press, 2008.

Stiglitz, Joseph E., Jose Antonio Ocampo, Shari Spiegel, Ricardo Efrench-Davis and Deepak Nayyar (eds), *Stability with Growth, Macroeconomics, Liberalisation, and Development*, The Initiative for Policy Dialogue Series, New York: Oxford University Press, 2006.

Subbarao, D. 'Impact of the global financial crisis on India collateral damage and response', *RBI Bulletin*, March 2009, www.rbi.org.in.

Subramanian, Arvind and John Williamson, 'The world crisis: Reforms to prevent a recurrence', *Economic & Political Weekly*, March 2009, www.epw.in/epw/uploads/articles/13344.pdf.

The de Larosiere Group, *Report the High Level Group on Financial Supervision in the EU*, Chaired by Jacques de Larosière, February 2009, www.ec.europa.eu/internal_market/finances/docs/de_larosiere_report_en.pdf.

The United States Government Accountability Office (GAO). *A Framework for Crafting and Assessing Proposals to Modernise the Outdated U.S. Financial Regulatory System*, January 2009.

The US Congressional Panel. *Modernising the American Financial Regulatory System: Recommendations for Improving Oversight, Protecting Consumers, and Ensuring Stability*, Special Report on Regulatory Reform, January 2009.

Trichet, Jean-Claude. 'Underpricing of Risk in Financial Sector', speech at the Coface Country Risk Conference, Paris, January 2009, http://www.bis.org/review/r090122a.pdf.

_____. 'Macro-economic Policy: Imbalances and the need to avoid going back to the status quo ante', address at the Annual Joint Parliamentary Meeting, European Parliament, February 2009, http://www.bis.org/review/r090218a.pdf.

_____. 'What Lessons can be Learned from the Economic and Financial Crisis', speech at the 5e Rencontres de l'Entreprise Europeenne, Paris, March 2009, http://www.bis.org/review/r090318b.pdf,

United Nations Conference on Trade and Development. *Trade and Developments Report*, various issues, Geneva: United Nations.

_____. Andrew Cornford, *Introduction of Basel 2: The Current State of Play*, Geneva, 17–19 March 2009, http://www.unctad.org/sections/wcmu/docs/c1mem3p13_en.pdf.

_____. *Basel 2 Agenda for 2009 Progress so far*, Geneva, 17–19 March 2009, http://www.unctad.org/sections/wcmu/docs/c1mem3p12_en.pdf.

_____. *Basel 2 and Banking in Emerging and other Developing Economies*, Geneva, 17–19 March 2009, http://www.unctad.org/sections/wcmu/docs/c1mem3p14_en.pdf.

_____. *On Risk, Rescue and Hazards: The Global Crisis*, Geneva, 17–19 March 2009, http://www.unctad.org/sections/wcmu/docs/c1mem3p18_en.pdf.

_____. *Sources and Symptoms of the Financial Crisis: The Aftermath of a Balloon Journey*, Geneva, 17–19 March 2009, http://www.unctad.org/sections/wcmu/docs/c1mem3p15_en.pdf.

United Nations General Assembly. 'Recommendation of the Commission of Experts of the President of General Assembly on Reforms of the International Monetary & Financial System', http://www.un.org/ga/president/63/commission/financial_commission.shtml (accessed 19 March 2009).

Venugopal Reddy, Y. *Monetary and Financial Sector Reforms in India: A Central Bankers Perspective*, New Delhi: UBSPD, 2000.

_____. *Lectures on Economic and Financial Sector Reforms in India*, New Delhi: Oxford University Press, 2002.

_____. *Economic Policy in India: Managing Change*, New Delhi: UBSPD, 2003.

Williamson, J. 'The Management of Capital Inflows', *Pensamiento Iberoamericano*, January–June 1995, available at the Peterson Institute for International Economics, www.iie.com/publications/papers/williamson0195.htm.

Working Group on Financial Reforms. *Financial Reform: A Framework for Financial Stability*, Washington: Group of Thirty, http://www.group30.org/pubs/reformreport.pdf.

Yongding, Yu. *The Management of Cross-Border Capital Flows and Macro-Economic Stability in China*, TWN Global Economy Series 14, Penang, Malaysia: Third World Network, 2009, http://www.twnside.org.sg/title2/ge/ge14.pdf.

Yu, Y. D. 'Managing Capital Flows: The case of the People's Republic of China', ADBI Discussion Paper 96, Tokyo, 2008.

Index

composition of 264
computing quasi-fiscal cost of
262–3
regulations, relaxation of 91
stabilisation funds of 265–6
Foreign Exchange Dealers'
Association of India 214
Foreign Exchange Management
Act (FEMA) 91, 235
Foreign Exchange Regulation Act
(FERA) 1973 91, 235
foreign financial enterprises,
presence of 55
foreign financial investors (FIIs) 90
Foreign Institutional Investment
(FII) 290
foreign investments, foreign banks
and 60
in Indian companies 292
foreign investors, in India 301
Foreign Investments Promotion
Board (FIPB) 110, 290
Free Trade Agreements 359

Group-7 countries 286, 351
Group-20 countries 351, 356–8, 363
Group-30 countries 286
Gangopadhayay, Shubhashis 245,
Ganguly, Ashok S. 244n, 245n
General Credit Cards (GCC) 229
Global Competitive Report, 2004 71
Global Depository Receipts (GDR)
268
global economic integration 41–4,
47, 52
global economy 3, 136
dependence of US dollar reserve
currency 342, 343
India and 1, 8, 41–63, 93–5, 279
global financial imbalance,

emerging market economies
(EMEs) and 299–311
global financial turbulence, and
financial sector in India 135–
53
'global greenbacks' proposal 268
global imbalances 37, 354
and crisis 35–8
impact on India 367–9
global perspective on 313–17
impact on India 321–3
India's perspective on 313–27
causes of 314
features of 313–14
globalisation, concept of 41–2
costs and benefits of 330
and financial sector 333–5
of monetary policy 204, 331–3
money, and finance 328–37
Goldman Sachs 335
Goswami, Omkar 245n
governance, reforms in 115
standards of 9
government debt market 127
government intervention 44
government-owned investments
(GIVs) vehicles, and capital
flows 286–95
government securities–24, 111, 143,
161
market 107
Government of Singapore
Investment Corporation
(GIC) 265
Greenspan, Alan 262, 326, 332
Group of Ten (G-10) 58
gross domestic product (GDP) 2,
96, 114
growth 93, 100, 102, 210, 301, 319
per capita, of India 97

Tanzi, Vito 245n
Tarapore, S.S. 109, 225, 245n, 254
Tarapore Committee 55
Task Force on Financial Market
    Regulations 11
Task Force on Revival of Cooperative
    Credit Institution *see*
    Vaidyanathan Committee
Task Force on Supportive Policy
    and Regulatory Framework
    for Micro-Finance 177
Tata, Ratan 245n
tax, concessions 21
  heaven 365
  regimes 13
Technical Advisory Committee on
    Money, Foreign Exchange
    and Government Securities
    Markets (TAC) 167
technology, change and economic
    growth 67
Temasek Holdings, Singapore
    265
Tendulkar, Suresh D. 244n
'threshold', importance of 53, 60
Topalova, 'Petia' 70
total factor productivity (TFP)
    growth 66-7, 69, 70, 71,
    101
trade, deficit 301
  growth in 2
  integration 65
  liberalisation of 50
  policy 191
  reforms in 90
  restrictions 50-1
transparency 286-7
Tregillis, Shane 245n
Trivedi, Pushpa 69

United Kingdom (UK), regulatory
    policy in 346
UK Hedge Fund Working Group,
    report of 286-7
UNCTAD 330, 343
Union Budget, of 2004-5 50, 51
United States of America, current
    account balance of 323
  current account deficit of 47,
    314, 328, 340
  excess liquidity in 340
  Federal Reserve in 220
  financial system in 328-9
  monetary policy of 340
  recovery and reforms in 351-2
  regulatory policy in 346
  sanction on India 222
  saving-investment balance in
    314
  sub-prime lending for housing
    in, and crisis 343, 349
  warning on asset bubbles in 349,
    350
urban cooperative banks (UCBs)
    110, 231
Users' Consultative Panel 167-8

Vaidyanathan, A. 244n
Vaidyanathan Committee 182
  recommendations of 187
Vasudev, C.M. 245n
Verma, M.S. 245n
Virmani, Arvind 70, 101
Vyas, Mahesh 245n
Vyas, V.S. 245n

Wadhwani, Sushil 245n
wage rates 71
Walker, David 287